HORRIBLE WHITE PEOPLE

Horrible White People

Gender, Genre, and Television's Precarious Whiteness

Taylor Nygaard and Jorie Lagerwey

NEW YORK UNIVERSITY PRESS

New York

NEW YORK UNIVERSITY PRESS
New York
www.nyupress.org

References to Internet websites (URLs) were accurate at the time of writing. Neither the author nor New York University Press is responsible for URLs that may have expired or changed since the manuscript was prepared.

Library of Congress Cataloging-in-Publication Data
Names: Nygaard, Taylor, author. | Lagerwey, Jorie, author.
Title: Horrible white people : gender, genre, and television's precarious whiteness / Taylor Nygaard and Jorie Lagerwey.
Description: New York : New York University Press, 2020. |
Includes bibliographical references and index.
Identifiers: LCCN 2020016516 (print) | LCCN 2020016517 (ebook) |
ISBN 9781479885459 (cloth) | ISBN 9781479805358 (paperback) |
ISBN 9781479805341 (ebook) | ISBN 9781479805334 (ebook)
Subjects: LCSH: Whites on television. | Sex role on television. | Gender identity on television. | Television broadcasting—Social aspects—United States.
Classification: LCC PN1992.8.W47 N95 2020 (print) | LCC PN1992.8.W47 (ebook) |
DDC 791.45/652909—dc23
LC record available at https://lccn.loc.gov/2020016516
LC ebook record available at https://lccn.loc.gov/2020016517

New York University Press books are printed on acid-free paper, and their binding materials are chosen for strength and durability. We strive to use environmentally responsible suppliers and materials to the greatest extent possible in publishing our books.

Manufactured in the United States of America

10 9 8 7 6 5 4 3 2 1

To Clay

CONTENTS

AUTHORS' NOTE, OR, A NOTE ON BEING HORRIBLE

This book began as a series of casual conversations between us on the rare occasions we happened to be in the same place: chats about shared viewing, similar frustrations. We found that both of us—often—had experiences that went something like this: We would be sitting around a dinner table with a group of educated, affluent, liberal or progressive, mostly White professionals in their late thirties and forties; and, since we study and teach television, someone would ask what television shows we thought they should watch. This is always a loaded question for television scholars. We clearly have personal, subjective, sometimes deeply private preferences in genres and particular shows, which can range from the more "guilty" (food appreciation, home makeover programming, or reality soaps in our case) to the more critically appreciated or blockbuster shows like *The Sopranos* or *Game of Thrones*. But we can also feel added pressure to display or (to be frank) *flaunt* our knowledge and critical sensibilities in order to signal our high cultural capital in the face of a group with obviously high economic capital—capital that as academics (one of us still feeling the effects of being hired during Ireland's austerity and the other a precarious academic with no job security)—we don't have. That complex affective burden of shame, failure, pride, knowledge, and caution makes this utterly mundane question surprisingly difficult to answer. It was also this gross emotional stew that we began to recognize in the often despairing characters on the comedies we found ourselves naming during these conversations: *Fleabag, Catastrophe, Casual, You're the Worst, Broad City, I'm Sorry*—the list kept growing.

These characters faced genuine problems: lost jobs, unaffordable rents, broken or unsatisfying relationships, grief and mental illness, but their reactions were despicable. They were mean and selfish, destructive and often very funny. And the thing that took us too long to notice was that they were all White. We felt far too implicated by liking them. It's that identification with the characters we began calling "Horrible White People" that led to this book. In the chapters that follow, we interrogate the centralization of this White, despairing, despicable affect—an affect apparent in our recommendations and in media culture more broadly. We are feminist, antiracist scholars, and writing is our activism. We began writing when Donald Trump was campaigning, and we are finishing as his impeachment begins; yet somehow his reelection still seems likely. We want to understand some of the cultural forces that brought us here. We are White and middle-class and ricocheting in and out of the wallowing and despair we see in these characters. We identify with many of them as much as we are repulsed by some. And that complicated dynamic of revulsion and attraction is easily masked by the ambiguity of laughter, whether we are laughing *with* or *at* someone or, in this case, their Whiteness. This book confronts what we were cringing at—that set of affective reactions we learned to call White precarity. And it interrogates television's role in perpetuating or excusing its central role in narratives that are marked as prestigious—the kind of shows TV scholars would recommend.

The title *Horrible White People* might evoke, for White readers, something other than what we have just described. One's first thought might be the violent White supremacists wielding torches and chanting hate during the rise of the Alt-Right or the psychotic White male gunmen involved in the hundreds of mass shootings across America or even the more seemingly naïve or uneducated perpetrators of explicit racism and anti-immigrant rhetoric repeated on rural reality shows featuring conservative protagonists like those on *Duck Dynasty*. We would unequivocally characterize these White people as terrible, some even evil; yet our classification of well-meaning, floundering, seemingly suffering, self-identifying liberals as "horrible" is meant as a provocation. It's meant to promote White racial humility and self-critique. We want to challenge readers to think about the insidious "horrible" nature of the White supremacy inherent in these suffering yet still incredibly privileged characters, which despite good intentions, center their perspective, their suffering, and their needs above all else.

This book is therefore first and foremost about naming Whiteness, interrogating and deconstructing contemporary representations of

Whiteness, because as the rather mundane but habitual dinner-party story attests, White people—including well-meaning, left-voting, antiracist, feminist White people like ourselves—continue to let their Whiteness and the Whiteness of their media consumption remain invisible and uncommented on. The subject matter of this book extends an invitation for deep personal inquiry and collective change. At our most optimistic, we hope it can be used as a tool for authentic, honest dialogue and action. Throughout this book, we use the terms *us* and *we* to refer to a White collectivity. We are White, and we are addressing common White representational dynamics; and "rather than retreat in the face of discomfort, we can practice building our stamina for the critical examination of white identity" and its complicity in maintaining enormous, frequently violent, structural inequalities (DiAngelo 2018; xiv).

In *Why I'm No Longer Talking to White People about Racism*, Reni Eddo-Lodge writes, "You have to be careful about the white people you trust when it comes to discussing race and racism. You don't have the privilege of approaching conversations about racism with the assumption that the other participants will be on the same plane as you" (2017, 91–92). Our hope is that in confronting White supremacy on TV—some we love, some we hate, but all made *for us*—we become more trustworthy. The danger Eddo-Lodge describes when talking to White people about race is a danger we as two White women don't face and in fact benefit from every time we have a pleasantly banal conversation with a person of color, every time we forget to listen before we speak. Also, conversations with White people about race are not dangerous for us. They can be stressful and exhausting and frustrating; they can demand that we speak slowly, with great care to massage or step around other White people's feelings as we try to persuade. But part of the power of Whiteness that we hope we illustrate in this book is its forgiving nature—forgiving *of its own*, including only until it becomes too difficult. We hope readers, especially White readers, are patient as they approach our critiques of these prestigious, often beautiful and sometimes poignant, but still complicit shows. And we hope that our readers of color will have more language with which to critique contemporary media, especially media that is often singled out as the best, most innovative and "quality" available today.

Introduction

The Fraying Fantasies of White Supremacy

The day before US President Donald Trump's inauguration on January 21, 2017, Abbi Jacobson and Ilana Glazer, the writers and stars behind *Broad City* released a video about inauguration day as part of their off-season "Hack into Broad City" YouTube series (Comedy Central 2017). The video opens with a panicked Abbi waiting for Ilana to answer her video call. Mimicking disaster films, Abbi is stuck in an unmoving elevator, and Ilana is standing in a dark locker in what appears to be her apartment building's underground storage space. Both women are dressed for the apocalypse with warm beanies covering messy hair, sweatpants, and no makeup. Abbi wears plaid flannel and a shearling vest, carries a massive backpack, and is desperate to maintain her weak phone signal. Ilana wears camouflage and waits for Abbi in front of stocked shelves, a hiker's backpack, and camping lanterns (although she reveals she forgot to collect food and batteries). The scene is apocalyptic, but the girls are counting down not to asteroid impact or nuclear Armageddon but to the minute Trump is sworn in as president. Despite their obvious agitation, Abbi reveals that she got stuck leaving a laser-hair-removal appointment, which she had prepaid and could not pass up, even for the end of the world. As the dramatic countdown ends, Abbi and Ilana realize their lives won't be immediately impacted: Abbi's elevator starts functioning normally, and the New York City stalwart *Law & Order: SVU* shoots a scene outside Ilana's window. Their race and class privilege becomes palpable as they pause, confused and unsure how to act; Abbi decides she will come over to Ilana's as planned, while Ilana says, "And you know what? We'll just Google how to Google our local representatives."

The girls' fear and rage at Trump's election is the guiding theme of the scene, but throughout, their lack of real urgency (forgetting food, worrying about hair removal) belies the inherent security of their position as White middle-class characters.[1] Their incompetence dealing with the realities of political unrest also reflects the limits and ineptitude of millennial White allies and White identity in comedic televisual representations that are the subject of this book. The video illustrates how the series engages in explicit critical political discourse while, like the other programs we examine in *Horrible White People*, aligning itself with the ultimately ineffectual White shock, dismay, and panic at the election of Donald Trump that dominated liberal reactions in social, fictional, and nonfictional media. *Broad City* is part of a prolific cycle of transatlantic television comedies we analyze in this book and call "Horrible White People" shows. They emerged mostly between 2014 and 2016 and target affluent, liberal, White audiences through prestige aesthetics and innovative, progressive representations. Yet they also reflect the complicity of the White Left, obsessed with its own anxiety and suffering, in the rise of the Far Right—particularly in the mobilization, representation, and sustenance of structural White supremacy on television.

How to Read This Book: Our Structure and Argument

We have created a parallel structure in each chapter that opens with an indicative example like the *Broad City* sequence just presented. From there, we lay out the argument of the chapter and proceed to outline extensive background and contextual information about that chapter's key concepts. Our chapters are based on a research model that combines media industries studies' concerns with political economy and cultural studies' concerns with identity, power, and inequality. Through the combination of these methodologies, we seek to expand our understandings of a significant trend in contemporary televisual representation and interrogate how industry and culture relate to and constitute each other. Each chapter begins by mapping how the Horrible White People cycle extends or breaks from historical legacies in industry, genre, and representation and concludes with close textual analysis that draws out the ideological implications of those extensions and breaks. This methodology insists on the importance of tracing historical trajectories of genre, identity, and political representation to contextualize how contemporary representations can be considered either progressive or regressive, while also acknowledging how television industrial logics, both cultural and economic, impact those trajectories.

This book may challenge readers because it analyzes the workings of structural White supremacy in a beloved cultural institution (television). As we discussed and presented this work in progress, readers and listeners often responded emotionally, as though confronted or implicated. That feedback illustrated how painful it can be to grapple with the idea that prestige TV shows, programs that wear progressive social credentials on their sleeve and—maybe most of all—characters with whom readers (perhaps especially White readers) might identify, are complicit in maintaining unequal, rhetorically and physically violent structures of power. We had to deal with that reaction in ourselves as well, and it became central to the theoretical underpinning of this book. As we explain in detail later in this introduction and throughout the book, White people's emotional reactions to conversations about racial inequality—often reactions of anger, denial, or flight—are what Robin DiAngelo (2018) calls "White Fragility." White fragility is on prominent display throughout the Horrible White People programming cycle, and the tone of despair is in fact a constitutive element of our definition of it. Only by diving in, wading through, having the patience to feel that denial or anger and then trying to keep reading, thinking, and writing with an open mind will readers get the most out of our arguments and hopefully join us in the project of acknowledging and thus working to dismantle White supremacy. Our argument is that even television that is culturally and socially relevant, award-winning prestige TV, technologically innovative, and generically, representationally, and artistically progressive— even that beautiful television—can function to sustain and perpetuate White people's cultural centrality and power. *Horrible White People* thus contributes to the growing field of Whiteness studies, expanding beyond the more mainstream focus on lower-middle-class rural masculinity (see Garner 2017, 1591) to expose the hypocrisies and invisibilities of other complicit intersectional White identities during the global conservative turn of the early twenty-first century; particularly that of upper-middle-class or affluent, liberal White women.

Horrible White People: Defining a Cycle

The particular iteration of the kind of progressive television that we define and analyze here is what we call "Horrible White People" shows, like *Broad City* in the example at the beginning of this introduction. Horrible White People (HWP) shows are a group of programs that proliferated after the Great Recession and peaked between 2014 and 2016. They are thirty-minute comedies or satires. Perhaps obviously, they star mostly White actors. Most of them also engage directly with discourses of liberal political progressivism and racial inequality, albeit from the distinctly White perspective of their main characters. They are serialized, single-camera, narratively complex (Mittell 2015) programs that engage, reference, satirize, or critique traditional comedic televisual modes or genres, most often the sitcom (see chapter 2). As the strategic products of contemporary streaming platforms and narrowcast or cable networks in a highly competitive television environment (mapped in chapter 1), they foreground aesthetic and stylistic innovation. Many of them have a strong authorial voice or are marketed as the products of an auteur, often starring their writer/creators as fictionalized versions of themselves. Unlike traditional sitcoms' focus on families or workplace or friendship families, these shows take on elements of romantic comedy and focus on romance or failed romance, frequently critiquing hegemonic ideologies of family. As a result, they feature female protagonists or complicated women in complex relationships with men and engage with contemporary discourses of "emergent feminism" or "the unexpected, and seemingly sudden, resurfacing of feminism" and its "renewed *mattering* to popular culture" (Keller and Ryan 2018, 2). They thus mark a break in television representation from the dominant postfeminist sensibility (Gill 2007) that rejected the utility or necessity of feminist politics. They focus instead on exploring changing norms around sex, gender, and relationships, especially a new, seemingly progressive "feminist antiaspirationalism" (Silverman and Hagelin 2018) or "light-hearted endorsement of 'imperfection'" (McRobbie 2015) that contrasts with the postfeminist aspirationalism of the previous two decades. The shifting distinctions and definitions of emergent feminism and postfeminism are detailed in the last section of this introduction (and in chapter 3), but the fact that these shows so explicitly engage with political issues, like the insidiousness of gender inequality, has led to their outsized cultural meaning, evinced by prolific critical attention and prestigious awards, noted throughout the book, where they are continually praised for their representational and stylistic innovations. Horrible White People shows are also hyper self-aware. Finally, perhaps most definitive of the cycle is the bleak grimness, black humor, and ethos of failure that unite these disparate comedies in their centering of White precarity.

TABLE I.1. Horrible White People Shows

Louie (FX, 2010–2015)	*Better Things* (FX, 2016–)
Girls (HBO, 2012–2017)	*The Detour* (TBS, 2016–2019)
Bojack Horseman (Netflix, 2014–2020)	*Easy* (Netflix, 2016–2019)
Broad City (Comedy Central, 2014–2019)	*Fleabag* (BBC Three; Amazon, 2016–2019)
Girlfriends' Guide to Divorce (Bravo, 2014–2018)	*High Maintenance* (HBO, 2016–)
Transparent (Amazon, 2014–2019)	*I Love Dick* (Amazon, 2016–2017)
You're the Worst (FXX, 2014–2019)	*Lady Dynamite* (Netflix, 2016–2017)
Casual (Hulu, 2015–2018)	*Love* (Netflix, 2016–2018)
Catastrophe (Channel 4; Amazon, 2015–2019)	*One Mississippi* (Amazon, 2016–2017)
Crazy Ex-Girlfriend (The CW, 2015–2019)	*Search Party* (TBS, 2016–)
Difficult People (Hulu, 2015–2017)	*You Me Her* (Audience, 2016–2020)
Looking (HBO, 2014–2015)	*Big Little Lies* (HBO 2017–2019)
Togetherness (HBO, 2015–2016)	*Friends from College* (Netflix 2017–2019)
Unbreakable Kimmy Schmidt (Netflix, 2015–2019)	*Divorce* (HBO, 2017–2019)
UnReal (Lifetime, 2015–2018)	*I'm Sorry* (TruTV, 2017–)
Younger (TV Land, 2015–)	*Russian Doll* (Netflix, 2019–)

Not every program we put in this category or analyze in this book fits every single element of our definition. *UnReal* (please see the appendix for brief descriptions of all the shows we reference throughout the book) is an hour-long satire rather than a thirty-minute comedy; *Search Party* incorporates elements of mystery and suspense thriller that disrupt its easy categorization in comedy; *Louie* is a key precursor to the shows we discuss but is male-centered, which contradicts our focus on female-centric shows. *I'm Sorry* focuses on a loving, economically stable nuclear family and therefore lacks the despair of other shows we associate it with. Nonetheless, as with TV genre study, our aim is not to make a definitive list but to put a name to what we see as a "cultural category"

(Mittell 2001) with revealing thematic, character, aesthetic, and tonal consistencies.

Horrible White People shows feature explicitly liberal, well-off (middle and upper-middle-class by broad American definitions), young or youthful (characters range from midtwenties to forties; see chapter 3) White women and the men they are related to or in relationships with. *Horrible* is a purposefully broad, intentionally provocative term and refers to the characters' attitudes and behaviors as well as to the "cringe" response they might induce in viewers (Havas and Sulimma 2018). Their "horrible" behaviors are often shocking, revolting, or purposefully heinous in part to stand out in a sea of "too much TV" (see chapter 1) and in part to appear progressive by challenging dominant norms of civility, gendered decorum, and middle-classness. *Girls* is perhaps the first Horrible White People show, and creator/writer/star Lena Dunham's character, Hannah, embodies the multiple levels of horrible that we wish to evoke. She is rude to her parents and irresponsible at work, treats her friends appallingly, but also wallows in bodily abjection. While seeing her frequently naked, nonconforming body does important work to challenge extremely narrow beauty standards (Ford 2016), it is also purposefully "unlikeable" and gross (Silverman and Hagelin 2018). In one memorable moment, she stabs a cotton swab so far into her ear that she ruptures her eardrum. A visual and aural representation of her obsessive-compulsive disorder, the event is punctuated by extreme close-ups and an internal diegetic soundtrack of excessively magnified sucking, slurping, and plunging noises as she tries to impose order on the interior of her own body. Hannah also represents a key Horrible White People character trope, the "well-meaning White lady," a common label for White women trying to be inclusive and antiracist but falling short by overemphasizing their own emotional reactions to other people's suffering or by asking for people of color to educate and support them on their journey to understand inequality and advocate for change (see especially *Girls*, S2E1–S2E2, featuring Hannah's Black Republican boyfriend played by Donald Glover).

The self-obsession shared by all the main characters in this group of shows leads to destructive behavior that is leveled at themselves and those around them. This destruction offers a harsh critique of dominant middle-class norms that have Whiteness embedded in them but also in the end shifts focus back onto White suffering. When faced with losing access to the jobs, housing, and relationships they thought were their automatic due, they wreak havoc instead. That destruction is most often emotional but can be negligent (Gretchen burns down her apartment building with her vibrator on *You're the Worst*) or veer into the criminal (Rebecca stalks her friends on *Crazy Ex-Girlfriend*, and Fleabag steals from her stepmother on *Fleabag*). These characters are frequently viciously mean, always floundering personally and professionally, and almost never capable of solving their problems.

Throughout this book, in identifying shows as part of a cycle tied to the particular industrial changes and cultural tensions of a specific time period, our goal is to define and discuss an especially insidious iteration of intersectional Whiteness. We discuss how Horrible White People shows privilege Whiteness in their aesthetics, in the uneasy tensions of mixing comedy and drama, and in narrative conclusions that always return to the emotionality of the central White characters while silencing the impact of the racism that the shows (sometimes) represent and (supposedly) critique. We see Horrible White People shows as a cluster of programming that is big enough to be significant and represents a left-leaning, ostensibly "woke" version of Whiteness that has not been analyzed before. The concept of the cluster or cycle helps us work through the relationships among televisual representation, an evolving TV industry, and a period of dramatic cultural change that continues to disproportionally centralize affluent Whiteness and White suffering in an era of growing income inequality, highly visible racial inequality and violence, rampant anti-immigrant rhetoric, and persistent gender and sexual discrimination against marginalized communities. We have compiled a list of HWP shows we see as complete, but we encourage readers to add to our choices, particularly with shows that may be emerging only as we finish writing. It would not be productive to enumerate why we have excluded every show we have left out, but what we have tried to do is create a name for a block of programming we see proliferating in specific cultural, political, and TV industrial circumstances. While we hope this book is illuminating of this cultural moment, we also hope that the term might be a useful tool for thinking through television Whiteness in the future or in other modes of TV. Therefore, while we set shows like *Two and a Half Men* (CBS, 2003–2015), and *Big Bang Theory* (CBS, 2007–2018) outside our scope for reasons of periodicity, shooting style (multi-camera as opposed to single-camera), mass audience address, and male-centricity, perhaps another author will find the work we have done here adaptable to help understand those programs as well. Conceptualizing this as a cycle puts boundaries on our analysis, but we hope the *concept* of Horrible White People—well-intentioned, self-identified liberal White characters who are floundering and who emphasize their own precarity in "quality," often self-critical, innovative programming—is portable and can help students and scholars understand Whiteness in other cultural contexts, historical moments, or genres. Although we see this cycle tapering to an end as we write, just like Whiteness itself, this programming cycle, with new entries like *Russian Doll*, may prove flexible and accommodating of difference just enough to maintain durability.

Defining a Historical Conjuncture

We began work on this project in the middle of Donald Trump's nasty and divisive 2016 US presidential campaign when we started to see thematic parallels between Trump's rhetoric of White victimhood, the anti-immigrant language of the Brexit campaign for the United Kingdom to leave the European Union, and an abundance of cynical, often emotionally brutal series on narrowcast and streaming networks featuring twenty- and thirty-something White people navigating faltering romance, friendship, marriage, and career in an era of cultural crisis and so-called White precarity. This section outlines the specific cultural-historical circumstances we understand to underlie HWP shows and our critical race and gender analysis of them. As table I.1 illustrates, this programming cycle includes a plethora of transatlantic television programs like *Casual, Catastrophe, Love, Fleabag, Better Things, You're the Worst, UnReal, Crazy Ex-Girlfriend, Difficult People*, and many others that emerged mostly between 2014 and 2016. It is their stories, and the cultural weight of their stories taken together as a collection of similar programs, that recenter Whiteness and thus contribute to the social, political, and representational milieu that has supported the rise of the Right and contributes to sustaining structural White supremacy. This recentering of Whiteness is based on the historical conjuncture or "the coming together of often distinct though related contradictions" (S. Hall 1979, 14) that include White precarity, liberal White feminism, and crisis White masculinity brought on by the political and social realities of the devastating global recession, the resurgent hypervisibility of racial inequality and racial violence, and emerging feminisms. This introduction situates these contradictions in the context of White supremacy, recession, postracial fantasies, and conflicted notions of postfeminism and popular feminisms. Throughout the book, we examine how distribution (chapter 1), genre (chapter 2), aesthetics, and representation (throughout) work together to culturally recenter liberal White failure and victimhood while usurping attention from the plight of minorities whom these liberal and progressive White people supposedly seek to help. We examine how all the contemporary social-political and industrial circumstances outlined here operate in relation to one another to create Horrible White People shows *as well as* utopian sitcoms featuring families of color (chapter 2) and what we call "Diverse Quality Comedies" (chapter 4), the shows like *Master of None, Atlanta, Insecure,* and *Dear White People* that are so generically and aesthetically similar to HWP shows but are created by and star men and women of color. While these seemingly disparate programming clusters might suggest an ideological dispersion across fragmented programming options, we illustrate an intertextual centering of Whiteness and particularly of White precarity in the 2010s.

In doing this analysis, we are joining the conversation that the press began in unpacking the economic and political reasons behind the now-infamous statistic that 53 percent of White women in the United States voted for Donald Trump and continue to vote for other conservative leaders, while failing to show up for progressive initiatives around racial injustice. Our contention is that while this cycle of programming seems different, distinct, or separate from the rise in partisan niche programming like Breitbart News, which increasingly fragmented audiences consume in their own self-curated bubbles of agreeable programming, there are nonetheless striking ideological similarities across broader television and media content that need to be interrogated in order for us to fully understand the ideological forces shaping public opinion in this divisive and contentious political climate.

This cycle both mirrors and constructs the ideological tensions and anxieties of this historical conjuncture. Thus, the proliferation of Horrible White People shows, along with the industry that produces them, is complicit in the rhetorical shift toward White suffering that has helped sustain structural White supremacy and worked to support the rise of the political Far Right in the United States and elsewhere where these shows are produced, distributed, and consumed. These programs foreground race and identity by centralizing the plight of well-meaning White characters who are newly confronted with undeniable evidence of racial and economic inequality but are unwilling to sacrifice their own comfort to support others' civil rights. In so doing, the shows address the rise of the Right with a darkly comic critique that calls out the failures of those on the political Left but alleviates their characters from responsibility by making them alternately emotionally suffering or incompetent adults who are willing to joke about their failures in order to show that they understand but are not willing to take action. This programming cycle centralizes Whiteness in a way that sustains its representational dominance and, by force of repetition, provides representational models or justifications for emphasizing relatively affluent White liberals' affective despair.

Furthermore, there is an important gendering of this precarious Whiteness that we work to unpack in the chapters that follow. Horrible White People shows are almost always set in the domestic sphere, and dysfunctional romantic partnerships (or breakups), alternative family structures, and control of domestic space are primary drivers of narrative conflict. The traditionally feminine gendered spaces of home and romance (see, for example, Spigel 1992; and Radway 1984) demand interrogation about why and how White *women* in particular bear the representational burden of White precarity, as well as how the men whose stories are intertwined with theirs are shown to be in crisis by becoming overemotional or overinvested in domestic chores, settings, and conflicts—by becoming feminized. Nira Yuval-Davis maintains that because women are associated with the body and with private space, whereas men are associated with the mind and public sphere, women are typically "hidden" from various theorizations of political phenomena; the gendered spaces of home and romance are typically ignored as politically significant, and women are excluded from political discourse. But, she argues, "women play the roles of cultural transmitters as well as cultural signifiers of the national collectivity," symbolizing "its roots, its spirit, its national project" (1993, 627). Sarah Banet-Weiser (2018) provides further important context to this shifting representational burden by pointing out that over the past few years we have witnessed the rise of "popular feminism"—or the increased attention to women and women's issues in popular media that Horrible White People shows are part of. But she suggests that the same social and cultural circumstances that have led to this rise have also enabled and supported a parallel rise of popular misogyny, thus contributing to the contentious contemporary gender norms and expectations represented on these shows. Banet-Weiser argues that the emergence of both is based on "the twinned discourses of *capacity* and *injury*" in which gender inequality is recognized, but rather than collective, political, or structural change, popular media presents "individual capacity" as that which will suture the wound (2018, 4). Banet-Weiser tracks how women's individual capacity is typically nurtured and promoted in popular media and how men's capacity is conversely threatened by that same female capacity. Horrible White People shows offer a contrasting intersectional representation of this injury/capacity dynamic by centralizing floundering affluent White men and women, all wallowing in the collective "injury" of contemporary gender inequality, financial stresses, and intensified visibilities of racial inequality, which we map in the following sections of this introduction. Therefore, this book examines the gendering of complicit liberal Whites, represented by Horrible White People characters obsessed with their own suffering, in the maintenance of the status quo in racial and gendered power structures, thus contributing to the cultural milieu that elected misogynistic right-wing populists like Donald Trump and his ultra-socially-conservative vice president, Mike Pence. We analyze in particular the ways this programming cycle and the industrial forces that produce it mobilize, represent, and sustain structural White supremacy through specific gendered characterizations, thematic consistencies, and aesthetic concerns on television.

Ambivalent Whiteness, White Supremacy, and White Precarity

In presenting this material at conferences and in online forums, we have often received feedback from listeners and readers who felt upset or even implicated by our critiques of these avowedly liberal and frequently self-critical or satirical shows. Indeed the relationship between the targeted viewer—an affluent, educated, urban-dwelling, White "quality" demographic—and the characters on-screen is complicated. As Stuart Hall laid out in the foundational theories of cultural studies that still guide our readings of these television shows, texts do not create fixed and universal positions; they are provisional and always sites of struggle. While we acknowledge and hope to inspire possibilities for more contradictory and contingent readings of these shows and their ideological effects, we present our interpretation of the construction of Horrible White People characters on the basis of substantial textual evidence and media-industry discourses of target demographics for these shows. And we do indeed implicate those White "quality" audiences—including ourselves—of complicity in the racist structures we describe. In chapter 4, we posit "quality" aesthetics as an aesthetics of Whiteness mobilized to target the unspoken but clearly present Whiteness of the most desired TV audiences. These assumptions underwrite the analysis of the entire book, and we refer to them continually because it is vital to persistently underscore how *all* White people benefit from White supremacy. Constant calling attention to Whiteness, which so often remains invisible and the default "universal" (Dyer 1997), is, in our view, one simple way to begin to combat that.

We find it crucial to note that people have most strongly disagreed with us when we have interpreted programs featuring Jewish characters as participating in the structural White supremacy that is an underlying assumption of this book. In response to this common reaction, we argue that part of the insidiousness of White supremacy is its limited inclusiveness (which we discuss throughout the book; see especially chapter 2). As Robin James (2015) and other critical race studies scholars have acknowledged about Whiteness before, cultural specificity and a certain measure of difference are allowed and even encouraged in order to mask the durable systems of White racism. We can look to history as well for examples of the expansiveness of US Whiteness, which has first violently excluded and eventually embraced Italians, Irish, eastern Europeans, and other groups of light-skinned immigrants. In *How the Irish Became White*, Noel Ignatiev writes, "It follows, therefore, that the white race consists of those who partake of the privileges of white skin in this society. Its most wretched members share a status higher, in certain respects, than that of the most exalted persons excluded from it" (1995, 2).

Following this formulation, anti-Semitism can continue to exist alongside fair-skinned Jewish people benefiting from Whiteness. "Putting otherwise privileged people of color at the center of white supremacist institutions obscures the white supremacy (and the imperialism/coloniality), thus allowing it to run all the more efficiently. . . . *This inclusion is always conditional and always instrumental*" (R. James 2015, 13). James further extends this argument to all identity categories or oppressed groups. In this same vein, Jewish comedic traditions, once the purview of vaudeville and stand-up comedy, have been essential to forming contemporary American television comedy. As those comedic tropes and techniques have become mainstreamed and sitcom structures have shifted, Jewish characters have been encompassed in liberal/progressive versions of dominant Whiteness as one iteration of White supremacy's self-serving inclusiveness. This ambivalent relationship between skin color giving high status and ethnic or religious identity categorizing one as a subaltern is actually the fodder for jokes in many Horrible White People shows. Perhaps most overtly, the tension appears in *Broad City*, in which the stars make frequent jokes about their pale skin (S4E7) and the privileges it offers them at the same time that they foreground their Jewish identity through jokes about both physical characteristics like Ilana's hair (S4E1) and Jewish cultural practices (S2E4; S3E10). Yet, as we discuss in more detail in chapter 2, acknowledging that tension in a few jokes is not enough to fully undermine the show's and cycle's overall participation in centralizing White precarity and White fragility. It is also not coincidental that as the industry feels cultural pressure to diversify, it looks to include a once-marginalized but now-normalized White ethnicity.

The structural White supremacy we describe can be inclusive even toward characters with other skin tones, provided they operate within White people's cultural norms and mostly lack cultural specificity—in other words, if they're Whitewashed. *Friends from College* offers an excellent example of this. The eponymous friends are a group of six Harvard graduates, four White, one Korean American, and the star of the ensemble, played by the mixed-race comedian Keegan-Michael Key. While Key does make jokes about race once or twice in the series, those references are wholly dominated by the affluent White culture that pervades the rest of the show. As one Twitter user, @BeeBabs, put it, "Keegan-Michael

Key needs a black best friend in Friends From College to inform him that this is some white ghetto bullshit he has got himself involved in" (January 17, 2019). The entirely un-remarked-on difference represented by Key and Jae W. Suh, who plays the Korean American Marianne, functions as a marker of the whole group's inclusivity and not-racist-ness. The final episode of the show's first season illustrates the show's cultural Whiteness: Ethan (played by Key) and one of his friends play racquetball decked out in tennis whites; Sam and her husband have a modernist glass-and-concrete country home in the Connecticut woods; Sam's husband organizes a lavish birthday party "Night of Surprises" that includes an archery demonstration; and, finally, the couple's Mercedes SUV, accidentally left in neutral, runs slow-motion into the pool. The show matches every aspect of a Horrible White People show (affluent, liberal, urban-dwelling, highly educated characters; bleak, self-critical comedy; high production values on a streaming platform) save its two characters of color. We argue that shows like this and other individual or supporting characters of color like Edgar on You're the Worst, Leon on Casual, Jo and Delia on Girlfriends' Guide to Divorce, and Black boyfriends on Search Party and Broad City actually strengthen the centralization of Whiteness that we describe in this cultural moment with their assimilationist (Gray 1995) and mostly Whitewashed characters who demonstrate with their presence how not-racist the White characters around them are and thus participate in the overall maintenance of White supremacy.

Throughout the book, we use the term White supremacy to refer to the structural inequalities built into the economies, government policies, and cultural productions of the early twenty-first century. We use the term White supremacy accurately but also with a conscious eye toward its potential initial shock value for White readers. White supremacy in this book does not refer to violent, torch-wielding, Confederate-flag-waving, open racists. As David Gillborn summarizes, "White supremacy is not only, nor indeed primarily, associated with relatively small and extreme political movements that openly mobilize on the basis of race hatred (important and dangerous though such groups are): rather, supremacy is seen to relate to the operation of forces that saturate the everyday, mundane actions and policies that shape the world in the interests of white people (see Bush, 2004; Delgado and Stefancic, 1997)" (2006, 320). Gillborn goes on to quote the scholar Frances Lee Ansley to highlight the often-invisible structural power relations of White supremacy, "a political, economic, and cultural system in which whites overwhelmingly control power and material resources, conscious and unconscious ideas of white superiority and entitlement are widespread, and relations of white dominance and non-white subordination are daily reenacted across a broad array of institutions and social settings" (Ansley 1997, 592). Furthermore, the way White supremacy is more narrowly depicted in this cycle often adheres to what Eduardo Bonilla-Silva calls "racism without racists" or "color-blind racism": a set of beliefs in which White Americans profess not to see differences in skin tone and "have developed powerful explanations—which have ultimately become justifications—for contemporary racial inequality that exculpate them from any responsibility for the status of people of color" (2014, 14). This version of racism and participation in White supremacy implicates *all* White people, including those who espouse liberal, progressive, and even antiracist social and political views.

The set of historical circumstances just outlined and detailed in the following pages threaten the economic and cultural security of those liberal Whites, including their perception of the United States as postracial. That general lack of security and sense of threat is what we refer to throughout as *White precarity*. As one cultural response to these circumstances, Horrible White People shows centralize behaviors that Robin DiAngelo characterizes as "White Fragility":

> White people in North America live in a social environment that protects and insulates them from race-based stress. This insulated environment of racial protection builds white expectations for racial comfort while at the same time lowering the ability to tolerate racial stress, leading to what I refer to as White Fragility. White Fragility is a state in which even a minimum amount of racial stress becomes intolerable, triggering a range of defensive moves. These moves include the outward display of emotions such as anger, fear, and guilt, and behaviors such as argumentation, silence, and leaving the stress-inducing situation. These behaviors, in turn, function to reinstate white racial equilibrium. (2011, 54; see also DiAngelo 2018)

This racial insulation, as a function of structural White supremacy, again, applies to all Whites and is frequently structured in the small ensembles of White characters on these shows, particularly White girlfriends in this cycle (see chapter 3). Horrible White People shows feature a range of responses to economic, relationship, and racial stress, including jokes, excessive emotional performances, and actual physical flight. While not every problem confronting HWP characters explicitly confronts them with racism or racial inequality, we argue that their White precarity and resultant responses to all conflict are racialized and enact White fragility. Finally, while these terms have been theorized in relation to the United States or North America, as we argue in chapter 1, we see them as transatlantic phenomena (Garner 2017, 1588–1589).

We do not claim that the White audiences watching and enjoying these shows explicitly condone the politics and policies of the Far Right. Nor do we suggest that the shows' creators are purposefully propagating White supremacy in service of fascism or the Right's ascension. Rather, we understand these shows as part of a *progressive* swing in televisual representation, responding to critiques like #oscarssowhite and working to include pressing social issues into their narratives, while developing more diverse, complex representations of contemporary life. This is a socially progressive move, yes, but it is also a business decision to try to attract increasingly dispersed and distracted affluent, subscription-paying audiences, as we trace in chapter 1. These shows thus fall victim to familiar critiques of liberal political activism and its historical blind spots around race and intersectionality (see, for example, Crenshaw 1991; P. Collins 2012).

"Use a Coaster, Damnit!" The White Possessive Investment in Housing

The Great Recession—the global financial crisis precipitated in part by collapsing housing bubbles in places like Ireland and the United States in 2007–2008—is a convenient marker for the beginning of the era of cultural crisis in which Horrible White People shows emerged and that set the stage for the global resurgence of the Far Right. In its no-holds-barred attack on basic tenets of the middle-class American Dream—a heteronormative nuclear family, job security, and fair access to home ownership—the US version of the recession laid bare the foundational fictions of that dream. Horrible White People shows visualize that attack through symbolic aesthetic choices in the production design of characters' homes, like lighting, sets, and props. Far-Right political parties in the United States and Europe reemerged in part by appealing to voters through rhetorics of nationalism and anti-immigration that attempted to reclaim those fictions, best exemplified in Donald Trump's campaign slogan, "Make America Great Again," or Britain's Leave mantra, "Take Back Control." Those calls to action are most often presented as economic imperatives to take back jobs, reduce unfair foreign competition, and protect local workers from outsourcing or immigrants allegedly driving down wages, but they also tend to turn into racialized attacks on marginalized communities. "Festering resentment is transposed onto readily available others—elites, globalists, immigrants, Muslims—who can be figured as scapegoats and sacrificed to restore order and cohesion" (M. Richardson 2017, 749). So at the core of these calls to action is a racialized identity in which White people belong and anyone else is a threat.

The political Right might more or less openly acknowledge this racist rhetoric (or at least refuse to repudiate it, as Donald Trump did, for example, in the wake of a violent White-supremacist demonstration in Charlottesville, Virginia, in August 2017). But all White people have what George Lipsitz (1998) calls a "possessive investment in whiteness." Whiteness "never has to speak its name, never has to acknowledge its role as an organizing principle in social and cultural relations" (1). It is Whiteness's invisibility that exerts its power in the representations of White liberals on Horrible White People shows, where the economic consequences of recession create personal crisis and lead to racial consolidation. Lauren Berlant argues that fantasies like the American Dream are "the means by which people hoard idealizing theories and tableaux about how they and the world 'add up to something.' What happens when those fantasies start to fray—depression, dissociation, pragmatism, cynicism, optimism, activism, or an incoherent mash?" (2011, 2). That incoherent mash, dominated by depression and cynicism, is the prevailing affective mode for the main characters of Horrible White People shows who are confronted with frayed fantasies of secure, well-paid employment and affordable home ownership.

On *Girls*, the show that provoked the cycle, Hannah Horvath's fledgling writing career is based on her ability to work for free, and indeed the series opens with Hannah feeling betrayed when her parents say they won't continue to subsidize her New York City apartment (S1E1). *Girls'* themes of failure, "imperfection," and inadequacy have been written about extensively,[2] but its frayed fantasies are visible across the HWP cycle. *Search Party'*s pilot episode similarly includes twenty-something Dory's boring, unfulfilling work as a personal assistant to a wealthy Manhattan socialite, highlighting the generational gap in wealth and possibility. *Broad City* addresses the same clash between older, wealthy, postfeminist women and underemployed, ostensibly more progressive younger women. In "Stolen Phone" (S1E6), Abbi loses her phone and follows it to the Upper East Side, which she and Ilana describe as "a horrible, vapid wasteland," approaching it tentatively and clutching each other as they walk. There, they observe in horror middle-aged White women in tweed complaining about the problems of the excessively wealthy. One woman laments, for instance, "That makes ten horses I had to replace." The scene is one of many examples of how the girls' friendship works to highlight and critique affluent, out-of-touch Whiteness as well as race and class inequality (some people even read this scene as a subtle jab at postfeminist poster child *Sex and the City'*s celebration of upper-class White femininity), while distancing themselves from complicity in that Whiteness (for more on this, see chapter 3). In this example, and more broadly across the cycle, White central characters, mostly women, manage to align themselves against the indisputable evils of overt racism or wealth so vast that it seems useful for nothing other than replacing outrageously expensive pets. But while making that alignment, Abbi and Ilana, Dory, Hannah Horvath, and all of the Horrible White People we analyze almost always fail to acknowledge the much more difficult truths of the relative ease granted them by family wealth, college education, and other benefits of their middle-class White identity—a social status and level of cultural capital that does not disappear because they are broke at the moment we enter their stories.

While those girls might be excused for being a bit adrift in their early twenties, the trauma with which three thirty-something couples on *You're the Worst* confront their own losses of relationships and jobs makes the layers of class, race, and gender privilege of their characters explicit. "You Knew It Was a Snake" (S3E12) traps the show's six main characters in Jimmy's home—the expensive, "architecturally significant" house snares all three couples inside it like an underwater mortgage—and cuts between their arguments as all the couples break up. The otherwise visually dynamic show becomes static in this episode, cutting from medium close-up to medium close-up within and between arguments. The uniformly pale blue of the home's walls connects all the arguments and contributes to the episode's claustrophobia and the banality of each character's complaints implied by their interchangeability. The enormous windows overlooking the Silverlake Reservoir that frame much of the action could provide the image with the warmth of a sunny Los Angeles day. Instead, they provide an overexposed, almost white backdrop that, like the wall color, ties together the interior spaces and, by washing out the exterior that might offer an escape, amplifies the sense of being trapped in the circular cuts among the three arguments. Of the episode's three fights, Dorothy and Edgar's makes White liberal pain at sharing privilege completely overt. A thirty-ish struggling actress whose years of attempts to break into comedy writing have failed, Dorothy met Edgar, a Latino war veteran, when he enrolled in her improv comedy class. Arriving home from one of her many low-paid gig-based jobs, this one cleaning up after a "colonial bros and Nava-hoes"–themed fraternity party ("I cleaned up the vomit, but the racism and cultural appropriation are going to leave a stain," she reports), she wakes up Edgar, and they begin their episode-long dispute about Edgar's rapid success in comedy. "You know I'm happy for you," Dorothy begins. "I mean, shit, I'm a liberal. God knows I should applaud when an underrepresented voice gets heard." When Edgar challenges the idea that he was hired only because he is Latino, she responds with the cliché, "Of course not. I don't even see race." We dwell on the dialogue of this scene because it is so familiar; comments like these are common from White people who believe in their own antiracism and espouse the colorblind ideology of postracial "sameness," which Sarah Nilsen and Sarah Turner (2014) describe as enabling the continuation of racial apathy. If no one sees race, no action is needed now; throughout the cycle, characters' dialogue shows us their *awareness* of racial inequality and White privilege, which is thus represented as an end in itself.

As Dorothy and Edgar's argument continues, Edgar pushes back against Dorothy, this time by pointing to the pastries she has brought back from a Mexican bakery. For the rest of the episode, clearly upset

Figure I.1. *Top:* Gretchen and Jimmy argue in his bedroom, while Lindsay and Paul break up in the living room. *Bottom:* Edgar and Dorothy argue. (Stills from *You're the Worst*; screenshots by the authors).

by being confronted with her own negative reactions and assumptions about Edgar's success, Dorothy rants tearfully about the misogyny she has faced in a Hollywood obsessed with youth and a comedy industry dominated by men. For her, the argument becomes a competition about who has been the most oppressed, White women or men of color (mirroring the 2008 US presidential primary election between Hillary Clinton and Barack Obama in that respect). Blinded by her own frustrations and work-related failures, she rehashes every hypocritical liberal cliché: she supports affirmative action despite "slightly less qualified" people of color being hired over White candidates; she insists that women have it worse than men do, regardless of race or ethnicity; and finally she asserts that straight White men are the real villains. The argument is finally clinched when Edgar, standing in front of the American flag tacked to his bedroom wall, shouts, "Maybe you only like me when I'm struggling. . . . I mean, what if I did make something of myself? Hm? If I did rise up there to your level, why? Why would that be so bad?" Crying, and literalizing the sentiments of White precarity, Dorothy shouts back, "Because. I am not up there. OK? I am down. I am the downest that I have ever been." Dorothy embodies Robin James's argument that "inclusion [of people of color] is always conditional and always instrumental. . . . People of color are admitted to white supremacy only insofar as this augments white supremacy; the moment this becomes a bad deal for white supremacy, it ends" (2015, 13). Furthermore, Dorothy's characterization of affirmative action as hiring "slightly less qualified" people of color frames any action taken to remedy structural White supremacy as a gift given by White people to others. This frame imagines racial equality as a zero-sum game in which if someone gains, someone else has to lose (Norton and Sommers 2011). Dorothy knows she is meant to be supportive of her boyfriend's success but cannot envision it as anything other than causing her own failure. Diegetically, Dorothy is talking about her failure to secure a steady job in comedy, but her dialogue throughout the episode reveals exactly the arguments we want to make about liberal middle-class White characters confronted with precarity for the first time. This is precisely the position at the heart of White liberals' complicity with the rise of the Right: the inability of those self-professed White liberals to continue (or start) to enact their progressive politics when their own comfortably institutionalized power must be shared or relinquished to do so.

Similar to Dorothy, the young White characters on all these shows continually express their frustration at a lack of access to markers of middle-class status, like jobs and home ownership, which they presumed were their natural right. The location of Dorothy and Edgar's fight is noteworthy because Jimmy, a stalled novelist, used all the proceeds from his first book to purchase the beautiful midcentury-modern home in one of Los Angeles's affluent, hilly, east side neighborhoods. The home itself, as on many Horrible White People shows, works to quickly establish the characters' class status. Horrible White People's relationships to these homes—whether they rent or own them and whether they can comfortably afford them or are struggling to pay mortgages—reflect the diminished promises of the middle-class American Dream of home ownership. The trauma with which White characters meet the loss of easily accessible home ownership across this cycle reveals the internalized assumption that those homes were an unquestionable part of their class identity. That threatened feeling or realization of "cruel optimism" then becomes exploitable by Trumpian rhetoric about taking back jobs and restoring America to a fictional past in which White people don't have to struggle.

In Lauren Berlant's argument that "cruel optimism" is a defining affect of the early twenty-first century, she maintains that "the fantasies that are fraying include, particularly, upward mobility, job security, political and social equality, and lively, durable intimacy" (2011, 3). The narrative arcs of the shows in the cycle often place viewers in the middle of those cruel optimisms. The pilot episode of *Girlfriends' Guide to Divorce*, for example, begins with a long-married couple, Abby and Jake, clinging to the fantasy of heterosexual monogamy, despite their marriage being in shambles. This particular fantasy is also the basis of Abby's lucrative career as an author of relationship guides and thus by extension her higher-earning, higher-status position in the relationship that invokes contemporary corporate feminism as another culprit for the breakup of the relationship. The optimism of a nonpatriarchal marriage of equals is followed swiftly by the cruel revelation of its failure when Jake climbs back into bed in the early hours of the morning, fresh from sex with his girlfriend, in order to hide their separation from their kids. Abby's marriage and career and the fantasy they represent are thus destroyed in the program's first scene. In another example, a recently divorced mother and her teenage daughter have to move in with a brother recovering from a suicide attempt after cashing out of the tech industry in *Casual*. In the same vein, *You're the Worst*'s Gretchen, a late-twenties music promoter in Los Angeles, lives in a messy, barely furnished, typical LA concrete-box apartment, far from the enormous size and stylish production design of earlier single women sitcoms like *Friends* (NBC, 1994–2004) or *The Mary Tyler Moore Show* (CBS, 1970–1777). Lipsitz uses "the adjective *possessive* to stress the relationship between Whiteness and asset accumulation in our society, to connect attitudes to interests, to demonstrate that White supremacy is usually less a matter of direct, referential, and snarling contempt and more a system for protecting the privileges of Whites by denying communities of color opportunities for asset accumulation and upward mobility" (1998, viii). The lush, detailed production design and extravagant on-location houses central to the pleasurable appeal of these shows often explicitly visualize this possessive investment in the accumulative privileges of Whiteness. On *Casual* (S3E9), Alex lashes out at his coworkers for altering and ultimately (in his mind) disrespecting his lavish modern house when using it for a photo shoot with a popular YouTube vlogger. In an on-the-nose moment of self-reflexivity typical to this cycle, Alex's Asian Airbnb roommate tells him after his tantrum, "You know, it's actually kinda funny because your identity is so tied to this house, and it's like basically getting torn apart." Similarly, *You're the Worst*'s Jimmy is hyperprotective of his posh Los Angeles home, constantly telling guests to use coasters and pick up after themselves.[3] In a telling example of this obsession with domestic possessions, to convince Lindsay that Jimmy has indeed run away from his life after all the show's couples have broken up, Edgar points out that he has redecorated by adding house plants—a gesture of warmth completely contrary to Jimmy's personality—as well as haphazardly tacking an American flag to the wall of the living room, and Lindsay is immediately convinced that Jimmy has disappeared (S4E1). Together these examples tie White characters' possessive investment in material things to their sense of identity, worth, and self.

The shock with which characters on *Casual*, *You're the Worst*, *Catastrophe*, and *Girlfriends' Guide to Divorce* react when their ability to pay mortgages on impossibly expensive, gorgeous urban homes is threatened by divorce or lack of employment betrays their assumption that their class and their (invisible to them) racial privilege owe them home ownership. *Divorce* literalizes this fear, making Robert, the husband in the titular separation, a failed property developer forced to live in an unfinished house with no plumbing when he moves out of the family home. The fact that none of these White characters actually lose their luxury, architect-designed homes further emphasizes the housing privilege built into middle- and upper-class White identity as a result of long-term federal housing policies that openly discriminated against Black buyers and other people of color shopping for homes, as well as the familial asset accumulation common to middle- and upper-middle-class White families that allows *Casual*'s Valerie and her daughter to move into Alex's home. On the LA-set programs in this cycle, the houses featured are either midcentury-modern California homes (*Casual*, *You're the Worst*, *Transparent*) or larger, more contemporary homes that emulate that style (*Girlfriends' Guide to Divorce*). Of course, this is a prominent architectural mode in affluent areas of Los Angeles, but it is also noteworthy that these mid-twentieth-century homes reference precisely the post–World

War II historical moment in which the federal government subsidized suburban home ownership for Whites, while blocking the same advantages from Black and other people of color (Rothstein 2017).

Furthermore, even though Latino immigrants and working-class African Americans were the more direct targets of subprime lending that helped cause the housing bubble and subsequent recession (Oliver 2008), well-off White Americans, exemplified by these Horrible White People, got a real taste, perhaps their first, of capitalistic exploitation. That experience, newly forced upon them by recession and the sheer surprise of a challenge to rights that these characters, in their ignorance of their own White supremacy, assumed were universal, led to their increased sense of victimization. Significantly, the foregrounding of White people struggling with their sense of entitlement to home ownership is rendered quite relative and inconsequential when compared to the housing crises on shows like *Chewing Gum* (E4, 2015–2017) and *Atlanta* (FX, 2016–), where working-class Black characters face homelessness and eviction from their public housing or rental properties, after being kicked out by parents and losing their job, respectively. Nevertheless, however bleak or dark the Horrible White People shows get, they continue to focus on White precarity. And while this centrality is arguably the result of television's continued investment in fostering an "identification with the fictions of whiteness" (Lipsitz 1998, 99), it also has to do with the cycle's engagement with postracial discourse, or more specifically the *sense* of victimization experienced not by Black people but by White people, which was exacerbated by continuous news and representations of undeniable racial inequality and racialized violence across television culture. It is not coincidental that fictional beleaguered, exhausted White people spread across television screens at the same time as images of black and brown children victimized by state violence spread across the news.

Liberals Who "Don't See Race": The Breakdown of the Postracial Mystique

The media environment in which Horrible White People shows exist also includes film and television that makes visible precisely the structures that retain privileges for White people while actively disenfranchising people of color. One prominent example is Ava DuVernay's documentary *13th* (Netflix, 2016), about the history of continued mass incarceration of Black people (mostly men) in the United States. The film was so widely praised as essential viewing for people interested in racial justice in the United States that Netflix made it available to stream free of charge for "classrooms, community groups, book clubs, and other educational settings" (McNary 2017). On more traditional television channels, programs like *The People v. O. J. Simpson* (FX, 2016) and a remake of the 1977 docudrama *Roots* (History, 2016) address racist histories and consequences directly, while shows like *Master of None* (Netflix, 2016–), *Black-ish* (ABC, 2014–), *Jane the Virgin* (CW, 2014–2019), *Being Mary Jane* (BET, 2013–2019), *Fresh Off the Boat* (ABC, 2015–), *Queen Sugar* (Own, 2016–), *Insecure* (HBO, 2016–), and *Atlanta* (FX, 2016–), among others, represent culturally specific experiences of people of color in the United States with varying degrees of sharp critique. These programs also help clarify, in sheer numerical terms, how much *more* Horrible White People content exists than content that centralizes culturally specific people of color (M. Ryan 2016; Fallon 2016; Smith, Choueiti, and Pieper 2016).[4] The televisual industrial logics of this inequality are discussed in detail in chapters 1 and 4, but these relatively few programs that overtly address their characters' racial identity, regardless of context, contribute to the definitive conclusion that the always-false ideology of a postracial America is no longer believable. This disruptive shock for White people, coupled with the bleak realities of the recession, produces characters that cling more tightly to their possessive investment in Whiteness.

To fully understand the representation of White people's sense of victimization and failure in these shows, we need to highlight their interest and investment in being postrace, which was seemingly confirmed with the election of the United States' first Black president in 2008 but was quickly destroyed by 2015 when Donald Trump began his explicitly racist presidential campaign. Postracial ideology, what Catherine R. Squires (2014) calls the "post-racial mystique," had, for at least a decade, perpetuated a fantasy that the United States had finally solved its "race problem" once and for all. In 2012, however, seventeen-year-old Trayvon Martin, who was Black, was murdered by George Zimmerman; Zimmerman was acquitted for shooting the unarmed teenager. The story was national news for months and ignited protests online and rallies and marches in over one hundred cities across the United States (Williams 2013). It was Martin's death and Zimmerman's acquittal that spurred the activists Alicia Garza, Opal Tometi, and Patrisse Cullors to found Black Lives Matter, "an ideological and political intervention in a world where Black lives are systematically and intentionally targeted for demise. It is an affirmation of Black folks' contributions to this society, our humanity, and our resilience in the face of deadly oppression" (Garza, n.d.). By the summer of 2014, grass-roots organization, occasional protests, and a deep fatigue with the constant barrage of police violence against unarmed Black men reached a head. When Michael Brown, another unarmed Black teenager, was shot by Darren Wilson, a White police officer, in Ferguson, Missouri, the protests that followed lasted weeks and shaded into violence in Ferguson, while angry but peaceful protests spread across the country again (see Buchanan et al. 2015). It was the violent rebellion in Ferguson, perhaps, that finally extinguished even the most optimistic or willfully blind belief in a postracial America. Yet White people clung to the postracial mystique by propagating the reactionary, out-of-touch "All Lives Matter" refrain, not in an explicitly racist way but rather under the guise of being more inclusive and "beyond race."

Squires notes that the term "postrace" "emerged in popular discourse at a time when the human genome project 'proved' that there aren't 'different races'; that we humans are more alike than different; that race is a social construct, not a constituent element of humanity" (2014, 5). This story fits comfortably with decades of neoliberalism that sometimes actively discards protections won by the civil rights movement with the argument that because everyone is equal, voter protections and affirmative action, for example, unfairly advantage people of color over White people. These arguments are based on a logic that assumes that everyone has equal opportunity and equal access to resources like education and employment that help foster class mobility. But those false assumptions are part of the postracial mystique that, Squires notes, fails to recognize the complex variability of race; the historical realities of people of color in the United States, including the differences among those histories; and an inability to understand the intersectionalities of race with other identity factors like class, gender, and sexuality. Indeed, Squires notes the long-standing frustration from the Left with so-called identity politics as a distraction from affiliation by class. Narratives of racial identity, or race-based inequality, Squires argues, disrupt neoliberalism's emphasis on personal achievement and hard work as the sole necessary traits to succeed in a meritocratic culture (2014, 6–9). What is essential here is that the postracial mystique, like the possessive investment in Whiteness, benefits all Whites and was endorsed or at least understood as a reality by White people across the political spectrum.

If President Obama represented the apotheosis of postracial America, even he was forced to carefully negotiate his performance of racial identity. The *Washington Post* (2016) marks the arrest of the Harvard professor Henry Louis Gates Jr. from inside his own home in Cambridge, Massachusetts, in July 2009, just six months after Obama's inauguration, as the end of Obama's ability to present himself as the postracial president. The *Post*'s 2016 recap of Obama's presidency cites this incident as the one that sent his approval ratings among White men plummeting, never to recover. And that was simply because, discussing the arrest of his personal friend Gates at a press conference, Obama criticized the White arresting officer and said, "What I think we know separate and apart from this incident is there is a long history in this country of African-Americans and Latinos being stopped by police disproportionately. That's just a fact" (Cooper 2009). This is a fact also reflected in story lines about the almost casual arrests or dodgy traffic stops of Black characters on shows like *Atlanta* (S1E2) and *Insecure* (S2E4), the Black-cast counterparts to Horrible White People shows that not only acknowledge but even normalize this racial discrimination as undeniable fact.

The key to this reporting of Gates's arrest is that even the *Post*'s analysis frames it and Obama's reaction to it in relation to White voters' responses. White men, according to this polling data, responded emotionally to a single mention of racial inequality and could never be persuaded back to Obama's corner, regardless of policy goals or outcomes. This centrality of Whiteness and sensitivity to White people's reactions to being confronted with their—often comfortably invisible to them—racialized identity and privilege is fundamental to why we are writing about Whiteness when our goal is to help dismantle White supremacy.

Ironically, this postracial mystique often expresses itself as a performance of hyperawareness of race. Returning again to *Broad City*, Ilana adheres to this form of millennial colorblind ideology in the way she "consumes" diversity through a kind of cultural tourism. When she halts a hookup with her doppelgänger because she suddenly realizes they look the same, Ilana explains that, in bed, she craves difference: "Different colors, different shapes, different sizes. People who are hotter, uglier. More smart; not more smart. Innies, outies! I don't know, a Catholic person" (S2E9). In another episode, she masturbates in a mirror wearing big gold-hoop earrings that read, in lacy script, "Latina" (see Nussbaum 2016). She fantasizes about sex with the Black pop star Rihanna, and in one episode, when she is craving "a pink dick" (i.e., a White guy), she wonders aloud to Abbi, "What could be better than a pink dick with a sense of humor?" She answers her own question with, "Well, a Black dick with a sense of humor." Together, these examples are what bell hooks calls the commodification of Otherness, which is "offered as a new delight, more intense, more satisfying than normal ways of doing and feeling. Within commodity culture, ethnicity becomes spice, seasoning that can liven up the dull dish that is mainstream white culture" (1992, 21–22). While Ilana's appreciation for diversity is often meant to signal her progressive stance on equality for all, her obliviousness to her own Whiteness and White privilege renders her politics superficial and ultimately ineffectual.

In another episode of *Broad City* (S2E2), Ilana's boss at the group-sales coupon company she is temping for tells her that she needs to make a sale or she will be fired. Even though she has no idea how to do her own job, Ilana hires four interns to do her work. In celebration of that work success, Ilana dons a white-colored 1980s-style power suit, which she proceeds to refer to for the rest of the episode as her "white power suit" as she bosses around what she calls an "ethnic smorgasbord of unpaid workers." Ilana finally becomes self-reflexive when she finds her Black female intern crouched on the floor apparently sweeping up trash and singing "Swing Low, Sweet Chariot," an African American slavery-era hymn that served as "a surreptitious alert on the Underground Railroad" (Keh 2017). Upon the realization of the intern's exploitation, Ilana, shocked, questions, "What have I become?" and quickly tells her interns to leave while promising to send their "reparations" (or payment) in the mail. Ilana's performance in the episode and the whole series is so excessive and detached from common sense that it is clearly meant to be comedic, and the bizarreness of her story lines cannot help but build polysemy into the text. Nonetheless, her exploitation of minority labor is left somewhat hanging as the episode concludes by recentralizing Ilana's struggle, as of course every episode recentralizes her and Abbi's emotional struggles and bond (see chapter 3 for more on their friendship). After Ilana becomes resigned to do the work on her own, she laments to her boss, "I was a capitalist pig, rolling around in my own fucking shit," thus focusing on her own sacrifice to work within the capitalist system, as opposed to further interrogating her complicity in the interns' oppression or the lack of real job opportunities for people of color. After all, despite incompetence, racism, and exploitation, Ilana keeps her job while her interns go home unpaid and unemployed.

The rendering of complex historical, political, and economic factors into *affective* responses from White people is also a feminizing move reminiscent of the ways television melodrama often operates as a sort of release valve for complex, taboo social issues by recasting them as personal problems, targeting female viewers and hoping for emotional responses.[5] While most of our Horrible White People shows are comedies—albeit some of them very grim comedies—in their focus on their protagonists' despair or even mental illness, they perform this same displacement of social problems onto individual, feminized, Whitened, emotional performance. *Fleabag*'s primary promotional image, a close-up of writer-star Phoebe Waller-Bridge's face, apparently immediately after a cry, her cheeks covered in trails of black mascara, is iconic of this trend. *Crazy Ex-Girlfriend*, *UnReal*, *Catastrophe*, and *You're the Worst* all exaggerate the racialized privilege of White women wallowing in emotion and the historical mandate that women of color take care of White women, by giving their protagonists long-suffering women of color as therapists. Most of these shows thus continue to perpetuate the racial hierarchy of femininity established during slavery, described by Angela Davis (1981), that allows White women to appear vulnerable and fragile, while women of color are represented as inherently tougher, never being perceived as victims on the same level as White women. Meanwhile, the longer-term non-White characters in shows like *Casual*, *Girlfriends' Guide to Divorce*, and *Crazy Ex-Girlfriend* are in fact complex, fully developed characters. They are often much more than the typical television characterization of the BBFF or what Kristen Warner

(2017b) calls "plastic representation." Sarah E. Turner (2014) coined the term "BBFF" for the "best black friend forever," who lives only to support her (or his) White friend and sacrifice her happiness or even her life to help her White friend fulfill her story arc. Part of the liberal appeal of these shows is precisely the creators' efforts to develop more diverse and complex representations of people of color beyond the BBFF. These characters are fully developed but still always secondary to the central White characters. Their explicit critique of television's politics of representation functions the same way as the characters' hyperawareness of racial inequality: to perform progressivism and mask the need for further substantive change.

Several of the shows in this cycle code themselves as progressive through their dynamic characterizations of characters of color. Edgar Quintero on *You're the Worst*, for example, explicitly critiques the trope of the BBFF. First, he gender-flips the usual feminization of the emotionally supporting and caretaking person of color, historically embodied in the mammy stereotype. Edgar cooks for Jimmy, the White male half of the show's central couple, chauffeurs him all over Los Angeles, and is routinely rebuffed when he asks for the most minor emotional support like attendance at his first improv show (S2E5). But *You're the Worst* further highlights this destructive character trope by making Edgar a nuanced character with a detailed backstory and his own plotlines. Because viewers know and sympathize with Edgar (unlike the stock-character therapists of color on some other Horrible White People shows), the emotional abuse he receives from his "best friend," Jimmy, in return for the emotional and concrete service he offers is visible and egregious; his palpable emotional pain and the inequality of his relationship with Jimmy makes the more typical "BBFF being supportive for a self-involved White friend" trope visible in a way that it may not ordinarily be. Edgar is a war veteran who is recovering from addiction and struggling with PTSD; he moves in with Jimmy because those afflictions, plus the lack of support from a Veterans Affairs health system represented as utterly dysfunctional, have left him homeless. The show's title tells viewers how to interpret the protagonists: they're the worst. So when Jimmy constantly berates and humiliates Edgar, demands his driving, cooking, and cleaning services, makes fun of his mental health problems, and never offers support apart from the grudgingly provided bedroom, viewers know that there is no oppositional reading of this relationship: Jimmy is a terrible person. On the one hand, signaling the show's liberal address, making Edgar a nuanced, sympathetic character disrupts the mammy trope that he inhabits by illustrating via contrast how pervasively gendered and lifeless a stereotype it is. Furthermore, during the show's first three seasons, we see Edgar cry, relapse into both addiction and homelessness, and calmly ask Jimmy for support. And we see the devastating emotional consequences of Jimmy's harsh denials, which always come with a bruising (but funny: it is a comedy, no matter how dark) insult. On the other hand, even when this kind of relationship calls attention to damaging representational trends by making it explicit how much Edgar is hurt by Jimmy's rebuffs and making the White protagonists look like jerks, the White characters are still clearly narratively central.

This continued centrality of White characters and their affective responses despite self-reflexive critique of liberal failure and ineptitude is the key point of our analysis in this book. In Mikhail Bakhtin's theories of the carnivalesque, he posits comedy as a vital space to work through political and social tensions, but laughter potentially also fills the void and smooths over those tensions, allowing viewers to acknowledge but not act on that which they recognize as problematic (Lachmann, Eshelman, and Davis 1988). Stuart Hall argues that "how things are represented and the 'machineries' and regimes of representation in a culture do play a *constitutive*, and not merely reflexive, after-the-event role" (1996, 443). Representational media, then, work to sustain cultural norms and maintain or even create the ideological structures in which we live. So a character trope like the mammy or the BBFF is a cultural structure, a repeated ideological representation that impacts viewers' understandings of others, particularly those with whom they don't have material experiences. These cultural structures—repeated patterns of representation—run parallel to the economic structures (for just one example) that keep people of color with less access to home ownership and intergenerational wealth accumulation than is available to White Americans. So *seeing* those structures is important. When characters on Horrible White People shows chastise middle-class White men for their attachment to their beautiful houses, as happens on *You're the Worst* and *Casual*, or when the casual racism of character stereotypes become the topic of conversation among White characters, as they often do on *Broad City* and *UnReal*, those cultural structures can become apparent even to those who benefit from them and from not acknowledging them. This kind of visibility and critique are part of the pendulum swing away from postracial and postfeminist ideology on television that denies race or gender as determining factors in success, or indeed in any life experience. We celebrate these representational moves. What this visibility or awareness does not do, however, is dismantle the power relations inherent in the original stereotype. Being a Horrible White Person, a patently despicable character, does not take away a White person's power, as we saw with Ilana's regrettable internship scheme. When confronted with Edgar's problems, Jimmy does not feel bad about being a jerk; he feels imposed on. Furthermore, Jimmy and his girlfriend, Gretchen, are still the primary couple on the show. They begin and end the title sequence; it is their love story that precipitates all other story lines; their homes are the primary sets; even when other characters have their own plotlines, they must eventually address the way their lives impact Jimmy's and Gretchen's. It is the preponderance of these kinds of story lines that centralize suffering White characters throughout the programming cycle that gives it the cultural heft that indicates it is not in fact "just entertainment" but a powerful ideological force.

Edgar offers a prominent example of the ways in which people of color are denied autonomy, support, and equality in their relationships with these shows' White protagonists, for whom they often do enormous loads of care work. While Edgar calls attention to the gendered nature of this timeworn character trope by gender-flipping it, most Horrible White People shows have women as protagonists. Casting a plethora of White women in vulnerable positions and emphasizing their excessive emotional performances are part of the common occurrence that women's bodies disproportionately express and bear the consequences of political battles but also tie this programming cycle to the decline in happy postfeminism and the emergence of multiple new feminisms in the beginning of the twenty-first century. The emotional trauma expressed by the young White women in this cycle, who are unable to find lasting heterosexual romance, well-paying jobs, and affordable home ownership, is often explicitly articulated as the result of economic crisis but is also clearly responding to a cultural shift from postfeminism to emerging feminisms and the contemporaneous changes to norms of female behavior and institutions like dating and marriage. These multiple, concurrent, interrelated cultural crises have caused upheaval among liberals and a resurgence of feminisms, a collection of circumstances that, as Sarah Banet-Weiser (2018) argues, are inextricable from and equally intertwined with the reactionary antifeminism and racism of the rising Far Right.

Dystopic Domestic Fantasies and Emergent Feminism(s)

As several feminist media scholars have noted, when Beyoncé opened the 2014 VMAs with the word "Feminist" emblazoned behind her, the spectacle seemed to signal for many a newly emerging "feminist zeitgeist" (Valenti 2014), where feminism was no longer a "dirty word" for mainstream celebrities and could even be considered "hip" (Gill 2016; see Banet-Weiser 2015). Together with other prominent stars like Emma Watson, Amy Schumer, Tina Fey, and Amy Poehler, these "celebrity feminists" (Hamad and Taylor 2015), among many others, reflect what Jessalynn Keller and Maureen Ryan describe as emergent feminism(s): "a visible shift in the relationships between feminism, identity, and politics in popular media culture" (2018, 1), a shift that is also apparent in many of the characterizations and thematic concerns of Horrible White People shows that feature complex female leads who often explicitly identify as liberal feminists or are at least constructed by the text as urban progressives. Some of the characters explicitly label themselves feminists with statements like Rachel Goldberg's "This Is What a Feminist Looks Like" T-shirt in the opening shots of *UnReal* (S1E1) or Dorothy's "I'm a liberal" statement on *You're the Worst* (S3E12). In addition, the characters' social liberalism frequently expresses itself via the embodied femininity and sexuality that are often prominent in feminist discourses. The central female characters on *Broad City*, *Fleabag*, and *You're the Worst* are all sexually active, sex-positive women; *You're the Worst* includes a nonjudgmental abortion (S3E10), while *Catastrophe*'s third season features an ongoing story line about the morning-after pill emergency contraception. *Better Things* and *One Mississippi* offer images of complex women in their forties (old for Hollywood representation) who still have romance, heartache, and sex in their lives. *One Mississippi*'s protagonist is a lesbian; *Better Things* explores a young girl and her mother beginning to discover the child's transgender/nonbinary identity and coping with that transition with love and understanding.

Prior to this shift toward explicit feminisms (a shift we, following Keller and Ryan 2018, refer to as *emergent feminisms*), the media cultures of the past two decades had reflected what Rosalind Gill (2007) describes as a "postfeminist" sensibility. Despite some contestation, most definitions of "postfeminism" united under Judith Stacey's (1987) original description of "the simultaneous incorporation, revision, and depoliticization of many of the central goals of second-wave feminism" (quoted in Dow 1996, 87). Postfeminist discourse is operationalized, then, to describe the representations of "empowered girls" (who are almost always White, straight, feminine, and upper-middle-class) in media texts that were simultaneously marked by specific themes and ideologies that seemed to run counter to the collective political goals of feminist activism. These media texts included women's magazines, advertisements, films like *Bridget Jones's Diary* (see McRobbie 2008), and TV series like *Sex and the City* (see Negra 2004), which all focused on individual empowerment, a revaluing of hegemonic femininity and heterosexuality (especially through consumerism), and an overall sense that the goals of feminism had been achieved and the political movement was no longer needed. These representations thus led to a general repudiation of "feminist" as an identity and feminism as a necessary politics in mainstream media texts for and about women. Yet, as the past few years have seen more celebrities and media makers embracing a feminist identity, drawing attention to feminist issues, and producing a heightened visibility around feminist political activism, many feminist media scholars are interrogating the potential impacts and limitations of this increased visibility and cultural attention to emergent feminism, wondering how strong a break from the dominance of the postfeminist sensibility it signals (Banet-Weiser 2015; McRobbie 2015; Gill 2016; Keller and Ryan 2018). *Horrible White People* adds to this interrogation by questioning the progress narratives that are too often associated with emergent feminism and highlighting the continued centrality of Whiteness in these emerging progressive representations.

Relatively affluent Whiteness was a key component of the postfeminist sensibility, and similarly mediated representations of feminism have always centralized the plight of heterosexual White women. As an offshoot of neoliberalism, postfeminist media representations tend to prop up the "individualized and depoliticized empowerment of girls and women, who are hailed as productive feminized workers, citizens, and mothers" (Keller and Ryan 2018, 4). And, while the "can-do" postfeminist girl (Harris 2003; see also Angela McRobbie's [2007] "top girls") is still apparent in television programming, the global economic crisis disrupted the myths and fantasies of postfeminist success in neoliberal societies, particularly the role of consumerism in displaying or exercising one's success and power. Diane Negra and Yvonne Tasker (2014) argue that recession-era media culture simply refashioned the familiar gender tropes of postfeminism into the resilient working mother (Leonard 2014) or the recessionista blogger (Nathanson 2014) while "avoiding meaningful critique of the privileged White male or the destructive aspects of Western capitalism" (Negra and Tasker 2014, 26). Yet, if Carrie Bradshaw's $400 shoes and $20 cosmopolitans were a sign of her postfeminist independence and power in *Sex and the City*, the material conditions and lived experiences of the recession made access to those fantasies seem untenable. In much the same way as secure home ownership is no longer a given for Horrible White People, a "can-do" attitude and individual entrepreneurship no longer lead to class mobility, financial stability, or happily ever after for striving young postfeminist women. Rather than save up and splurge on designer shoes, the always-broke misanthrope Gretchen steals a blender from the gift table at a wedding on *You're the Worst*. The girls on *Broad City* steal office supplies and clean a stranger's house in their underwear to try to pay for concert tickets. And Laura, the teenaged daughter from *Casual*, illustrates both her urban progressive politics and her need for money when she takes a job collecting petition signatures for ten cents a name, in order to save up for tattoo removal. The seamless mixture of ultimately meaningless liberal outrage (Laura learns the environmentally friendly ballot initiative that she thought she was supporting is actually fronted by an oil company) and frivolous or cosmetic personal pursuits reminds us of Abbi's laser hair removal on inauguration day and represents the uneasy transitions between consumerist postfeminism and more politically engaged emergent feminisms that may yet yearn for the lost easy access to consumerist satisfactions. Another, more desperate financial gambit happens over the course of several episodes of *Fleabag* when the unnamed protagonist steals a small sculpture from her stepmother's home to try to sell it to raise cash to support her failing café.

Fleabag's empty, financially draining London café is a symbol of the character's complete emotional breakdown, as well as serving as a representation of the impossibility of the neoliberal fantasy of emerging from austerity and financial crisis via individual resilience and entrepreneurship. In a review of Amy Schumer's 2015 romantic comedy *Trainwreck*, Anne Helen Petersen (2015) finds similarities between it and a series of postrecession women's media such as *The Mindy Project* (Fox, 2012–2015; Hulu, 2015–2018), *Young Adult* (2011), *Bachelorette* (2012), *Girls*, and *Bridesmaids* (2011) that she describes as "postfeminist dystopias," which have collapsed the mythology that women can find happiness through depoliticized consumer identities or traditionally coupled, happy heterosexuality. She writes, "What used to be the narrative backbone of the perfect rom-com looks increasingly gnarled, unseemly, undesirable." Petersen is one of many critics to notice a changing affect in media representations or the way political, economic, and cultural transformations are changing the realm of social identities and interactions (Ticineto Clough and Halley 2007) and the ordinary dimensions of everyday life (Stewart 2007). As Keller and Ryan summarize, affect theories constitute a reckoning with what neoliberalism, and by extension postfeminism, makes people into and how they rationalize, cope with, or adapt to the feelings of precariousness that neoliberalism produces (2018, 10). Horrible White People shows wallow in the negative emotional consequences of precarity. They break from the utopian fantasies of family sitcoms, focusing instead on what Sianne Ngai (2007) calls "ugly feelings," or negative affects that speak directly to the disillusionment with postfeminism and neoliberalism more broadly as a result of the recession and the dissolution of other sociopolitical myths like the postracial mystique and the American Dream. This cycle of programming almost universally dwells within Petersen's dystopic vision of the world, in which domestic settings and romantic coupling no longer provide financial or emotional security.

Out of all the moments of domestic dystopia in the Horrible White People cycle, perhaps none is more symbolic than the conclusion of *You're the Worst*'s season 3 premiere. In this episode Lindsay, newly pregnant with her first child, is so horrified by the vision of decades of mundane married life ahead of her that she stabs her pudgy and pain-fully boring yet loyal husband Paul. Earlier in the episode, Paul teased Lindsay with a large gift-wrapped box he won't let her open until the special evening he has planned. When Lindsay prances into the kitchen that evening, dressed for a night out, she is devastated when she learns her gift is to cook a meal "as a family." As she prepares a "hominy and poblano-pepper pozole" ordered from Red Napkin (a thinly veiled refer-ence to Blue Apron, the meal kit delivery service incredibly popular with affluent white working professionals), Lindsay's distress is clear on her face as she chops mushrooms without watching what she's doing. When Paul says, "I'm so happy I get to do this with you, forever wife," Lindsay is not comforted by the postfeminist dreams of a comfortable suburban life, impending motherhood, and long-term stability. Instead, she's dis-appointed and frankly terrified at her lost independence, feeling trapped into an ideal to which she is utterly unsuited—encapsulated by the fact she doesn't know what an apron is and mistakenly calls it a nape-ron. As the scene builds, Lindsay's chopping becomes angrier and more frantic, the camera closes in on her face and cuts more and more quickly be-tween her face and the still image of a happy-looking older couple on the iPhone docked nearby playing a podcast about birdwatching. The now frantic pace cuts between close-ups of the couple and Lindsay's face, punctuated by the loud, blind, rhythmic chopping of her knife on the cutting board, with Paul quietly droning on in the background. Abruptly the chopping sound drops out as the scene cuts to a wide shot of the kitchen as she turns silently, shoves her chopping knife into her unsus-pecting husband's side and returns to her task, finally looking calm as Paul screams from behind her and outside the frame. In this moment, violent action is the only escape Lindsay sees from the postfeminist vi-sion to which she is supposed to aspire. Over the course of the rest of the season, she has an abortion without consulting her husband, she and Paul divorce, she suddenly realizes she'll have to get a job, and she becomes briefly homeless, crashing at Jimmy's before moving into Doro-thy's abandoned studio apartment. Lindsay's storyline thus neatly sum-marizes the conjuncture of all the dominant fears of the era of White precarity central to this cycle of programing.

Horrible White People shows focus on liberals confronting the struc-tures keeping their hegemonic power in tact while seeing the normal-

Figure I.2. Paul and Lindsay prepare a meal kit before she stabs him. (Still from *You're the Worst*; screenshot by the authors).

ized neoliberal dreams, to which they have aspired for decades, collapse around them. In wallowing in their despair, these characters consolidate their identity around a gendered Whiteness, often obscuring or overshadowing the plight of characters of color around them. The large scale of this programming cycle and its address to middle- and upper-class audiences highlight how educated, urban-dwelling, White liberals, who are presumed to mobilize for civil rights and vote for left-leaning politicians, often react with an ineffectual fear that neither returns them to their former status and security nor leaves room to organize for those whom they claim to support. The rest of this book looks more closely at the intertwined narratives of representations of White victimhood and emotional responses to hardship, TV's generic patterns, and shifting industry norms of production and distribution. Ultimately, we argue that these representations and business practices mirror and help reproduce the ineffectual responses of liberals and progressives to growing class- and race-based inequalities and that they are indeed part of a broadly neoliberal economy and ideology that continue to worsen those divides.

1

Peak TV and the Spreadability of Transatlantic Horrible White People

The first-season finale of the Horrible White People show *Fleabag* follows the unnamed protagonist (played by the writer/creator Phoebe Waller-Bridge, referred to throughout as "Fleabag") to her godmother-cum-stepmother's "Sex-hibition." At the art show, Fleabag experiences a series of brutally comic affronts by the people in her life—her self-aggrandizing and passive-aggressive godmother, her cuckolded ex-boyfriend, her dumb but ridiculously attractive date, and especially her distant and disbelieving sister—affronts that together culminate in the final reveal of Fleabag's heart-wrenching betrayal of her beloved friend Boo; that betrayal led to Boo's accidental suicide and spurred Fleabag's guilt-ridden cycle of grief underwriting the series' whole first season. The season finale thus reflects the dark, bleak humor of the Horrible White People cycle, in which disturbing subjects like suicide, depression, and grief are probed for humorous effect to appeal to a discerning demographic of television viewers looking for complex or intelligent comedies. The art gallery where the exhibition takes place is all blue light and cold white angles. The modernist architecture of the glass wall interrupted by steel girders frames an expansive view of London, with St. Paul's Cathedral forming the center of the backdrop.[1] The architecture is noteworthy because it forges an aesthetic link to the domestic architecture of midcentury Los Angeles homes in *You're the Worst*, *Transparent*, and *Casual* that represent both the class address and symbolic representations of the possessive investment in Whiteness (discussed in the introduction and chapter 2) common in Horrible White People shows. The episode also lampoons the self-indulgent and pretentious (in these representations) high-art setting, where, for example, the stepmother's first piece is the bidet that accidentally gave her her first orgasm at age eleven and a half and where her self-described most "profound piece yet" is simply an empty pedestal with the title card "A Woman Robbed"—standing literally for a stolen sculpture of a naked woman's torso that now supposedly symbolizes "all the women of the world who have been robbed of their freedom, of their happiness, and in the saddest of cases, of their bodies." This parodic pretension parallels that in *I Love Dick*, where, for just one example, a single brick on a pedestal is revered as a work of art, and when that same brick is knocked over, its broken pieces are simply collected and retitled as an entirely new sculpture. On *Better Things*, the protagonist overtly discusses and navigates high- and low-art taste cultures in her role as an actor and acting teacher, distinguishing between mass-market commercial work and what she sees as more fulfilling "artistic" work, often joking about how rare the latter really is (S2E6). Continuous references to specific cultural knowledge and taste, as in these examples, applies to the entire Horrible White People cycle. In particular, Fleabag's condescending, self-reflexive judgment of her godmother and her art reproduces the tenor of snarky pop-culture references and declarative judgments of taste across the cycle and even implicates viewers directly in those judgments with the taboo-crossing intimacy (which often celebrates social, bodily, and physical abjection, another feature of the cycle) of its direct address (Woods 2019). The art installation is pretentious, but the understanding of it as pretentious is the basis for the shared taste culture of the Horrible White People cycle. Because the show's comic sensibility makes fun of an elitist aesthetic posturing, audiences are expected to understand the art discourse in order to then understand or appreciate the joke's critical lens. This kind of "inside joke" has the "the capacity to create in-groups and out-groups" and is usually particularly important at the level of nation (Jensen and Sienkiewicz 2018, 239), because comedy plays a key part of uniting diverse people into an "imagined community" (B. Anderson 1991) that shares common mores and ideas. Yet, even though these shows stem from different national contexts, they all explicitly acknowledge this shared comedic taste culture. The subject of this chapter is the creation of taste cultures based on race and class that supersede national borders and align with changing contemporary TV technologies and production models that emphasize quality television programming and transnational distribution.

Examples like *Fleabag*'s art installation suggest how television comedy, often relegated to the inferior cultural position of superficial entertainment rather than serious art (Mills 2004; Double 2005), as well as being understood as nationally specific and somewhat untranslatable across national cultures (Mills and Horton 2016, 38), has become a strategic transnational export. As nuanced modes of distinction become ever more important in the era of "Peak TV" (see especially Lotz 2018), a specific type of bleak television comedy is being mobilized as a way for cable networks and streaming portals to target an emergent "imagined community" or "coalition audience" (J. Collins 1992)[2] of upper-middle-class comedy consumers: "those who have assembled high cultural capital resources via socialization, education and occupation, [and] are activating these reserves through distinct modes of comic consumption" (Friedman 2011, 367). The introduction situated the renewed possessive investment in Whiteness in the context of recession, postracial fantasies, and conflicted notions of postfeminism and reemergent feminisms. In this chapter, we argue that increasingly international models of TV distribution via streaming video on demand (SVOD) contribute to the creation of a transnational collective identity based on shared taste cultures and feelings of White precarity and that the version of horrible self-proclaimed liberal Whiteness we analyze is a transatlantic phenomenon.

In the following sections, we establish comedy's traditional relationship to national identity and then argue that in the era of Peak TV and global streaming platforms, Horrible White People characters expand that national context, as they are designed to sell subscriptions on both sides of the Atlantic. Thus, in keeping with the arguments throughout the book, this chapter illustrates that the structural White supremacy represented and unconsciously supported by well-meaning, self-identifying liberal White characters is not a phenomenon confined to the United States but rather travels and grows along the same routes as distribution patterns necessitated by a changing twenty-first-century TV industry. Unlike popular-press common sense that frames SVODs as "disruptors" in the vein of other tech companies (Jarvey 2019; A. Richardson 2011), this chapter argues that Horrible White People shows reflect the persistent industrial logics that centralize "quality" TV and its historically presumed White audiences.

A Different Kind of Cultural Forum

As both casual consumers and media studies scholars can attest, television transformed dramatically in the 2010s. The technological innovations of internet-based TV and the resultant upheavals in the industry's processes of development and distribution have created oceans of content and a constantly updating collection of ways to watch. Amanda Lotz (2018) characterizes this as nothing short of a revolution. As the sheer quantity of television programming and distribution outlets has continued to increase, it can feel impossible to find shared cultural reference points. In that milieu, older formulations of television as a cultural forum (Newcomb and Hirsch 1983), a place where an entire nation shares cultural experiences and hashes out complex or taboo ideological changes or differences, have fallen out of favor.[3]

Nonetheless, despite a massive surge in the quantity of programming and a proliferation of ways to watch and subscribe, a certain ideological cohesion is particularly apparent in the spread of Horrible White People shows across a variety of television distribution platforms and national contexts. Rather than the mass national audience of historical broadcasting models, these seemingly niche programs nonetheless create an imagined community based on associations of class, taste, and race rather than local geography. Faye Woods (2019) writes about these shows, which she calls "comedies of discomfort," as a specifically transatlantic phenomenon, albeit with clear roots in their specific national comedy histories. Despite the dispersion of this type of comedy, it is highly sought after by networks and online streaming portals seeking viewers to support their services and/or advertisers on both sides of the Atlantic. Pierre Bourdieu argues that taste is a key marker of social status: "all cultural practices . . . and preferences in literature, painting, or music, are closely linked to educational level . . . and secondarily to social origin. . . . Taste classifies, and it classifies the classifier" (1984, 1, 6). Similarly, Herbert Gans (1974) suggests that individuals who make similar aesthetic choices aggregate into what he calls "taste publics." Taste publics are based on consumers' choices and are rooted in similar values and aesthetic standards, which are connected to shared subcultural backgrounds or taste cultures. Affiliated groups then flaunt their moral and aesthetic preferences (as Fleabag does with her conspiratorial but contemptuous direct-address asides about her godmother's art) through similar selections in reading, music, TV, movies, painting, brunch (as we will see later), and other arts and entertainment. Bourdieu and Gans, then, posit a collective identity based on the cultural products people consume (or advertise that they consume) and signal identity factors like class and education, to which we add race in order to name and render visible Whiteness's typical invisibility or tendency to presume its own universality (Dyer 1997). Television studies scholars mobilize the concept of a taste public (albeit without necessarily using Gans's or Bourdieu's words) in the discourse of "quality" TV and audiences. That discourse has existed in the US TV industry at least since the 1970s, when Nielson ratings began disaggregating viewer numbers into increasingly specific demographic categories, enabling the creation of programming specifically designed to target an imagined "quality" audience (Gitlin 2000; Feuer, Kerr and Vahimagi 1985). The quality audience, as historically imagined, is relatively affluent, educated, politically and socially left-leaning, and—although typically unspoken—White. As TV regulation and technology have massively increased distribution outlets, that imagined "quality" audience has shifted to incorporate, for certain "edgy," aesthetically innovative shows, a transnational identity paralleling contemporary distribution and, we argue, emphasizing the durability and spreadability of the version of self-proclaimed liberal Whiteness analyzed in this book.

In a study analyzing British comedy taste and modes of cultural distinction, building on Bourdieu's theories of the social stratification of aesthetic taste, Sam Friedman suggests that culturally privileged comedy consumers—those consumers with "cultural capital resources" obtained through "the 'structured' conditions of an individual's *habitus*, the process of cultural socialization, whereby children from the dominant classes (middle and upper-middle class) are inculcated with certain cultural dispositions that orientate them towards a 'natural' and embodied understanding of 'legitimate' art" (2011, 349)—look for comedy that is "intelligent," "complex," "intellectual," and most of all "clever." He adds, "They were looking for more than 'cheap pleasure,' for comedy that was not *just* funny" (359). "Good" comedy for them "provoked a wide range of emotions, and many expressed preferences for 'dark' or 'black' comedy where disturbing subjects are probed for humorous effect" (360).

For Friedman's respondents, "an inability to appreciate 'darker' humor usually indicated a less critical and nuanced comic appreciation" (360), so for him this focus on and appreciation of dark and resonant comedy has "strong echoes" of Bourdieu's (1984, 32–48) "disinterested aesthetic" of the privileged classes. The elements of dark or black comedy, and comedy that is more or other than "just" funny, are definitive elements of Horrible White People shows. The understanding of people who appreciate that kind of grim humor as sophisticated and critical also mimics the collusion between Fleabag and her viewers around the taste on display at her stepmother's art exhibit. The structures of cultural socialization that create the dominant class and its taste are also historically racialized structures that elevate culturally White taste to "good" taste, and while Friedman writes about British comedy consumers, we posit that the taste culture he maps is a transnational one.

Supporting our argument for a British/American taste public, Michele Hilmes (2012) argues that the "Anglo-American axis" is constitutive of the two nations' entire broadcast history, making this transatlantic cycle just one iteration of that complex web of influence. The promotional trailer for season 3 of the Horrible White People show *Catastrophe* acknowledges this when one half of the central, London-based catastrophic couple tries to explain her erratic behavior to her American partner, spluttering, "It's a tough time. There's a lot of—Brexit, you know. Your new president." Her quip illustrates the tight cultural ties between Donald Trump's election and Britain's secession from the European Union, which are often discussed in the same breath, reflecting a sort of commonsense understanding that the allies' "special relationship" extends to the similar economic, social, cultural, and political circumstances that led to these two right-wing, supposedly populist votes (see Ouellette and Banet-Weiser 2018; Graff, Kapur, and Walters 2019). Hilmes further argues, "British and American broadcasting together constitute a unified system, a powerful symbiotic machine of cultural influence that has spread long tentacles around the globe and affected the ways that culture is practiced and understood far outside the boundaries of these two nations alone: what I call the *transnational cultural economy* of British and American broadcasting" (2012, 4). While our focus in this book is primarily on the US television industrial context, the texts we analyze are crafted within a consciously transnational television industry and

Hilmes's transnational cultural economy. *Catastrophe* and *Fleabag* are our primary examples of programming developed and produced in the United Kingdom, and it is noteworthy that both had additional financing from Amazon, with much (though not all) of their international distribution contracted for release via the streaming portal. Faye Woods (2019) makes it clear that British programming, and *Fleabag* in particular, cannot be uncritically assimilated into US cultural discourses, and while cultural specificity of both content and production contexts is key, the raced and classed position of "quality" television is similar on both sides of the Atlantic. Hilmes (2012) illustrates the history of the US industry borrowing the terms and conditions of "quality" wholesale from Britain, while Brett Mills and Erica Horton highlight the ways that US TV's cultural status in Britain shifted in the 1980s when Channel 4 in particular used imports to build "a younger more affluent" audience that came to associate its carefully chosen US imports with "quality" (2016, 36). This long history of exchange argues for a transatlantic understanding of "quality" programming, and the version of well-off, self-professed liberal Whiteness that we analyze throughout the book appears not just in the United States and Britain but around the globe.

In the same vein, the title of this chapter references Henry Jenkins, Sam Ford, and Joshua Green's (2013) concept of "spreadable media," which describes circulations of media content in a networked culture and particularly the changing technological and industrial dynamics that make content easy for people to access and disperse. The "revolutionary" technological disruptions of internet streaming platforms are a key aspect undergirding the spreadable appeal of Horrible White People shows. Following Jenkins et al. (2013, 259), we use the terms "transnational" or "transatlantic" rather that the commonly used "global" in recognition of the uneven nature of media flows, particularly the flow of comedy, which "flows globally, if generally only in one direction," and where "American and British comedies have, for decades, succeeded in finding success in a variety of global markets, with relatively little material traveling in the opposite vector" (Jensen and Sienkiewicz 2018, 240). Significantly though, early readers and commenters on this work have found Horrible White People shows in Ireland, Canada, and Australia in addition to our list of US and British programs. So, as with the whole book, we hope this chapter provides tools that others can use to expand our analysis to regions and products beyond our scope. The depictions of Whiteness in Horrible White People programming and the conception of the White "quality" audience are a demonstrably global phenomenon—one that parallels Keith Feldman's concept of the "globality of Whiteness in post-racial visual culture" (2016, 289–290). The historical legacies of colonial modernity and resultant global White supremacy (Moraña, Dussel, and Jáuregui 2008) and the often purposely veiled symbolic dynamics of postracial recentering of Whiteness that Feldman traces inform Horrible White People shows' comedic taste cultures, which foreground explicit social and political progressiveness yet also center a White precarity that shores up the hegemonic structures of White supremacy.

Significantly, the centrality of this transatlantic imagined community of elite comedy consumers and their taste culture emerges during the "postnetwork" era, that is, after the proliferation of channels and modes of distribution fractured what was once very clearly a national broadcast audience. Elana Levine wonders whether the expression "postnetwork" works in the same ways as the terms "postfeminism" and "postrace" function to cover over important work still to be done: "In this respect, postnetwork logic would argue that now that the dominance of the Big Three broadcast networks is behind us, there is no longer a need to think about television as a site of cultural struggle" (2011, 180). That is, if representational power is no longer consolidated in or monopolized by three dominant institutional voices in the United States or a public broadcaster in the United Kingdom, postnetwork television becomes more democratic and diverse (this common line of reasoning is critiqued further in chapter 4's discussion of independent and web-based TV production). Questioning this logic and the motives behind the prominence of this discourse, Levine quotes John Fiske, who argues that "television-as-culture is a crucial part of the social dynamics by which the social structure maintains itself" (Fiske 2011, 1). Extending this point, we argue that TV's contemporary technologies and business practices help maintain the social structures of White supremacy by prioritizing and centralizing the concerns and tastes of smaller, elite audiences over a mass, national audience. As George Lipsitz reminds us, television was, and we argue remains, a key venue unifying certain subjects into "an imagined community [of whiteness] called into being through appeals to white supremacy . . . and the shared experience of spectatorship" (1998, 99). This "unification" is a by-product of the historically conservative television industry grappling with the collision of new technologies, changing business strategies, and innovative storytelling that has led to a precarious era of transformation or even "revolution" called "Peak TV" (Lotz 2018).

Peak TV: The Industry of Too Much TV and "Not TV"

Speaking to both the postnetwork trends and cultural influence of the contemporary television industry, in the summer of 2015, the FX network CEO John Landgraf declared to a room full of TV critics that we had reached "Peak TV in America" (M. James 2015). "Peak TV" quickly picked up traction in the industry presses as another hagiographic descriptor, circulated by critics and academics alike, encapsulating television's evolution for the better since *The Sopranos* debuted in 1999 and even more rapidly in the 2010s. Other such titles include "The Golden Age of Television" (a term used to describe two or three previous eras as well), "The Platinum Age," "Neo-Network," "TVIV," and even the "Gilded Age" (see R. Thompson 1997; Bianculli 2016; Polan 2007; Jenner 2016; Adalian 2018). Together these labels point to a celebration of original scripted television content being distributed across broadcast, cable, and increasingly streaming video platforms, which is said to be revolutionizing the textual characteristics, industrial practices, audience behaviors, and cultural understanding of contemporary television. So, for some critics, the definition of "peak" as "the highest level or greatest degree" (*Merriam-Webster Online* 2017) captures the status of quality programming, like Horrible White People shows, ushering in another superior era for television—a far cry from the "vast wasteland," as it was once notoriously known (Minow 1961).[4] These critics praise the innovation in genre and technical effects of shows like *Game of Thrones* (HBO, 2011–2019) and *Stranger Things* (Netflix, 2016–), the intelligence and wit of *Master of None* (Netflix, 2015–) and *Silicon Valley* (HBO, 2014–2019), and the social relevance of *Veep* (HBO, 2012–2019) and *Orange Is the New Black* (Netflix, 2013–2019). Yet, in citing statistics revealing that the number of original scripted shows nearly doubled from 2009 to surpass four hundred by the end of 2015, Landgraf cautioned that the TV industry might be in a bubble (M. James 2015). If we are at the peak, he claimed, we have no place to go but down. Landgraf was suggesting that the TV industry is heading into a period of maximum output, "where it's becoming almost impossible for most viewers to keep up with all of the worthwhile things to watch, and, as a corollary, where financial pressures, increasingly fractured audiences, over-production, proliferation of streaming services and platforms, or some combination of all these, will soon bring about some kind of falling off of interest, or attenuation in quality" (MacDuffie, n.d., 1). NPR's Linda Holmes (2015) illustrated, for example, that you could devote each day of 2015 to watching all the episodes of a different comedy or drama and not have time to finish them all.

In this overwhelming "peak" of television content production, the sheer quantity of programs means that a cycle like Horrible White People could easily go unnoticed despite individual shows (notably *Girls*, *Transparent*, and *Fleabag*) within the cycle winning awards and being cited as part of the superiority of this peak.[5] Ultimately this cycle reflects Peak TV in two ways. First, it reflects the peak's high-level scripted content. Most of the shows in the cycle have the high production values, smart writing, formal innovation, and social relevance that tend to be labeled "quality" by mainstream critics and audiences, while also receiving generally positive reviews and awards (we cite awards and critical praise throughout the book as we discuss specific programs in order to illustrate their outsized cultural impact despite the fact that many early readers of this book and conference respondents had never heard of most of the shows we analyze). But second and more importantly, this cycle reflects Peak TV's insatiable demand for and attempt to use those quality aesthetics to appeal to ever-diminishing audiences of White, relatively affluent, tech-savvy, educated, urban viewers described by traditional discourses of quality audiences (see chapter 4 for a discussion of quality aesthetics as an aesthetics of Whiteness). Those White consumers' inflated importance to a still-dominant cultural force and incredibly lucrative industry thus becomes one of the cultural structures that maintain and support White supremacy, reflected in seeing characters who mirror those imagined viewers over and over again in the central roles in the most prestigious and culturally valued programming.

In Landgraf's warning to critics and industry personnel in the summer of 2015, he implied that the TV bubble might not burst but slowly deflate, because the rate of growth was unsustainable. Nevertheless, several years after his caution, the output continues to grow, with an estimated five hundred shows produced in 2017 (Frankel 2017). This is arguably because for many people in the industry, the era of Peak TV is great for business. More shows equals more work for industry labor, from writers to craft service providers. The past decade or so has seen the expansion of production centers all over North America beyond the typical hubs of Los Angeles and New York to include Vancouver, Atlanta, North Carolina, New Orleans, and New Mexico, among others (Adalian and Fernandez 2016). There are so many original scripted series being produced that a major point of contention in the most recent Writer's Guild of America (WGA) negotiations was for writers to be able to work on multiple series simultaneously, since writers were being denied the opportunity to cash in on the mushrooming number of writing jobs because their contracts tied them to one series at a time, even when it was in limited production for years (Frankel 2017). This growing prestige and labor expansion tends to lead to more celebration than criticism about the trajectory of contemporary television. Nevertheless, even as the industry talks about itself in relation to progressive narratives, the industrial shifts of transnational television distribution remain linked to the historically problematic ideological centralizing of Whiteness through appeals to White audiences and elite taste cultures, highlighting how TV has not actually changed as much as the discourses of Peak TV would have one believe.

SVODs: Not-So-Disruptive Disruptors

Much of TV's celebrated growth and focus on innovative progress is credited to the expansion of internet-distributed television or streaming video on demand (SVOD) over the past five years on platforms like Hulu (US only), Amazon Prime Video, HBO Now (US only), NowTV (UK, Ireland, and Italy), and Netflix that all operate on a subscription basis. These "portals" (Lotz 2017) include both original and legacy fictional films, documentaries, and television series in their content offerings. In fact, since entering the original content game, portals have inspired a great deal of confusion about whether their programming can be considered "television" at all, allowing them to capitalize on that confusion to help build prestige brands for themselves. Matt Zoller Seitz (2013) was one of many media critics contemplating whether Netflix shows like *House of Cards* (2013–2018) and *Arrested Development* (2013, 2018) should be eligible for the US TV industry gold standard Emmy Awards. In arguing against their classification as "television," he highlighted their different production contexts (often filmed all at once like a film production instead of in weekly installments), audience viewing practices (binge-watching the whole series when it is released all at once), and textual qualities (higher production values, less repetition, complex serial narratives). The bickering over definitions ultimately repeats similar debates that circulated around HBO programs like *The Sopranos* (1999–2007) and *Sex and the City* (1998–2004) in the early 2000s, shows that many people claimed were not television because they did not have to follow the same rules of scheduling, censorship, and budget as traditional broadcast and cable television do (see, for example, Polan 2007; Leverette, Ott, and Buckley 2008). Horrible White People shows have been central to these debates, as they problematize typical generic lines between comedy and drama, as well as categories of series, miniseries, or limited series and, as we trace in this chapter, typical delineations between national productions.

Most importantly, these portals distribute, mostly for the first time, an enormous amount of content produced in the United Kingdom and other European and Asian markets to the United States, previously quite a closed TV market. At the same time, the biggest international portals, Netflix and Amazon, distribute US content more quickly than before to other territories and ramp up the quantity and speed of content licensed around the world, even in markets that imported a substantial amount of programming anyway. These diverse national production cultures have different sets of rules about censorship, scheduling, program duration, and production calendars, along with the more obviously different languages, comedic sensibilities, and cultural norms prevalent in the narratives, characterizations, and aesthetic tendencies of their content. Yet all these differences are strategic in helping the portals brand their content offerings as "quality" or prestigious, in that the programs' distinctions, uniqueness, or foreignness are emblematic of that which viewers can't get on traditional television-distribution outlets and are therefore worth paying extra for (Polan 2007). So, while much of the banal terrestrial

TV—sports, news, chat, game shows, and reality TV, what Frances Bonner (2003) calls "ordinary television"—retains distinctly national (or regional or local) flavor, the content produced for and distributed by global portals is often framed as "not TV" and creates a transnational taste culture in which shared affluence, race, and mutually intelligible cultural references are the ties that bind, rather than national identity.

Netflix, the leader of the SVOD portals, remains notoriously opaque about media distinctions in its own content classifications, embracing the label "television" when it suits Netflix (to capitalize on the publicity or cultural and economic capital of the Emmys and other TV awards) and obscuring or blurring the label when it does not work to Netflix's benefit. When Netflix revived the Warner Bros. television series *Gilmore Girls* (The CW, 2000–2007) for a four-part miniseries, for example, the original series producer, Gavin Polone, sued the studio because Polone's deal with Warner Bros. entitles him "to receive $32,500 for each [*Gilmore Girls*] episode produced after 2003, plus a percentage of the show's modified adjusted gross and an executive producer credit" (Cullins 2016). The studio refused the payment, using a rebuttal claiming that Netflix was not "a traditional television network" and that the revivals were not considered "episodes" but rather ninety-minute movies (Pedersen 2016). While for many viewers and critics the revival was clearly an example of television, both Netflix and Warner Bros. took advantage of changing understandings of what counts as television to enhance their bottom line and to hail an elite taste culture by framing their content as prestigious. Indeed, Netflix admits that it targets elite audiences in international territories (Lobato 2017, 12), and as the other portals and networks with global syndication goals seek to compete with Netflix, they too will follow suit. Looking closely at these discursive framings is critical to understanding how the industry may strategically focus on the way its programming is innovative or unique in order to court praise, exclusivity, and prestige but how it also ultimately covers up the more traditional televisual methods it uses to attract and maintain television viewers. This conscious industry strategy runs parallel to unconscious representational strategies that promote diversity, inclusion, and stylistic innovation but also build those strategies around White central characters.

Definitions also blur on Netflix and Amazon Prime Video as they play fast and loose with their "Netflix Original" or "Prime Original" label, often slapping it on transatlantic imports like *Catastrophe* (commissioned by Channel 4 with additional funding and distribution outside the United Kingdom and Ireland by Amazon Prime and labeled on the portal as a "Prime Original") in the United States or *Riverdale* (a CW/Warner Bros. production) in the United Kingdom. Most likely, this is to emphasize the transatlantic series' claims to superiority over traditional broadcast and cable shows, thereby advertising "added value" for the portals, but it also emphasizes taste cultures over national identities. Nevertheless, despite these ongoing debates about definitions and the portals' purposeful opacity, as Lotz highlights, "in many cases, these [audio-visual] messages are still produced within industrial logics consistent with broadcast- and cable-distributed television" (2017, 3). She adds, "A medium [like television] derives not only from technological capabilities, but also from textual characteristics, industrial practices, audience behaviors, and cultural understanding" (3). Our analysis of the production contexts, genres, textual characteristics, and representations of Horrible White People shows (most eventually distributed by portals, if not produced by them, and their direct narrowcast competitors) supports their classification as television and specifically points to some of the more troubling televisual consistencies, like the possessive investment in Whiteness, in this era of change and innovation.

Despite Netflix and other subscription-based SVOD portals that distribute or heavily influence the shows analyzed in this book marketing themselves as disruptors or as radically new ways to watch TV, it is clear that they borrow from HBO's highly successful, decades-old brand playbook, especially its strategies for creating and hailing an elite taste culture by being strategically "Not TV" (see Polan 2007). Specifically, newer portals are creating compelling, original, scripted series in order to attract and maintain certain types of "quality" subscribers, while preventing "churn," or those subscribers who cancel their subscriptions at certain points during the year or after having watched a favorite series. Although the SVOD portals offer a variety of diverse programming options, like HBO before them, they are attempting to position themselves as alternatives to traditional network or broadcast offerings by consistently branding themselves as the premier sites for innovative or disruptive "quality" television.

Among the shows produced in this model are Horrible White People shows. They are all funny, and most of them are a half hour and focus on domestic spaces and families—loosely defined—but they are not necessarily comfortably labeled sitcoms. Chapter 2 explores in more detail how these series disrupt the utopic family-sitcom generic structures with serialized plots and replace the fantasy of familial unity and heterosexual coupling with self-destructive narcissism. Crucial to our argument here is *why* these SVOD portals produce certain types of what Avi Santo calls "para-television," "which purposely relies on mimicking and tweaking existing and recognizable TV forms" while staying within the institutional framework of classic televisual logics, instead of breaking cleanly from the representational norms, genres, and structures of traditional television modes (2008, 19). It has to do with courting very specific audience segments that the portals and networks think are most likely to subscribe to their platforms and services but who also fit their brand and values. These preferences tend to be based on highly gendered, raced, and classed biases that have structured television development for a long time, despite the networks denying or rendering those biases invisible. Furthermore, because the biggest SVOD companies (Netflix and Amazon) are global corporations, they seek out transnational taste cultures like that described earlier so that they don't have to make original content for every single market. That means for US-based companies like those two giants, the racist legacies of the US television industry and its conceptions of desirable viewers will be exported along with the original content. Mareike Jenner (2016) describes, for example, Netflix's strategy to produce and distribute original serialized drama in order to attract specific "cult TV" audiences. In particular, she argues, Netflix revived the series *Arrested Development* because it had the prestige awards, indie aesthetics, self-reflexivity, and witty commentary on contemporary politics that suggest all the markers of quality. But more important to Netflix was that the series also had loyal committed viewers who represented the class identity that Netflix was chasing and who were convinced that *Arrested Development*'s worth and especially its complex, intelligent, and bleak comedy had not been recognized by the network or "mainstream" audiences when it originally aired on Fox.

Like Netflix's strategy to reboot a structurally innovative yet still recognizable television property in order to attract an active and enthusiastic, affluent fan base, the shows in the Horrible White People cycle have their roots in tried and true television genres, particularly the situation comedy. Traditionally, one reason sitcoms were such an important component of broadcasting schedules is because their limited sets and casts, shorter duration, live tapings, and repetitive structures made them relatively cheap to produce (Mills 2009). In contrast, Horrible White People shows, even though they are (mostly) half-hour comedy or dramedy programming, mimic the serialization, aesthetics, and production values of those expensive quality or cult dramas that have proven popular on subscription channels and portals. All of the shows in this cycle break from the multicamera cinematography of traditional sitcom aesthetics, instead shooting on film, using long takes, filming with cameras on the move to various on-location sets, and ultimately favoring single-camera production in order to permit multiple setups and carefully composed mise-en-scènes similar to the aesthetics of cinema (O'Donnell 2007). Often embedded in those more innovative aesthetics are appeals to the elite taste culture we have been describing.

On *You're the Worst*, for example, the central couple and their best friends have a brunch ritual called "Sunday Funday" (S1E5). This episode opens with on-location shooting at a brunch café in one of Los Angeles's hipster East Side neighborhoods. After brunch, the friends take turns planning activities for the rest of the day. This episode features Edgar's list, which he promises is "the most underground, unique, and dope Sunday Funday ever." The gang then proceeds to eight more locations around town, shooting in a local record store; a green park overlooking downtown Los Angeles, where they receive "Zen massages"; a cemetery that is home to the most obscure taco truck in the city; a petting zoo; a marionette theater; a street closed for construction, where they hold shopping-cart races; a real estate open house, where they know there will be free cookies; and finally a backyard cocktail party. The physical spaces and distances between all these locations are emphasized with quick, stylish intercuts to a paper map of Los Angeles, with circles and routes drawn in marker to get from each spot to the next. The locations are carefully curated to create an image of these characters as loaded with cultural capital and to highlight the performative nature of their cool in-the-know-ness. This is emphasized by the other brunch crew who steals their Sunday Funday list and follows them to every activity until Edgar confronts their leader, who breaks down under the pressure of coming up with Sunday Funday ideas and admits that he had to cheat. The false uniqueness of the Sunday Funday activity list, and its predictable hailing of a specific elite taste culture, speaks to the constant repetition of a supposedly innovative aesthetic pattern in a classic genre with only slight variation in creating the whole body of quality programming under discussion. Horrible White People shows make for an ideal form of quality para-television (Santo's formula of repetition with limited innovation) with their blend of serial and episodic narratives, centered on the sitcom's familiar small group of protagonists dealing with everyday domestic and interpersonal conflicts. What is most striking, though, is that while this cycle proves innovative in its aesthetics, narratives, and sometimes scheduling, its centrality of middle- and upper-middle-class Whiteness persists.

As the industry propagates discourses of Peak TV and Not TV that focus on change, progress, and invention, they deliberately obscure how conventional some of the content remains and by extension how traditionally White and generically and aesthetically conservative some of the prestige programming actually is. This obstruction is particularly apparent in Netflix's 2018 marketing campaign "The First Time I Saw Me," which explores the history and relevance of viewers' nostalgia for seeing characters that looked like them reflected in the media. The first video of the series appeared on Netflix's Facebook page and featured Krissy, who saw herself in the Latino and Cuban characters and culture of Netflix's *One Day at a Time*. The campaign's lineup includes Netflix Original show actors like Logan Browning (*Dear White People*) and Selenis Leyva (*Orange Is the New Black*) and highlights many of their original programs as the #firsttimeisawme. The awareness campaign thus centers Netflix's efforts to foster more representational diversity and inclusion, and it calls creators and influencers to action to follow in Netflix's supposedly groundbreaking footsteps and foreground characters who represent broader intersectionalities of race, class, gender, and sexuality. The campaign also works to deemphasize how much money the portal spends on syndication deals for nostalgic, traditional, White-cast programming like *Friends, Full House, Gilmore Girls*, and *The Office*—acknowledging the importance of this traditional syndication to Netflix's brand and economic model might make the portal appear less innovative or disruptive. Through high-profile strategic marketing campaigns like this, the frequent circulation of Peak TV accolades in the press (see Garber et al. 2015) and on awards shows celebrating "the most diverse list of Emmy nominees ever" (see chapter 4) as well as through the deliberate obfuscating of whether these portals' content is "television," the industry strategically positions itself in a progress narrative that emphasizes its distance from past formulaic, derided, and racist legacies of TV. In doing this, the television industry rhetorically positions itself alongside other false ideological narratives like the postracial mystique outlined in the introduction or the enduring belief that the United States follows a constant trajectory of racial progress. Following Joseph R. Winters's (2016) call to critique progress narratives that gloss over more painful memories, histories, and legacies in favor of an imaginary and self-congratulatory world, we seek to expose how the industry still relies on culturally defined racist, classist, and gendered biases left over from the industry's origins as it develops programming. In doing so, we hope to emphasize all the effort, change, and activism that is still needed to actually live up to the progressive narratives being propagated in this era of Peak TV.

Transnational Comedy and Branding Disruption

These progress narratives are key to the portals as they establish global brands for themselves to attract as many subscribers as possible. As Christopher Anderson (2008) lays out in relation to HBO in a slightly earlier era, appealing to subscribers requires first establishing a consistent and identifiable brand and building a deeper and more durable relationship between subscribers and the brand by producing original series that have the potential to engender viewer loyalty. Catherine Johnson (2012) suggests that in a time of increased choice and interactivity, branding has become key to both UK and US networks' and portals' attempts to manage viewer behavior and the values associated with their channels, services, and programs. Yet, in the era of Peak TV, the relative youth of many of these distribution outlets and the diversity of content offered across them have made branding more challenging than on more traditional television networks. As Jason Lynch (2015) notes, all of the SVOD portals have a branding problem, and "while Amazon and Hulu are trying to compete with Netflix, the reality is that Netflix is the clear victor in the battle of the streaming services."[6] Lynch recounts survey data that indicate that Netflix's variety is most appealing to viewers and that although Hulu is known for a few standout shows (like the Horrible White People shows *Casual* and *Difficult People*), its reputation is hurt by its interruptions from advertising. What is most striking, though, is that despite brand distinctions across portals, subscription channels like HBO, more traditional narrowcast channels like FX, broadcast channels like FOX, and Britain's Channel 4—and their specific economic imperatives to produce distinctive programming—all these distributors have versions of Horrible White People shows. That is because, in addition to Santo's assertion that seemingly new TV formats are based on limited innovation to tried and true formulas, "quality" original programming helps channels define their identity, and by 2010, all television networks were experimenting with developing programs that were clearly distinctive from traditional broadcast norms (Lotz 2018, 29). Transnational comedies like Horrible White People shows became key to their disruptive branding, especially as internet distribution introduced new models and programs moved more easily across boundaries to gather global audiences (Lotz 2018, 96).

Horrible White People shows are branded as quality TV because of their elite taste cultures, production values, and generic and stylistic innovation but also because of their global appeal and their supposed ability to supersede limited national sensibilities. Because these shows are pricey to produce for half-hour comedies and have relatively small (compared to broadcast sitcoms or sports, say) audiences in any given market (although actual measurement is impossible thanks to portals' reluctance to release viewer data), coproductions, with their built-in brand-boosting international glamor, feature prominently in this cycle. Gillian Doyle (2016) points out how international financing and presales to international markets are key to getting high-end dramas made. It is these very expensive dramas, she argues, that drive viewers to SVOD platforms or subscription channels, making them a widespread programming trend. Horrible White People shows like *Catastrophe* that are coproduced and distributed by a SVOD portal (Amazon US) and commissioned by a more traditional broadcaster (Channel 4) work the same strategies as Doyle's examples: *Game of Thrones* (HBO, distributed in the

United Kingdom and Ireland via subscription-based Sky Atlantic) and *Fortitude* (commissioned by Sky Atlantic). The fact that many of these shows are internationally cofinanced indicates the ways that consumers defined by race, class, education, and urban location are targeted as a taste public rather than defined by national identity even when the shows' content is the kind of dark, critical comedy that might seem like it would have to be locally context-specific to make sense.

Horrible White People shows are precisely culturally specific, *but* that cultural specificity speaks more to the experiences of transatlantic racial and class-based affinities than to national location. That purposeful transnationalism is then positioned as part of the portals' disruptive branding. The intentional construction of that transnational audience is evinced by their international cofinancing, presales, and distribution platforms as well as by their particular blend of UK and US comedic sensibilities and often by the actors' and creators' own accents and mobility. Instead of national identity, the shows in the Horrible White People cycle foreground race and class identity extratextually with their marketing materials, audience address, and distribution strategies. The characters' Whiteness is obviously common across many of their promotional posters, but you can also see in the images the focus on hip urban settings, chic or hipster clothing, and other markers of cool (expensive) casualness (like in their postures), which are all central to a contemporary transatlantic, upper-middle-class taste culture (see figure 1.1). Like these markers and references to high art like the ones in the opening paragraph, brunch scenes are a common feature that signal the cycle's elite taste culture and its Whiteness. *You're the Worst*'s Sunday Funday ritual, described earlier, satirizes the desperation of trying to maintain a sense of constant innovation and displays of leisure and hip taste, but brunch or similar settings recur throughout the cycle. In season 2 of *Fleabag*, Fleabag's completely empty café is suddenly thriving, in part because of theme days like "chatty Wednesday," which requires patrons to chat with each other with every purchase (S2E5). Chatty Wednesdays are so successful that the café overflows and threatens to even make a profit. Elaborate home-cooked breakfasts with brunch staples of waffles and cocktails are a consistent feature on *Casual*. The *Search Party* gang embark on the series' central mystery (S1E1) over brunch and process the fact that they have murdered someone over breakfast cocktails and pastries as well (S2E3). Again,

Figure 1.1. Promotional posters for Horrible White People shows feature Whiteness and similar transatlantic class and taste cultures. (Promotional material for season 1 of *Casual*, screenshot from shortyawards.com; promotional material for season 2 of *Catastrophe*, screenshot from amazon.com; promotional material for season 1 of *Divorce*, screenshot from tvseriesfinale.com; promotional material for season 1 of *Love*, screenshot from rottentomatoes.com; promotional material for season 2 of *Difficult People*, screenshot from impawards.com; promotional material for season 1 of *You're the Worst*, screenshot from FXX.com; promotional material for season 1 of *Fleabag*, screenshot from comingsoon.net; promotional material for season 2 of *Transparent*, screenshot from amazon.com; promotional material for season 5 of *Broad City*, screenshot from hulu.com).

there are specific cultural inflections to brunch and breakfast on either side of the Atlantic. In the United States, the Whiteness of brunch is tied to urban gentrification (Doll 2012a, 2012b; Berger 2012; Schilling 2014) and often represents middle- and upper-class White incursions into formerly Black, Latinx, and immigrant neighborhoods, thus raising prices on commodities and real estate and forcing out the locals. It has also become pop-culture shorthand for "stuff white people like" (Post Staff 2008) and "synonymous with upper class, yuppie assholes and urban tourists" (Schilling 2014). Whatever the specific cultural backdrop, it implies leisure time to socialize over a typically excessive (often featuring enormous portions and morning alcohol) and relatively expensive meal (in breakfast terms) and therefore implicates the class and taste cultures we have described in this chapter so far.

In the same gentrifying move, the shift of the sitcom into "quality" discourses has also shifted its characters firmly into the middle and upper-middle classes. This is a departure from British sitcoms' often working-class norms and aligns the British-produced programs in the Horrible White People cycle with US sitcom's middle-class norms (Woods 2019). Even in the United States, though, the relentlessness of the striving for the so-called American Dream and the wallowing in despair when it is not achievable (prominent features of the cycle) disavow a long history of working-class sitcoms, including critical favorites like *Roseanne* (ABC, 1988–1997; with a controversial reboot in 2018) and *Roc* (Fox, 1991–1994), as well as early immigrant-family sitcoms that George Lipsitz (1986) discusses as explicitly functioning to draw post-Depression and postwar viewers into the new American ideals of consumption and credit. Nonetheless, the centralizing of a White elite taste culture in transatlantic sitcoms of the 2010s, reflected in formal and thematic characteristics, is merely an extension of Hilmes's transnational cultural economy of British and US broadcasting, despite its innovative-disruptor branding.

Transatlantic Horrible White People shows frequently feature characters from both sides of the ocean. *Catastrophe* and *You're the Worst* both feature transatlantic couples as the main series protagonists to explore cultural clashes but ultimately reveal more commonalities in demeanor and affect than differences. *Catastrophe's* Sharon and Rob banter in a constant stream of shared television references, and in *You're the Worst*, even when Jimmy mocks Gretchen's terrible taste in art and design ("You definitely shouldn't decorate your own house"; S3E12), the couple ends that particular argument by reading Jimmy's trashy romance novel together—the wildly successful follow-up to his critically praised, commercially ignored highbrow literary first novel. Gretchen's discerning taste is further validated by her boss in the show's final season when she discovers and signs the next big hip-hop star—thus throughout the series, taste, ranging from highbrow to hip or ironic, clearly delineates characters and their relationships to each other and to their work. Similarly, the bromance on *Casual* between the White American Alex and the Black British Leon is based on shared cultural consumption, even though it parallels the racial dynamics between *You're the Worst's* Jimmy, who is White and English, and the Latino American Edgar that is discussed in the introduction. Nevertheless, whether as central characters or supporting cast, Horrible White People shows centralize friendships, relationships, and general commonalities of taste culture and affect above national origin.

Speaking to this focus on an imagined community of transnational viewers, Karen Petruska and Faye Woods write about "Netflix Originals," the content that is marketed by the international SVOD giant as its own "original" content but that is frequently imported or exchanged between the United States and the United Kingdom, elsewhere in Europe, and South Korea. They argue that SVOD providers like Netflix are indicative of this transitional moment in the industry in which new methods and norms of distribution "dislocate the term ['original'] from its former association with national specificity" (2018, 50). Their argument applies to TV generally, not to a specific genre, but the comedic programming we are talking about is most often distributed this way and created and marketed as disruptive with an understanding that global capitalism has created a mobile, international middle-class that shares certain taste cultures. "This discursive application of 'Original'—claiming ownership over a series created entirely by a different channel in a different nation—homogenizes international productions under the ever-encroaching spread of Netflix, with Amazon in hot pursuit. The diversity of global content depends upon the continued success of a broad range of producers, and 'false Originals' potentially threaten their viability, as SVOD services subsume distinctive national broadcasters and their brands into production funnels that feed a monopolistic, global 'Netflix nation'" (Petruska and Woods 2018, 56). What Petruska and Woods describe as the monopolistic, global nature of SVOD giants puts a nationalist spin on a trend that could be understood as the logical extension of global media conglomeration and deregulation. And it leads, as they argue, to a Netflix- or Amazon-, or savvy-SVOD-consumer nation, as opposed to distinctively national TV cultures.

The type of purposeful transnationalism of Horrible White People shows is seen elsewhere in the television landscape through the proliferation of subtitles, multiple untranslated languages in a single text, and transatlantic coproductions (supplementing the more common European coproductions). Stand-alone streaming platforms and the global business models of Netflix and Amazon have transferred to US and UK television the blockbuster movie industry's international-first (or at least a close second) mentality (Miller et al. 2005), in which the appeal to transatlantic and more global audiences is built into the production and distribution models of quality TV that would garner smaller audiences in a single market. This kind of purposeful transnationalism is not necessarily new, although it might be newer to the comedy genre, thus connoting innovation or disruption for the portals. While some sitcoms, notably *Friends* (see Mills 2009; Cobb, Ewen, and Hamad 2018), have had large international audiences, common wisdom holds that comedy is a nationalized language, that it speaks too closely to local cultures and circumstances to be easily exported (see Bore 2011, which pushes back against this recurring emphasis on cultural difference in TV comedy). But with the constantly increasing niche-ification of audiences, comedy has become an exportable product as well—and not just any comedy but female-centered (romantic) comedy about White people obsessed with their own anxiety and suffering. With Horrible White People shows, this portability speaks to transatlantic patterns of growing inequality that reify Whiteness and entrench neoliberalism (J. Butler 2011; Spivak 2011) despite the fairly clear disasters of Brexit (negative economic consequences from trade and investment, political consequences from border changes and changes to free movement within Europe, etc.) and Trump's election in the United States (violent White supremacists rallying openly across the country; escalating conflict with North Korea, Iran, and others; refusal to support measures to fight climate change; etc.). In other words, disaffected White liberals are similar on both sides of the ocean, and the television industry banks on the fact that they like watching the same shows about their own suffering and victimization, "folded into mediated taste communities" (Banet-Weiser and Ouelette 2018, 2). Writing about the political realities and rightward shift of the early twenty-first century, Sarah Banet-Weiser and Laurie Ouellette argue that "political allegiance today is construed less through the winning of consent on a mass scale, than through the sense of political identity and consumer belonging offered by competing media outlets" (2018, 2). They are discussing highly partisan news-media outlets, but the organization of publics into mediated identities based on taste and media consumption applies broadly across contemporary popular culture and certainly describes the transatlantic taste culture created and hailed by Horrible White People shows.

Catastrophe and Transatlantic Horrible White People

In order to illustrate the purposeful spreadability of Horrible White People shows and their taste culture, this section puts one transnational comedy, *Catastrophe*, into the context of the ongoing climate of transition in the TV industry toward the dominance of SVOD disruptor or progress narratives and also into the context of some of the political, economic, and cultural continuities between the United States and the United Kingdom discussed earlier in this chapter and in the introduction. A story of two migrants living in London—the Irish schoolteacher Sharon and the American advertising executive Rob, played by cocreators Sharon Horgan and Rob Delaney—*Catastrophe* follows the couple's relationship as a weeklong tryst results in a surprise pregnancy and an even more unexpected marriage. Though they barely know each other and have little in common other than instantaneous sexual chemistry, they decide to have the baby and see if they can weather life's various catastrophes, big and small. The series works as an international text on the level of character as well as production and distribution. *Catastrophe* was commissioned for Britain's Channel 4 and distributed internationally by Amazon Prime. Because it is a coproduction with a gap in airdates of only six months, it had to be conceived as an international product—especially in subsequent seasons. The creators did this in part by merging British and American comedic sensibilities in the show's "unflinching depiction of marriage and family life" (Blake 2019). As one Amazon Studios executive put it, Horgan's "strong creative voice and storytelling sensibility have resonated with audiences globally and will make for outstanding shows for our Prime members" (Andreeva 2018).

The conception of a comedy audience as global might seem to challenge common understandings of comedy as national (Jensen and Sienkiewicz 2018; Medhurst 2007), but in the 2010s, the imagined community posited by scholars of comedy and sitcom shifted, as we have noted, to a transnational taste community. Brett Mills, for example, argues that comedy—"a prime testing ground for the ideas about belonging and exclusion"—is often key to the dynamics of establishing national collectivity. "The failure for those new to a country to properly 'get' [the jokes of] the imagined community can be used to suggest that they don't properly 'belong' and therefore should leave" (2018, 268). This aligning of comedy with *exclusion*, rather than the creation or identification of community, speaks to darker comedy and the more sinister political climate that Banet-Weiser and Ouellette establish in their discussion of early twenty-first century right-wing media but that is also central to the cultural climate that foregrounds White fragility both within and beyond the Horrible White People cycle. Simon Critchley further maintains that the difficulties associated with translating humor can offer a sense of "cultural distinctiveness or even superiority" (2002, 67–68). So when a viewer does not "get" Sharon's and Rob's TV references and pop-culture jokes, they are in essence conceding to the cultural condescension common to Horrible White People characters.

Despite *Catastrophe*'s intentional transatlantic address, conceptions of a "national sense of humor" persisted in describing its comic sensibility, especially its dark, bleak affect. "To Phil Clarke, the head of Channel 4's comedy department, *Catastrophe* is a kind of hybrid, 'aping what you did in the States' in terms of mixing drama, comedy, and season-long story lines, 'but also plundering some British comedy traditions, mostly of hatred, self-loathing, and repression'" (Paskin 2016). The TV critic Willa Paskin adds that *Catastrophe* is reflective of a broader trend in this transatlantic comic merging, claiming, "There's another way to understand what has happened to American comedy in recent years: it has become more British. The hallmark of the British sitcom is a quasi-unbearable protagonist who is an Everyman, only insofar as every man can laugh at him." Similarly trying to capture the Britishness of *Fleabag* and its comic lineage, Faye Woods (2019) explains the cultural history of abjection in British humor. Likewise, the comedian Ricky Gervais (2011) describes British humor as "more comfortable with life's losers. . . . We don't want to celebrate anything too soon. Failure and disappointment lurk around every corner." The British comedian Simon Pegg (2007) agrees in his elaboration of British comedians' more liberal and subtle use of self-deprecation and irony (than Americans), specifically "the need to bury emotion under humor." Yet these generalizations rather underestimate the appeal of *Catastrophe* and other Horrible White People shows; this is not a simple case of "media imperialism," in which the United Kingdom has infiltrated and reshaped the United States' sense of humor. Arguably, Homer Simpson and every specifically American sitcom character played by galumphs like Jim Belushi, Kevin

James, Tim Allen, or any of the cast of *Big Bang Theory* (CBS, 2007–2018) or *It's Always Sunny in Philadelphia* (FX, 2005–2012, FXX 2013–) are all at times quasi-unbearable everymen akin to Gervais's best known character, the boss in *The Office*. Furthermore, although these notions of irony, self-loathing, failure, complexity, and general bleakness seem to persist in mainstream-media descriptions of Britain's national sense of humor, Friedman's study of British comedy consumers suggests that within Britain as well, tensions over this vision of humor exist along class lines. British comedy consumers with high cultural capital, he notes, preferred clever, dark, more resonant comedy that evoked more complicated emotions like shame and despair alongside laughter, whereas those with lower cultural capital felt comedy "should not invoke negative emotions" because it would "defy the pleasurable spirit of comedy" (2011, 362). Horrible White People shows like *Catastrophe*, then, are not so much influenced by a bleak or dark comic style that is particularly British but rather are aligned with a specific transatlantic *classed* taste culture. *Catastrophe* reflects the way the feeling of White precarity embodied in these unlikable, often mean-spirited, and unhappy Horrible White People characters is an affect that unites them and viewers who are amused by them across national boundaries. That ethos of failure, reliance on snark, and celebration of abjection may have a shorter history in popular understandings of US comedy but indisputably draw together all Horrible White People shows.

Catastrophe was Sharon Horgan's follow-up to the critically lauded "dark and dysfunctional" *Pulling*, cowritten with Dennis Kelly and starring Horgan. The series with "a lack of a moral center" was inspired by the writers' own life experiences in their twenties living in shared accommodations with "nutters" and being in "rubbish relationships"; it follows three cohabitating women in their thirties "behaving badly, getting insanely drunk, sleeping with awful men" (Raphael 2009). As a precursor to the Horrible White People cycle, *Pulling* was celebrated (like a lot of HWP shows; see chapter 3) for countering "the dearth of strong female comedy roles" (Raphael 2009) and disrupting gendered behavioral norms and expectations. *Catastrophe* built on *Pulling*'s mildly autobiographical model, as "the show's premise was a sort of composite of their personal lives: Horgan got pregnant not long after she began dating her now-husband; Delaney is a recovering alcoholic and American expatriate raising a family in London." Describing the series' goal, Delany echoes the precarious affect of "cruel optimism" (Berlant 2011): "You might have a few months' rent or mortgage in the bank. You might have a partner that you feel you can depend on. But, really, there's just no certainty," he said reflecting on the end of the series (Blake 2019). This sense of dread and uncertainty pervades the cycle.

Catastrophe also illustrates how performers and producers both often have international sales in mind when they create products, selling not just their shows but their celebrity or auteur status abroad as well. Sharon Horgan parlayed *Catastrophe*'s success in the United Kingdom and the United States into *Divorce* for HBO in 2016 and has secured, like Phoebe Waller-Bridge, a lucrative first-look deal with Amazon Prime on the basis of the successes of their shows. Another Horrible White People show, *Divorce*, is frankly quite similar to *Catastrophe*, although aesthetically and tonally it is colder, as the whole series takes place in winter and Sarah Jessica Parker's repressed, mostly stoic lead performance seems to purposefully contrast with Carrie Bradshaw's ditzy postfeminist consumerism and with Horgan's self-centered, often shouty performance in *Catastrophe*. This time, instead of a couple that chooses to stay together despite a series of catastrophic obstacles, the couple chooses to break up.

As we have detailed earlier, comedy often "works" because of the close relationship between comedian and audience. "In-jokes rely more on the workings of that group dynamic than the specifics of the joke . . . so humor can be seen as a communicative act whose context is vital to its success" (Mills 2009, 15–16). But in a global television environment, that context is forced to expand and find commonalities other than geography. "As important as comedy can be in the creation of National identity, some aspects of it are quite apparently able to achieve international, if not quite global, appreciation" (Jensen and Sienkiewicz 2018, 239). Rather than national identity, the "in-jokes" or comedic context on *Catastrophe* is made up of Amazon Prime consumers, cord-cutters—elite audiences compared to mass broadcast sitcoms—who appreciate a certain type of complex, dark comedy (as Friedman's study suggested).

Catastrophe's in-jokes, like those of most Horrible White People shows, rely heavily on pop-culture references. But the specificity of their citations is telling. They are not mass-culture references but allusions to other transnational TV shows, including some of those mentioned already that have helped drive programming trends toward very expensive, niche-marketed dramas. *Game of Thrones* is a common reference, as when Rob describes Sharon's toenails as "white walkers." In conversation and argument, Rob and Sharon often mention *Lord of the Rings* (which is a film franchise rather than a TV show but is also a purposefully global product); they relate Rob's job in advertising to *Mad Men*; and when they are struggling to reconnect sexually after their second child, they try to reclaim intimacy by watching *The Walking Dead* and *Breaking Bad* together. These are sometimes nerdy or quirky jokes, but as a group, they represent precisely the taste cultures targeted by global streaming portals. Other shows in the cycle, like *Difficult People* and *Casual*, similarly reference this taste culture. In *Difficult People*'s "Pledge Week," the main characters, Billy and Julie, stage a successful roast of PBS, which traverses material that is hyperaware of the cliché understanding of the channel's nerdy, liberal, elitist target market. Later in the episode, at a premiere party for a new HBO miniseries, in a posturing move, Julie and Billy criticize and joke about HBO's blundering development passes on *Mad Men* and *Breaking Bad*, only to later plead to each other how much they want to pitch a series to the network. This desire to be associated with HBO's prestige brand was established in the previous episode when Julie's out-of-touch mother comments about the award-winning HBO comedy *Veep*, "Everyone on *Veep* talks too fast; I'm switching it to *The Big Bang Theory*," resulting in a frustrated eyeroll from Julie, clearly meant to distinguish her and her mother's TV tastes. In the same vein, *Casual*'s Alex, who was recently let go from his job as chief technology officer at a tech company, meets with a financial adviser (S3E3). As the adviser suggests cutting some seemingly unnecessary expenses from Alex's budget, she questions the $85 a month he spends on music-streaming services. Alex illustrates his savviness and good taste, defensively justifying his need for multiple versions of the same service: "'Lemonade' [Beyoncé's visual album] was a Tidal exclusive, and Taylor Swift is only on Apple Music," implying that consuming all the brand exclusives across platforms is essential to a music connoisseur, even one struggling to pay his bills. "As Philippe Coulangeon (2005) notes, the new culturally privileged consumers of pop-culture may be best characterized not as 'cultural omnivores' but as 'enlightened eclectics,' employing a distinctly 'enlightened' aesthetic lens to all cultural consumption [not just traditional 'high art' objects]" (Friedman 2011, 351). Together, these kinds of jokes emphasize the shared language of so-called quality TV and changing media-industry norms over that of local or nationally specific cultural or political references. Indeed, the political references on most of these shows are also international—justified perhaps by the different cultural origins of the main characters but with the obvious bonus of being legible to US and British audiences. Although these examples all stem from the shows' dialogue, the similar "quality" aesthetics that are prevalent across the cycle also hail this demographic through what we argue is an explicitly White quality aesthetic (see chapters 2 and 4).

Furthermore, the financial difficulties that *Catastrophe's* couple face when Rob loses his job while Sharon is pregnant with their second child mean that they are shopping for a smaller home because they don't feel able to afford their current London house. This focuses one of the show's central narrative arcs on the characters' possessive investment in housing, a common theme of this cycle, outlined in the introduction and discussed in more detail in chapter 2, that centralizes a perceived loss in middle-class White characters' status. Moreover, Rob's alcoholism and Sharon's generalized dissatisfaction with her career, with motherhood, and with marriage are all mirrored throughout this programming cycle, regardless of an individual show's national origin, adding up to a cycle of programming about White precarity. These themes all center on the trauma with which White characters meet their loss of access to markers of middle-class status, like jobs and home ownership, that they presumed were their natural right. This is the same threatened feeling or realization of "cruel optimism" that produces characters wallowing in despair and consolidating their identity around their possessive investment in Whiteness on both sides of the Atlantic.

But Look at All the Diversity on Television!

One of this book's central arguments is that contemporary quality television recenters Whiteness as part of an (unconscious) cultural drive to maintain structural White supremacy in an era when White people feel under threat. But, as any TV viewer might exclaim, look at all the new diversity on television! While the bigger, corporate SVOD portals and niche-market television networks develop and distribute this cycle of Horrible White People shows, it is important to note that contemporary online access to distribution outside of the traditional television system simultaneously provides unprecedented freedom for independent producers and marginalized communities, granting access to viewers and ideally allowing for increasingly diverse storytelling and subject matter (Christian 2018; see chapter 4 for a discussion of independent and web production's role in diversifying quality TV). Many networks and portals are in fact making room for more and more diverse voices as they look for ways to lure traditional television audiences to new ways of consuming television and to attract millennial cord-cutters or cord-nevers with niche, often short-run television series that catch the attention of viewers who otherwise would not watch prime-time TV on a consistent basis (Frankel 2017). Netflix has been particularly explicit about its investment in diversification, by luring the mega-successful television producers Ryan Murphy, Shonda Rhimes, and Kenya Barris to exclusive multihundred-million-dollar contracts. All three producers have been credited with "provid[ing] visibility where it didn't exist before" and "giv[ing] hero's journeys to people who get them far too infrequently" (Watercutter 2019). In order to appeal to audiences craving more distinctive voices, broadcast and cable networks as well as internet-distributed television portals are also looking for talent in new or unconventional places. For example, at the age of only twenty-four, Lena Dunham, on the basis of her appeal to tech-savvy millennial women whom HBO wanted to attract, was given a series deal for *Girls* after writing and directing only one independent feature film, *Tiny Furniture* (2010) (Nygaard 2013). Similarly, Issa Rae parlayed her smart writing and relatable performance on the YouTube webseries *The Misadventures of Awkward Black Girl* (2013) into a deal with HBO to create *Insecure*. And, sensing a new creative voice that could attract an underserved African American audience, FX gave Donald Glover a series deal to develop *Atlanta* after he had only previously served as a writer and guest actor on NBC's *30 Rock* (2006–2013) and starred on *Community* (NBC, 2009–2015). By giving headlining roles in front of and behind the camera to women and people of color who have traditionally been relegated to the sidelines or stereotyped, these new strategies are leading to unprecedented diversity on television. The television industry is celebrating itself for this diversity as well, noting in the 2018 broadcast of the Emmy Awards, for example, that the show that year featured the most diverse set of nominees ever (Television Academy 2018; the song-and-dance number celebrating this diversity is analyzed in chapter 4).

So, at the same time that Horrible White People shows proliferate, there are more diverse casts on US television than ever before. While Hollywood cinema continues to come under fire for overrewarding White producers, directors, and actors at the Oscars and for consistently Whitewashing major roles in blockbuster films, there has actually been a surge in people of color on-screen and behind the camera in television (Smith, Choueiti, and Pieper 2016). *The People v. O. J. Simpson* (FX, 2016), *Roots* (History, 2016), *Master of None* (Netflix, 2016–), *Black-ish* (ABC, 2014–), *Grown-ish* (Freeform, 2018–), *Mixed-ish* (ABC, 2019–), *Fresh Off the Boat* (ABC, 2015–), *Atlanta* (FX, 2016–), *Queen Sugar* (OWN, 2016–), *Insecure* (HBO, 2016–), *The Mindy Project* (NBC, 2012–2015, Hulu 2015–2017), *Jane the Virgin* (CW, 2014–2019), *Empire* (Fox, 2015–2020), *Power* (Starz, 2014–2019), and *Being Mary Jane* (BET, 2013–2018) all represent both culturally specific experiences of people of color and racial conflict. These relatively few series (within in the sheer bulk of Peak TV production) then come to serve as evidence for self-congratulatory narratives of racial progress. They become evidence for the dominant stories that the industry tells itself about how its technological progress goes hand in hand with social progressiveness. Like so much of what we have described in this chapter that is presented as radical innovation, even this rhetoric mirrors utopian technological determinism of earlier industrial shifts. The advent of widespread cable television and its spike in the number of TV channels in the 1980s was accompanied by "blue sky" thinking that heralded the opening of the airwaves to independent producers and underheard voices (Streeter 1997). But as Herman Gray (2005) has demonstrated, Black faces on- and off-screen serve a cyclical economic function and tend to disappear once they have lured the desired audiences to a new network or platform. Timothy Havens uses *Roots* (1977) to explain how this diversity strategy works within international distribution patterns as well: "The success of the original *Roots* miniseries proved there is an interest in Black stories abroad. But the pattern we've seen, again and again, is that Black shows break new ground that White shows benefit from. So *Roots* was followed by a number of White miniseries that were very successful abroad, *Fresh Prince* by White youth-oriented shows" (quoted in Roxborough 2016). "Industry lore" has long held that global audiences will pay to see White characters but not actors of color in lead roles (Havens 2013), despite the frequent global success of films like *Black Panther* (2018) or *Crazy Rich Asians* (2018).

Moreover, while some of these non-White-cast shows reflect the culturally specific experiences of people of color (*Master of None, Atlanta, Insecure, Queen Sugar,* etc.), many shows with multiracial casts are part of what Kristen Warner (2017) calls "postracial blindcasting" or "plastic representation," whereby "diversity became synonymous with the quantity of difference rather than with the dimensionality of those performances." The superproducer Shonda Rhimes's oeuvre on ABC is perhaps the most frequently cited example of postracial TV, diverse casting, and its commercial success. Starting with *Grey's Anatomy* (ABC, 2005–), Rhimes's blindcasting practices have made hits of shows with multiracial casts (*Grey's* and *Private Practice* [ABC, 2007–2013]) and created two of TV's first Black female leads (*Scandal* [ABC, 2012–2018] and *How to Get Away with Murder* [ABC, 2015–2020]) since Diahann Carroll starred on *Julia* (NBC, 1968–1971). Rhimes, Warner argues, deploys "race neutralization as a solution to racial inequity" (2015b, 633). That is, whatever conflicts the characters on her shows have, they are not "about" race but about other differences.

Despite the continued critiques of the limitations of most of these representations, especially from scholars and critics of color, when the 2016 Emmy nominations were announced, the television industry was lauded for its diversity, while other major media gatekeepers like the Oscars faced criticism from actors and filmmakers of color as well as public campaigns like #oscarssowhite for their persistent Whitewashing. The Emmys that year celebrated broadcast series like *Black-ish, Empire, Fresh Off the Boat,* and *Jane the Virgin,* all starring people of color, that had also received critical and ratings success with audiences. FX's *Atlanta,* in particular, has received extensive critical acclaim and various accolades, including two Golden Globe Awards for Best Television Series–Musical or Comedy, and Best Actor–Television Series Musical or Comedy for Donald Glover and two Primetime Emmy Awards for Outstanding Lead Actor in a Comedy Series and Outstanding Directing for a Comedy Series, making Glover the first African American to win the directing comedy Emmy (Turchiano 2017; Van Luling 2017). Overall, these recognitions appear to signal a shift away from the dominance, naturalness, normalcy, and persistence of Whiteness on television, with countless think pieces patting the TV industry on the back (Morris and Poniewozik 2016; King 2015; Poniewozik 2015a; and Rorke 2015). But we argue that these wins do the work of making White viewers and Emmy voters feel good about supporting underrepresented voices, while in fact the broader television landscape remains overwhelmingly White (M. Ryan 2016; Fallon 2016; Smith, Choueiti, and Pieper 2016).

Furthermore, when industry heads are pressed about their motives for supporting creators and performers of color, they often shy away from claiming altruism or commitment to the social good, instead insisting on the commercial motives noted by Gray and Havens. "'We recognized pretty quickly this was not about social good, this was about good commerce,' says Gary Newman, co-chairman of Fox Television Group. 'When you have a country as diverse as ours, you just have to have programming that appeals to different groups'" (Levin 2016). Courtney A. Kemp, the creator and executive producer of *Power*, a popular Starz series about a Black nightclub owner, echoes Newman's sentiments: "People have begun to recognize how much money they can make by targeting underserved audiences. The color that's relevant here is green. It's not about any kind of altruism, or a sea change in how people are feeling about diversity" (Levin 2016). Similarly, Courtney Jones, the Nielsen Company's vice president of multicultural growth and strategy, says that commonsense notions about content with diverse casts or themes being "niche"—therefore coming with inherent risk of limited audience appeal—are changing and offers as evidence a 61.5 percent nonblack audience for Issa Rae's Black-cast *Insecure* (Berg 2017b). These rhetorical moves rationalizing both more diverse programming and the spreadability and bankability of transatlantic Horrible White People as being commercially motivated are smokescreens, though. All of these decisions framed as exclusively financial or industrial are of course also cultural decisions. Whether producers are showing a commitment to diversity or sticking with the tried and true centrality of Whiteness, they focus on economic justifications, backing away from addressing why it might be socially or ideologically good to foster diversity in representation. Rarely does the industry seem willing to talk about the broad representational or ideological impact it can have, safeguarding itself instead so that even when programmers and development executives are doing the right thing, they do not have to feel pressure to *keep* doing the right thing. As Keith Negus summarizes, "What often appear to be fundamentally economic or commercial decisions . . . are based on a series of historically specific cultural values, beliefs and prejudices" (2002, 119). Whether these television executives admit it or not, they are engaging in a "contingent assemblage of practices" that are both economic and cultural (Du Gay and Pryke 2002, 2). While their decisions might be intended to increase sales and competitive advantage, "the complex ways in which cultural attitudes inform economic decisions cannot be fully regulated by the profit principle" (Santo 2008, 35). In this way, the contemporary discourses of the TV industry parallel the defensive discourse that political comedians like Jon Stewart and John Oliver use all the time: falling back to the position that "we're just comedians" relieves them of the pressures to acknowledge and therefore live up to the political and social influence they actually have (Gray, Jones, and Thompson 2009).

These contradictory discussions and framings of TV's upswing in people of color and justifications for the spreadability of Horrible White People programming in the 2010s bring us back to Elana Levine's question about the motives behind the label "postnetwork": "Whose interests are served by denying that television may still play a role as a site of cultural negotiation?" (2011, 181). We ask the same question about who gains or keeps power by using the language of Peak TV or discussing diverse production and casting decisions as solely financial choices. Television is unlike social media, where corporate control is exercised via algorithms that are unintelligible and invisible to most users and content appears to be user-generated and therefore benefits from a sheen of authenticity or interpersonal communication, rather than the public or mass communication that it actually is. The more visible corporate authorship of fictional television—branded by channel, portal, or producer—could lead one to understand it as a less "real" representation of contemporary cultural exchange. However, when in the space of only a very few years (around 2012 to 2018 or 2019), such a large collection of programming echoes the same set of characters, relationships, and conflicts, wins awards and sparks outsized cultural commentary, it coalesces into an undeniable cultural phenomenon. So who gets to keep power by calling TV "postnetwork" or at its "peak," thus denying its continued cultural role and persistent developmental logics? The same forces invested in postfeminism and postracial fantasies: those whose best interests align against relinquishing their position in the status quo—not necessarily individuals but those who benefit unconsciously from White supremacy, patriarchy, and capitalism.

2

Alternative Families and White Fragility

The Politics of the Dystopian Sitcom

In the pilot episode of *Transparent*, the titular transgender father, Mort Pfefferman, invites his three adult children over for dinner at their family's sprawling 1970s glass-and-timber house in the Pacific Palisades, a posh enclave on the West Side of Los Angeles. The Pfeffermans were the original owners of the architect-designed home by Buff, Straub & Hensman (as we are informed in a later episode), but a divorce twenty years before this evening's dinner has left Mort the sole inhabitant of the family home. The siblings bicker and speculate about what special announcement has sparked this dinner invitation as they approach the house. They guess, cavalierly, that Mort has cancer, and rather than display concern, only son Josh cynically suggests that Mort should begin gifting each child $12,000 per year until his untimely death in order to avoid inheritance taxes. The family finally sits around the table, eating not a home-cooked meal but messy take-out BBQ, anticipating Mort's news. In the end, the kids' nonstop overlapping, narcissistic chatter frustrates Mort into yelling "Stop it!" and then—rather than coming out as transgender, as he had planned—revealing to them that he is selling their childhood home. From this point forward, almost every character experiences shifting sexual or gender identities and falls in and out of marriages and stable-seeming relationships, and the home, its original décor, and its shifting ownership (from Mort, now Maura, to daughter Sarah to Josh, with a tense Airbnb era somewhere in the middle) become symbolic of the characters' fraught relationship to the idealized institution of a heteropatriarchal nuclear family. In this chapter, we examine the ways that sitcom—a genre fixated on representing each era's idealized norms of family, gender roles, and domestic spaces—shifts and evolves within the aesthetics of Horrible White People shows in order to reflect in the very structures of the genre the White precarity represented in characters' actions and the shows' tones throughout the cycle.

Horrible White People shows such as *Transparent* are centrally concerned with the loss of access experienced by middle- and upper-middle-class White characters to the trappings of the American Dream as laid out, among other places, in classic sitcoms from the 1950s and beyond: suburban home ownership; a stable, well-paying job; and lasting, secure family relationships (see, for example, Spigel 1992; Lipsitz 1986). This cycle of programming disrupts the aesthetic and ideological conventions of the genre, creating a dark, dystopian picture of hetero relationships and threatening the stable, brightly lit comfort of sitcom's domestic spaces. In order to deflect criticism of the characters, and the institutions they represent, this challenge to generic norms and even to generic classification assimilates as much difference as possible into the form, relying especially on the self-aware critical bite of Jewish comedy traditions and engaging with emergent feminisms. By situating the evolution of this cycle in a genealogy of sitcom's engagement with race and Whiteness and theorizing these dystopian families with Robin DiAngelo's concept of White fragility (2018), we argue that the ultimate effect of these challenges to sitcom conventions, like all elements of Horrible White People shows, recentralizes White suffering under the seemingly protective guise of liberal social critique.

Genre: Sitcoms, Family, and Utopian Whiteness

One of TV's oldest genres, adapted from vaudeville and radio, the sitcom is often "understood as an 'obvious' or 'straightforward' form of programming which is easy to spot and simple to define" (Mills 2009, 24). As such, Brett Mills writes, it is also usually considered a "hegemonic and conservative" genre (30). Michael Newman and Elana Levine add that the historical reputation of the sitcom has been two-faced: some of the most admired television programs ever work within the familiar or "obvious" conventions of the genre, but taken as a whole, sitcoms are frequently regarded contemptuously as among the most "conservative, formulaic, and artless of narrative forms" (2012, 59). Sitcom's dismissability is key to its ideological power. Unlike complex prestige dramas that reward careful attention, sitcom's appeal lies in laughs, repeatability, and simple plots that make for easy viewing. This understanding of the genre as simplistic and conservative remains in the era of Peak TV but is represented by a slew of aesthetically and generically traditional sitcoms that feature families of color helping reinforce the neoliberal ideal of the independent, self-sufficient family unit. *Black-ish*, *One Day at a Time*, and *Fresh Off the Boat*, for example, reflect how families of color are welcomed into this dominant generic space because they carry the burden of maintaining this national ideal and repairing its historical association with Whiteness. In contrast, White nuclear families, in the shows we discuss as part of the Horrible White People cycle, are rejected in favor of alternative relationships. Horrible White People shows and families have the aesthetic freedom of genre innovation but as a result create dystopias instead of happy family sitcoms. This chapter situates Horrible White People shows' innovation in a generic history in order to examine how generic experimentation and laughter function as enablers of White fragility.

In sitcom's oldest, most recognizable form, it is episodic; it creates and solves a problem within its short, weekly running time and resets all relationships to the status quo at the end of each thirty minutes. The most common version of a sitcom is set in the home of a husband and wife or small nuclear family (Butsch 2005). So when, at the end of an episode, the conflict is solved and the premise resets itself, sitcom reinforces the dependable solidity of those relationships and the reliability of their primary location: the family home. Structurally and aesthetically, sitcom repeats comfortingly familiar narratives of heteropatriarchal nuclear families with stable homes and relationships. In "Job Switching" (S2E1), one of the most iconic episodes of the classic sitcom *I Love Lucy*, for example, Lucy and Ethel reverse traditional gender roles with their husbands when they go to work in a candy factory while the men stay home and do the housework. Their escapades lead to hilarious spectacles of failure on both sides, and the episode ultimately illustrates that women are better at housework and men are better at public labor, reinforcing conventional gender roles and the stability of the patriarchal family structure.[1] In contrast, Horrible White People shows build on more recent character trends from innovative sitcoms like *Seinfeld*, *Sex and the City*, and *Friends* and stylistic trends from "quality" television to purposefully disrupt the narratives and ideologies on display in the *I*

Love Lucy example. In so doing, they react to or represent, in particular, emergent feminisms or new representational challenges to normative gender roles in the 2010s (see the introduction and chapter 3) via alternative family structures and representations of diverse sexualities.

While chapter 1 discussed these generic innovations as industrial strategies to garner labels of "quality," to build brand identities, and to attract specific transnational audiences in the era of Peak TV, this chapter focuses on how substantial departures from generic norms, especially in such an old, prolific, and consistent genre as sitcom, can contribute to, as well as react to, moments of cultural upheaval. Lauren Berlant posits the shifting terrain of genre, where conventional formats struggle to adjust to the present, as a key venue for the painful affect she calls "cruel optimism." She focuses "in particular [on] older realist genres . . . whose conventions of relating fantasy to ordinary life and whose depictions of the good life now appear to mark archaic expectations about having and building a life. Genres provide an affective expectation of the experience of watching something unfold, whether that thing is in life or in art" (2011, 6). So for Berlant, the expectation of watching the same pattern repeat itself over and over in a particular genre creates an assumption or anticipation of seeing that thing unfold in real life. That optimism becomes cruel when that anticipation is thwarted and, in our examples, White millennials are not able to access long-lasting, fulfilling relationships; reliable, well-paid employment; and suburban home ownership. The relationship of sitcom fantasy to ordinary life can be seen in US TV's early iterations of the genre, such as *Donna Reed* (ABC, 1958–1966), *Father Knows Best* (CBS, 1954–1955; NBC, 1955–1958; CBS, 1958–1960), *Leave It to Beaver* (CBS, 1957–1958; ABC 1958–1963), and many other classic sitcoms that presented an idealized White nuclear family in their newly constructed postwar single-family suburban homes as a symbol of the American Dream that often diverged from the bleaker realities of television audiences' lived experiences or "the way we never were" (Spigel 1992; see also Coontz 1993).

Historically one of TV's defining characteristics as a medium has been its domesticity. Domesticity in this case means within the home but also speaks to well-marketed post–World War II conceptions of privacy, individualism, and romanticized versions of nuclear families. Indeed, the TV as an appliance rearranged domestic space around itself, helping reinscribe women's role as caretakers and homemakers—private roles in direct contradiction to the public labor they had been asked to do during the war (Spigel 1992; Douglas 1994). As an extension of this focus on domesticity, television has always been obsessed with depicting family, and US sitcoms in particular were integral to painting a vision of suburban, middle-class, White families as the norm. The sitcom's aesthetics and formal features were vital to underscoring and, in many ways, constituting this utopian fantasy. The traditional static, multicamera shooting style meant a limited number of sets facing a proscenium; these were most often communal domestic spaces like the living room or the kitchen. Because editing was done live in-camera, the classic version of sitcom is flooded with light to avoid having to reset lights in between shots, a setup that contributed to the sitcom's happy, upbeat atmosphere. For similar practical reasons, colors of props, furniture, and wardrobe were often very bright. Most often shot with live studio audiences and sweetened with laugh tracks, sitcoms created an experience of communal laughter, shared jokes and experiences, helping to contribute to the "imagined community" of prosperous post–World War II American nationhood (B. Anderson 1991; chapter 1 of this book). As Brett Mills notes, "the laugh track reaffirmed the collective nature of consumption, aligning viewers with unarguably funny moments of mass comedy" (2018, 269). Absolutely central to that imagined community was a collective sense of Whiteness in the face of the beginnings of the African American civil rights movement. Sitcoms became key cultural products for manufacturing a "unified white racial identity through the shared experiences of spectatorship," and that identity was grounded in "an identification with the fictions of whiteness" (Lipsitz 1998, 99).

As Lynn Spigel notes, the genre's focus on domesticity and family was key to attracting large audiences in US TV's early years: "In merging vaudeville with theatrical realism, the sitcom created a middle-ground aesthetic that satisfied television's overall aim in reaching a family audience" (1992, 144). Since White people held a monopoly of access to television in the early years, most broadcasters, looking for the mass audience required to repay the expense of producing network programming, tended to erase racial and ethnic difference, favoring a broad, fictionalized version of aspirational middle-class Whiteness that would please advertisers rather than representing the heterogeneous makeup of actual television viewers. While many early sitcoms were based on the ethnic (often Jewish) humor of stand-up comedians and vaudeville stars like George Burns and Gracie Allen (*The Burns and Allen Show*) or Gertrude Berg (*The Goldbergs*), the genre's reliance on domestic settings and episodic structure ultimately contained representations of racial or ethnic difference that may have threatened the dominance and exceptionalism of this fictionalized and aspirational American Whiteness (see Spigel 1992, 2001; Mellencamp 2003).

Spigel offers the example of the fall of Milton Berle to demonstrate this ultimately racist work of the sitcom. Berle was the vaudeville star *cum* variety-show host of *Texaco Star Theatre* (NBC, 1948–1959), or *The Milton Berle Show*. The show had ratings so high that it was perhaps the first to spawn rumors of electricity spikes or municipal plumbing issues because everyone in the United States opened the fridge or flushed the toilet at the same time during commercial breaks. But, as Spigel delineates, Berle's humor was spontaneous, physical, sometimes crude, and very much based on a "New York" sensibility that was code for traditions of Jewish humor. As TV moved from live to filmed, from New York–based production to Los Angeles, and into a properly mass national medium, "the sitcom format, [in contrast to the variety show] with its preplanned storylines that mitigated against the comic's spontaneous displays of 'adult' humor and ethnic in jokes, was a particularly apt vehicle for television" (Spigel 1992, 150–151). Classic domestic sitcoms "thus worked to contain the overly aggressive, and often adolescent, masculinity of the variety show, while also placing men such as Cuban Desi Arnaz and Lebanese Danny Thomas [stars of *I Love Lucy* and *Make Room for Daddy*, respectively] into safely middle-class settings where their ethnicity was just one more running gag" (Spigel 1992, 154). As the strict episodic structure of the genre has loosened, men of color have often remained captured in those safe, middle-class settings. White men, in contrast, have fled those domestic spaces when their relationships are threatened or when they are asked to bear too much responsibility for others. On *You're the Worst* (S3E13), for example, the serialized romance between Jimmy and Gretchen eventually produces his marriage proposal at the top of Griffith Park in Los Angeles. When she says yes, he leaves to retrieve something from his car and flees Gretchen, his job, and the entire city without a word and lives incommunicado in an upstate trailer park for several months. This act of fleeing is a key dynamic of Robin DiAngelo's conception of White fragility. In this instance, it is enabled by an infusion of serial narrative structures into the half-hour comedies of the Horrible White People cycle, thus allowing White protagonists the privilege of escaping the containment of the classic sitcom's episodic structure, which reined in ethnic challenges to the sitcom's ideological centralizing of conservative White families.

Furthermore, while the domestic settings and episodic structures of early sitcoms softened the ethnic difference of major television stars or made race the butt of the joke, George Lipsitz (1986) points to the ways in which urban, ethnic, working-class comedies also operated as a kind of instruction manual for assimilation into a new White American identity and consumer economy after World War II. He suggests that ethnic sitcoms like *The Goldbergs* (CBS, 1949–1956), *Mama* (CBS, 1949–1957), and *Life with Luigi* (CBS, 1952) "provided one means of addressing the anxieties and contradictions emanating from the clash between the consumer present of the 1950s and collective social memory about the 1930s and 1940s," when the Great Depression and the war era had fostered "cultural ideals based on mutuality and collectivity" alongside a mistrust of capitalism (1986, 358). TV was vital to the new postwar commercial economy because buying a TV set, a substantial purchase at the time, was a marker of ascension into the new middle class and the object of much consumer spending. Once in the home, the box in its American commercial form was a prodigious marketing medium for a great many newly available mass-market commodities.

TV in general, but the sitcom narratives and thematic concerns of the ethnic, working-class subgenre in particular, also paralleled and supported contemporaneous government policies, from freeway construction to subsidized mortgages, that encouraged atomized suburban living and acquisitiveness. This process also disrupted or disbanded urban immigrant neighborhoods in favor of individualized home ownership in suburbia—a process that included shifting European ethnic identities (*The Goldbergs* was about a multigenerational Jewish family; *Mama* a Norwegian family; *Life with Luigi* an Italian family) to a broad, flattened "White." This expansive inclusivity of Whiteness, as we discussed in the introduction, continues to be an important feature of real-world racial power dynamics as well as an ongoing cultural function of sitcom. And indeed, in this Whitening process, many sitcoms moved their families from their urban apartments to single-family homes "in the country," as *I Love Lucy* put it, in later seasons. Lipsitz uses an example from *The Goldbergs* in which the matriarch, Molly, first questions the financial risks of buying something on an installment plan, only to later give in to the ideology of "living above her means, the American way" (1986, 362). So, within the conventions of the classic American sitcom, all ethnic or racial difference becomes contained, subsumed, or redirected toward the aspirational goals of middle-class suburban Whiteness and consumer practices, producing a utopian vision of the good life in which "property is sacred, the family is eternal, the parents are always right, and authority always wins" (Grote 1983, 169). Ethnic, working-class characters, argues Lipsitz, were able to express the anxieties associated with the collective memories of economic deprivation during the Depression, only to be controlled and ultimately transformed by the sitcom's simplistic narrative structure into aspirational American consumers in much the same way Spigel describes the containment of "ethnic" performers like Desi Arnaz and Danny Thomas.

The fictionalized utopian Whiteness and aspirational ideology of the sitcom discipline ethnic and racial difference in these ways throughout the history of the genre. Thus, in the 1980s, *The Cosby Show* (NBC, 1984–1992) was at first seen as a significant break from the genre's dominant representational Whiteness. Conceived of as a purposeful contrast to another trend in sitcom's representations of race—its reliance on stereotypical racial traits for demeaning humor in series like *Amos 'n' Andy* (CBS, 1951–1953) or the predominantly poor and working-class Black families of 1970s sitcoms like *Sanford and Son* (NBC, 1972–1977) and *Good Times* (CBS, 1974–1979)—*The Cosby Show* was developed as a "social corrective" to the negative representations of African Americans on fictional TV and in the media more broadly (Gray 1995). The show therefore follows a wealthy, highly educated African American nuclear family, the Huxtables, that just happens to be Black. *Cosby* adheres to the logics of colorblindness, a representational philosophy that ignores a particular group's race and ethnicity in order to highlight similarity to the dominant (White) norm and to promote notions of equality via that similarity (Warner 2015a). Yet, in deemphasizing the fictional Huxtable family's race, the show fails to address the social and economic inequities that continued to plague the Black community. Sut Jhally and Justin Lewis (1992) deemed this "enlightened racism," an ancestor to the self-aware hipster racism prevalent in Horrible White People shows. Herman Gray explains how *Cosby* functioned under the conservative neoliberal regime of Reaganism: "The appearance of upper middle-class Blacks on television ideologically announced and politically legitimated the end of structured social inequality based on race. In the 1980s, under the hegemonic bloc that some have termed Reaganism, the Huxtables both humanized Blacks (for Whites) and affirmed that it is possible to make it in an America with an open opportunity structure. By staging a program like *The Cosby Show* under Reaganism, television and the (corporate) network system that produced it played a vital role in representing and legitimating the 'disappearance' of structured social inequality based on race (and class)" (1994, 118). Key to this "disappearance" was the way the show focused on familiar domestic settings, moral and ideological conservatism, and the classic aesthetics of conventional sitcoms. Aside from a few "very special episodes," there was nothing, other than skin color, distinguishing the family at the center of *The Cosby Show* or its episodic narratives reconfirming the idealized nuclear family from utopian White sitcoms of earlier eras like *Father Knows Best*.

In the 2010s, a similar process of assimilation and legitimation was enacted via utopian sitcoms starring families of color that offered a stark contrast to the rejection of the heterosexual nuclear family on so many Horrible White People shows. Whereas Desi Arnaz occasionally ranted in Spanish for comic effect and in keeping with the "fiery Latin" stereotype, the Johnsons, the Black American family on *Black-ish*, often portray a certain amount of cultural specificity or even acknowledgment of racism. But in return, so to speak, the program adheres to traditional sitcom aesthetics and narrative structures and features an affluent suburban family much like the Huxtables. Even when an episode deals explicitly with racism, the Johnsons too reset their happy-family premise at the end of every episode, erasing any conflict with White neighbors or coworkers by showing the whole family happily together in their kitchen at the end of an episode and beginning the following episode as if the racial tension or conflict left no residual effects. In fact, these generic limitations eventually led to conflict between the show's creator, Kenya Barris, and the network, resulting in Barris's exit in favor of the lucrative deal with Netflix discussed in the previous chapter (Holloway 2018; Goldberg 2018). Furthermore, the neoliberalism of the Reagan era has only been exacerbated in the new millennium, despite global financial crisis and conflicts over health care, minimum wages, and the cost of education (for just a few examples) demonstrating its ultimate untenability because of the ways it enshrines inequality. *Black-ish* and *Fresh Off the Boat*, the story of a Korean American family moving to a predominantly White area of Florida and establishing themselves via the neoliberal hallmark of entrepreneurialism (they establish a restaurant), illustrate immigrant and Black families as succeeding in a neoliberal framework and insulating themselves from racial prejudice via a happy, utopian family togetherness that contrasts drastically with the neoliberal failure and breakdown of the family structure in Horrible White People shows.[2]

Both *Black-ish* and *Fresh Off the Boat* are part of a small surge of half-hour TV comedies, also including *One Day at a Time*, that could be fairly characterized as the opposite of HWP shows: mass-market sitcoms with non-White families that are the generically and aesthetically conservative counterpoint to Horrible White People shows' generic experimentation. If generic change or experimentation signals a disruption in the genre's classic, consistent representation of the heterosexual nuclear family, these shows' adherence to generic norms and traditions result in an embrace of the nuclear family as the site of all problems' solutions. Their very traditional sitcom aesthetics help construct them as utopian families. They use multicamera setups (albeit somewhat updated and more flexible than older shows in the genre), and all three shows rely on an abundance of shot/reverse-shot conversations to set up jokes and move the plot forward. They utilize the bright, uniform lighting associated with that shooting style, and they have almost entirely contained episodic structures (there is some serialization, but you would be able to jump in and understand any episode in any order). *One Day at a Time* still relies on a laugh track, and other shows, like *Black-ish*, make heavy use of musical cues to the same effect. These shows have limited sets with an emphasis on domestic space, especially kitchens and living rooms. Even the color palettes are bright and cheery.

The pilots to both *Black-ish* and *Fresh Off the Boat* begin by acknowledging the fictionalized and highly constructed idealized utopia of the White suburbs. On *Black-ish*, the father, Dre, talks in voice-over about their family being the only non-White people in the neighborhood, while the image makes a visual analogy of bus tourists looking on in awe; on *Fresh Off the Boat*, the kids explicitly comment on all the White people and how different their Florida suburb is to the DC Chinatown neighborhood they were leaving behind. Commentary on assimilation into utopian suburban Whiteness is the guiding theme of both pilots, yet those elements of racial diversity, cultural specificity, or critique are often contained via the traditional sitcom format. In *One Day at a Time*'s second-season opener, for example, the usually well-mannered Cuban American teenage son, Alex, gets suspended from school for punching a kid who told him, in a racially charged insult, to "go back to Mexico." The central focus of the episode is a family discussion on the living room's couch, interrogating the personal and social impact of racial slurs and stereotyping—one that takes into account intersectional differences in racism, including generation, as the grandmother discusses her experiences, and the privileges of racial passing from the light-skinned daughter. While the episode tackles a lot of the complexity of race relations in the United States and the lack of easy fixes, it ends with the mother, Penelope, reassuring her son of his worth and her unwavering support in him as the family comes together over ice cream, which in Penelope's words is "the one thing that completely stops the effects of racism." So, while *One Day at a Time* is rightly celebrated for depicting a Latinx single-mother household and tackling important sociopolitical issues, the genre's utopian and ultimately conservative format allows for the incorporation of some progressive social and political representations only to safely contain and depoliticize them with the reconstitution of the family and the episodic structure.

As discussed in chapter 1, this small surge of half-hour TV comedies— along with other culturally specific programming discussed in chapter 4—is often propped up by industry discourses at awards shows and in the trade and popular press to illustrate how inclusive and diverse television representation is becoming, as it seems to allow overt and specific commentaries about different cultural experiences, including experiences of racism. We put these shows in conversation with Horrible White People shows because the self-identifying liberal characters on HWP shows would see themselves understanding the racial conflict represented on these more utopian sitcoms and supporting these families of color. HWP characters would think they were "on the same side" and part of the same cultural drives as the Johnsons, the Alvarezes, and the Huangs. Significantly, however, in exchange for culturally specific representations of racial conflict, you often get a beautiful, happy, comforting, almost nostalgic (generically speaking) vision of the American family. Robin James (2015) has argued that White supremacy is as inclusive as possible, right up until it becomes a bad deal for White people—or until White people might have to relinquish some of their privilege to make room for others. These sitcoms featuring families of color work in the same way: they have complexity and cultural specificity; they have extended families; they even have a certain amount of critique of the racial order couched in comedy. But they also do the work Lipsitz describes in relation to an earlier generation of more diverse sitcoms, reproducing the assimilationist neoliberal ideal of self-sufficient families living independently.

The conventional utopian diverse-cast sitcoms are an important part of the ideological field (Fiske 2011) of the entire televisual landscape that contributed to the centralization of White precarity in the 2010s. While the contemporary diverse-cast sitcoms we compare to the HWP cycle avoid the critiques launched at *The Cosby Show* by representing the lives of people of color with cultural specificity, the parallel trends in TV comedy of White-cast dystopias and people-of-color-cast utopias create two very different sets of norms or expectations for the meaning of home and family—one safe and secure, one grim and threatened. This is a divergence of genre as well: the utopian, diverse-cast programs adhere much more closely to static traditional modes of sitcom, while Horrible White People comedies consistently challenge the aesthetic and structural borders of the genre. This undeniably racialized distinction renders families of color resilient and forgiving in the face of racism, and this category of White people (most often not inhabiting traditional families) sad, confused, and threatened.

Horrible White People comedies, in a dramatic stylistic and representational contrast, have bled into darkness, seriality, melodrama, and even the musical (*Crazy Ex-Girlfriend*) to the extent that their primary identifying characteristics seem to be their focus on family and snarky wit rather than any stylistic, thematic, or even character consistency with the classic sitcom. Thus, as expectations of the "good life," to recall

Lauren Berlant's words, erode, so too do the conventions of one of the oldest and often most conservative television genres. Given the genre's intrinsic relationship to idealized aspirational Whiteness, that Whiteness, like the genre's historical norms, appears fragile and precarious. What emerges, then, is a half-hour format shaped, of course, by shifts in television distribution and consumption (as discussed in chapter 1) but also reacting to the ideological failures of the present.

The "Yiddishification" of American Comedy

The beginning of the Horrible White People cycle coincides, as we mapped in the introduction, with a particular historical conjuncture of cultural upheaval and changing industry practices. Yet the cycle is not a complete revolution in the thematic and aesthetic conventions of the sitcom. Rather, it represents a culmination of particular aesthetic and representational challenges to those norms over the years, including the gradual assimilation of nontraditional family structures, nonhetero sexuality, and Jewish humor into the postwar vision of the White American family. The latter is significant in that it represents how Jewish ethnicity has been strategically incorporated into Whiteness and that, in particular, the mainstreaming of Jewish comedy was a key signal of that assimilation.

In addition to race, throughout television's evolution, the sitcom has both mirrored and constructed changing social and political ideas about family and American culture more broadly (Taylor 1989). The prevalence of suburban-dwelling, White nuclear families in the 1950s presented that family structure as an immutable norm. That ideological work was so powerful that the norm remains dominant today, with only a modicum of additional inclusiveness. Historically, the most common alternative families in sitcoms have been workplace families, where co-workers take on gender roles similar to a clichéd nuclear family (Taylor 1989), ultimately merely substituting work settings for domestic settings, such as the newsroom on *Mary Tyler Moore* (CBS, 1970–1777), the military hospital on *M*A*S*H* (CBS, 1972–1983), the bar on *Cheers* (NBC, 1982–1993), or the paper company on *The Office* (BBC Two, 2001–2003; NBC, 2005–2013). The other, now common, alternative to suburban nuclear domestic bliss is the (typically urban) friend family. *Mary Tyler*

Moore and *Laverne & Shirley* (ABC, 1976–1983) in some ways had both workplace and friend families; *The Golden Girls* (NBC, 1985–1992) had a friend family; but *Seinfeld* (NBC, 1989–1998) and *Friends* (NBC, 1994–2004) really solidified friend families as a common alternative to sitcoms' utopian nuclear family. *Seinfeld* and *Friends* are essential predecessors to Horrible White People shows because they address and begin to embrace the failure at work and in romance—albeit without the bleak, despairing affect and, for *Friends*, with a contrastingly chipper, bright, and colorful palette—that are central to the dystopian ethos of Horrible White People shows.

Alternative-family sitcoms of different eras have been vital to helping mass television audiences grapple with and eventually accept changing social relationships and political policies. According to Bonnie Dow (1996) the utopian and ultimately conservative format of the genre allows for the incorporation of some progressive social and political representations, like feminism, while safely containing and depoliticizing them, in much the same way that Spigel and Lipsitz argue that sitcoms could contain and depoliticize racial difference in the 1950s. In the 1970s, televisual families broadened to incorporate the impacts of feminism by normalizing a woman who focuses on her career over marriage with *Mary Tyler Moore*'s workplace family. Later, sitcom assimilated rising divorce rates, disillusion with marriage, and acceptance of LGBTQ identities with the alternative friend families of 1990s sitcoms like *Seinfeld*, *Will and Grace* (NBC, 1998–2006, 2017–2020), and *Friends*. In the 1990s, *Will & Grace*'s friend family—made up of straight Grace; her roommate and best gay friend, Will; straight Karen; and gay Jack—helped expose "straight panic" and normalize a limited range of gay families (Becker 2006). Adding political efficacy to changing representational norms, Julia Himberg (2018) notes how the commercial success, activism, and production cultures surrounding *Modern Family* (ABC, 2009–2020) and its central gay couple, Mitch and Cam, played a part in building support for gay rights, including marriage equality in the 2010s. The friend families of *Friends* and *Seinfeld*, in particular, with their often-unlikable central characters and their narrative innovations, like *Seinfeld*'s relatively complex episode-long jokes and *Friends*' serialized will-they-or-won't-they romance between Ross and Rachel, are key moments in the genre that paved the way for Horrible White People shows. Like a lot of HWP shows, through their alternative-friend-family structures, both programs significantly critiqued dominant norms of American culture, particularly its idealized nuclear families, yet made those critiques palatable by carefully excluding any challenges to the dominant racial order.

Seinfeld is a particularly important parent of the shows in this book. Its polarizing series finale on May 14, 1998, with an audience of seventy-six million viewers, predicted some of the ideological complexities and comedic tensions around race and ethnicity that plague Horrible White People shows. At the same time, it reset character norms and comedic targets of mainstream sitcom humor through what Jon Stratton (2006) calls the "Yiddishification" of American comedy. The final episode put its four iconic main characters, Jerry, George, Elaine, and Kramer, on trial for "criminal indifference" and a violation of the "duty to rescue" law after they mock an overweight man named Howie rather than helping when they witness him getting carjacked at gunpoint. The ensuing trial serves as the perfect frame to trot out a variety of "character witnesses" or cameo appearances by favorite recurring characters from the series' nine seasons. Ultimately, these witnesses underscore that however appealing or relatable audiences found the characters and their antics, the four friends are actually "really bad people," as Babu Bhatt, a Pakistani former restaurateur (S3E7 and S4E15), testifies. After finding the four guilty, the judge summarizes in his sentencing, "I do not know how or under what circumstances the four of you found each other, but your callous indifference and utter disregard for everything that is good and decent has rocked the very foundation upon which our society is built. I can think of nothing more fitting than for the four of you to spend a year removed from society."

This episode, of one of the most commercially successful sitcoms ever made, earned notoriously divided reviews and landed high on many lists of the worst finales of all time. It was criticized by many people for labeling the main characters so grossly antisocial that they actually belonged in prison. By extension, the show seemed to indict the millions of viewers who identified with the characters' witty (if also snarky or cruel) commentary on the frustrating minutiae of everyday life (Morreale 2003). This uncomfortable implication of viewers in their beloved characters' bad behavior is central to the affective register of pleasurable disgust or "cringe" common to many Horrible White People shows (see, for example, Havas and Sulimma 2018 on the aesthetics of cringe; and Hargraves, forthcoming, on the irritation of watching *Girls*). Regardless of the polarizing finale, *Seinfeld* cemented the idea that sitcom characters did not have to be sympathetic or aspirational and by extension that the genre need not be utopian in order to illustrate American norms—or evolving standards—of home and family. Many HWP shows explicitly frame their protagonists as "bad people" through various elements of narrative exposition but most obviously in the titles of many of the shows: *You're the Worst, Fleabag, Difficult People*, and *Crazy Ex-Girlfriend* all highlight the more deviant or negative characteristics of the leads, whereas *Casual, Catastrophe*, and *I'm Sorry* more subtly point to the shows' glibly self-critical ethos.

This zenith of unlikable characters owes a debt to Norman Lear's satirical bigot Archie Bunker from the critically and commercially successful *All in the Family* (CBS, 1971–1979) as well.[3] But Bunker illustrated a fundamental problem with characters designed to provoke: while he was structured by Lear, the narrative, and CBS's targeted marketing to liberal, educated, upper-middle-class "quality" audiences as a character to critique and ridicule (Feuer, Kerr, and Vahimagi 1985), some audiences admitted to identifying and agreeing with working-class Archie's conservative, frequently racist, social and political views (Rosenberg 2014). *Seinfeld*, unlike *All in the Family*, had no foil or contrasting character like Archie's much more liberal and idealistic daughter and son-in-law for viewers to choose to identify with. Instead, *Seinfeld* encouraged empathy and identification with its four antisocial main characters, a strategy so successful that its language, jokes, and characters became embedded in American popular culture well beyond the show's run. Yet, as the *Seinfeld* finale illustrated, the often ambiguously satirical framing of Horrible White People shows and their questionably parodic character constructions leave them open for a variety of interpretations, empathies, and readings depending on viewers' standpoints. We argue that the wiggle room in that interpretation lets viewers potentially identify with the *attempt* to not be racist or the *awareness* of White liberal racism, allowing that awareness to the take the place of confrontation that might threaten the series' humor or viewers' own comfortable position of laughter.

If viewers identify with "really bad people" on-screen, formulating characters' self-aware bad behavior as a punch line lets characters and

the viewers who identify with them off the hook for often terrible behavior. In Robin DiAngelo's (2018) definition of White fragility, when
White people's sense of racial comfort (postracial beliefs or ignoring
structural racism in favor of more easily solved or ignored individual
racism) is challenged, they flee the situation rather than cope with the
confrontation—and given their racial privilege, they are easily *able* to
simply exit the situation and move into a space of racial comfort. In
TV comedy, laughter functions as a mechanism of this kind of flight.
In an episode of *I'm Sorry* titled "Racist Daughter" (S1E2), for example,
White, liberal, middle-class, suburban Los Angeles parents arrange a
play date between their five-year-old daughter and the new Black student at her school. When the mother, Andrea, tells her daughter, Amelia, about the get-together, Amelia says very matter-of-factly that she
doesn't like the color of Elsie's skin. Challenged by her shocked and
uncomfortable parents, she repeats this in three or four different ways.
The parents' facial expressions are emphasized by close-ups and cuts
that show the panicked/embarrassed/caught-off-guard eye contact they
make with each other as they try to shift their daughter's opinion without scolding her. Mom stutters; Dad's forehead creases and uncreases
repeatedly while he mutters "yeah" after Mom's every attempt to spit out
versions of "I think her skin is very beautiful." Daughter Amelia finally
ends by holding out her arm, stroking the pale skin on the inside of her
forearm and saying, "See this color skin? This is the color skin I like."
Andrea consults her daughter's young White teacher, who assures her
that racism is a common phase and that most kids grow out of it very
quickly. Andrea recruits her Black male friend Brian, another father at
the school, to approach Amelia at the park and, in his words, to "be a
good role model for her." "Don't sweat it," he says. "I am a lot of people's
Blackest friend."

Throughout the episode, as when Brian fails to convince little Amelia and then says that he is going to text all the parents and tell them
about Amelia's racism, the problem is framed as rich comedic territory
for Andrea's friends and primarily as embarrassment for Andrea. The
incident culminates when, during father Mike's dinner party with colleagues, Amelia arrives in the living room covered in self-applied black
paint and, holding out her arms as if around a rotund belly, quotes, "Hey
hey hey, I'm Fat Albert." The full circle from disliking dark skin to appro-

priating it for her own play encompasses a range of White racism from overt hatred to appropriation.

The endless amusement of Andrea's friends and the laughter spurred by Andrea's awkward embarrassment turn White racism into a childish phase so outré that it is absolutely clear that it is not shared by the adults. Yet, by displacing racism onto a child and turning it into the episode's running joke, *I'm Sorry* presents it as a problem solved or passed through briefly before education. While perhaps the intended reading of this episode is how horrifying racism is for liberal White people (even if that horror is mild embarrassment rather than the psychic pain endured by actual victims of racism) and how they strive to correct it in their children, there is also the fact that overtly racist statements create some of the episode's biggest laughs. A viewer could watch Amelia's blackface appearance, see how funny Andrea's comedy-writing partner, Kyle, finds it, and call to mind recent celebrity blackface incidents, thinking of them as funny rather than rhetorically violent acts of cultural appropriation.[4] Kyle could be taking cruel or ironic pleasure in the adults' discomfort (the dominant or intended reading), but he could also, like Archie Bunker, be providing an opportunity to enjoy a White child's blackface performance. Like a lot of Horrible White People shows, *I'm Sorry*'s lack of a laugh track—which typically encourages a more unified response to its comedy—opens a potentially wider range of interpretations (Mills 2018, 269). Yet perhaps the key to understanding this episode is the end of the dinner-party scene. Immediately after Amelia's Fat Albert impersonation, the camera cuts to a close-up of Julie, Mike's Black coworker and the only non-White person in the room. Her look of discomfort and dismay is part of the punch line of the joke. But rather than addressing Julie, the remainder of the scene features Kyle's wisecracks and laughter. The camera lingers on Julie's silent displeasure because she is seated next to Amelia, but she is speechless while the comedy comes from taking pleasure in the discomfort of hosting a dinner party where someone commits a faux pas—in this case of middle-class White parents having a racist daughter. The effects of racism on people of color is dismissed by characters like Brian and Julie who are ultimately unaffected by the child's behavior and serve to illustrate by association that the White parents are not racist. Thus, just like Archie Bunker and the characters on *Seinfeld*, viewers can identify and empathize with the White characters' narcissism, cruelty, ineptitude, well-meaning liberal racism, or displays of White fragility. The critique of those attitudes is embedded in the scenes as well but is potentially dismissed by cathartic laughter and Black characters either getting the joke (like Brian) or being silent (like Julie). Viewers then are offered the option to laugh with Kyle or Brian, rather than sympathizing with Julie.

This tension around interpretation points to another way that *Seinfeld* is an important precursor to the Horrible White People cycle: its success and popularity helped entwine Jewish humor and culture into that of mainstream humor, thus normalizing and centralizing the traditional Yiddish self-deprecating critique of modern bourgeois "civility" or norms of appropriateness and boundaries between public and private (Stratton 2006), found in so many sitcoms that followed it, especially HWP shows. In the *Difficult People* pilot, for example, the character of the show's creator, Julie Klausner, an aspiring comedian, exemplifies both the challenge to civility and this self-deprecating critique when she receives a lot of pushback after firing off a controversial tweet: "I can't wait for Blue Ivy [Beyoncé and Jay Z's toddler daughter] to be old enough for R. Kelly [a musician accused of urinating on and raping underage girls] to piss on her." The joke (which received shocked and disgusted reactions from fictional characters in the show as well as from viewers watching who expressed their disgust via Twitter [see Yahr 2015]) establishes the series as one that will continually push the boundaries of appropriateness, while also representing (and perhaps critiquing) the extreme desperation that Julie's character will go to for a laugh or to find any semblance of success as a comedian: mainly the abjection she performs as a result of her feelings of professional precarity (see chapter 3). Similarly, in the pilot episode of *Fleabag*, the unnamed protagonist gets caught by her boyfriend masturbating to a speech by Barack Obama. Her boyfriend is so horrified with her mixing of public political figures and private sexual pleasure that he breaks up with her on the spot. These moments exemplify the cycle's often cringeworthy (see Havas and Sulimma 2018) yet purposefully self-critical ethos, one of its defining attributes stemming directly from the influence of Jewish comedy. Many of the Horrible White People shows are, in fact, created by Jewish writers and feature Jewish characters, but significantly the influence of Jewish comedy traditions extends beyond those specific shows to underlie the comedic sensibility of the whole cycle.

According to Jeremy Dauber (2017), there is a long, diverse history of Jewish humor that stems back to the Bible, but an important theme within those traditions takes the form of self-deprecating commentary on Jewish culture itself—humor that shields against anti-Semitic stereotypes by exploiting them first. This type of comedic critique derives from Jews' long history of persecution and subordinate status, but the same comedic mode is used in Horrible White People shows to exploit critiques of well-meaning liberal White people in order to shield them not from anti-Semitism or racial violence but from accusations of White privilege or complicity in structures of White supremacy. In the history of Jewish comedy, this tack is meant to deflate pomposity or ego of those people who consider themselves high and mighty (like middle-class White people in the 2010s) and often does so by focusing particularly on defending the poor against the exploitation of the upper classes or other authority figures (threats of unemployment, broken relationships, and the failed promise of the American Dream), ultimately serving as a social catharsis to their subaltern status (an entirely *perceived* subaltern status in the updated Horrible White People version). One of the comedic-character traditions that embodies Jewish humor's self-deprecation is the *schlemiel*—or the stupid, funny loser—known for his foolish weakness, which in many iterations transforms into a naïve innocent, a man (or woman) imposed on by the unreasonable and threatening forces of the dominant culture. The schlemiel thus provides the subaltern community with an opportunity to laugh at its own circumstance and at the dominant society that has placed it in this circumstance (Stratton 2006, 126). Jon Stratton, among many other scholars, notes that George is the schlemiel on *Seinfeld*, even though the show represents his Jewishness (and that of all the characters) rather ambiguously (see Carla Johnson 1994; Krieger 2003; Gillota 2010). His habitually lazy, foolish performances and repeated failures at work and in relationships ultimately serve to challenge norms of white-collar professionalism and middle-class ambition, work ethic, and appropriate behavior.

The self-deprecating critique common in Jewish comedy, Stratton notes, is often directed at conceptions of the family or heterosexual relationships because "the nuclear family, after all, is thought of as the point of imbrication of civil and cultural codes of behavior" (2006, 122) as well as being central to the cultural function of sitcoms. The family, in other words, is both the buffer between public and private and the place where people are socialized into public norms and mores. So, when the family is disrupted or critiqued as it is by prioritizing platonic friendship groups over reproductive, heteropatriarchal nuclear families, as it is in the friend-family sitcom, "civility" and the dominant cultural order are also threatened. *Seinfeld* routinely criticized modern dating rituals, monogamy, heterosexuality, and the concept of settling down with a nuclear family, especially through the ups and downs of George's relationship with Susan Ross, which highlighted their obvious incompatibility and the lack of fulfillment offered by marriage.

More than anything else, this type of self-deprecating humorous critique of dominant culture reflects *Seinfeld*'s influence on many sitcoms that followed it, especially Horrible White People shows that are openly critical of their protagonists. Significantly, while Stratton reads this critique as distinctly Yiddish—an example of what he terms "a Jewish moment," adapting Alexander Doty's (1993) "queer moments"—he nonetheless points out that after years of integration into American comedy through comics like Lenny Bruce and Woody Allen, and especially *Seinfeld*, the schlemiel "has lost his status as expressing the ambivalences of feeling of a subordinate group as Jewish attributes become Americanized" (Stratton 2006, 126). He highlights how that onetime subaltern perspective is now subsumed within dominant American comedy, and thus Whiteness, mirroring the limited inclusiveness of White supremacy. *Difficult People* acknowledges this link explicitly when the struggling stand-up comedian Billy sarcastically tells a casting agent, "I know, a Jew in comedy; how will I ever defy the odds and make it?" (S1E2).

While the schlemiel was at one point an outsider position, a distinctly Yiddish perspective, Jewish comedy has been so influential, Stratton says, as to have become the dominant form of *American* comedy. It is now a mainstream comic trope, seen in many HWP shows even with characters who are not Jewish. On *You're the Worst*, for example, Lindsay's critique of heteropatriarchal marriage, which culminates in her stabbing her husband with a kitchen knife, aborting his child without consulting him, and ultimately divorcing him, is not dulled by the fact that she is an explicitly dumb and utterly incompetent adult.[5] Furthermore, the comic Jewish subaltern perspective is particularly complex in the US social and cultural context because even outside of comedy, Jews' skin color was crucial to their success (trumping even religious difference), leading, like Italian and Irish immigrants, to the eventual social reality of their racial inclusion, despite many Jewish immigrants and their children finding the process of identifying as White Americans ambivalent, filled with hard choices and conflicting emotions (Goldstein 2008). So, while American Jews may feel equivocal about their position in relation to Whiteness, even being seen to repress Whiteness in favor of identifying with other subaltern groups (Michael Alexander 2007, 98), they cannot negate the way that Jewish comedy has been subsumed within American comedy in general or the way that the Jewish circumstance has been "displaced into an apparently universal possibility of modern identification" (Stratton 2006, 135). The Yiddish critique of Anglo-American civility has laid the foundation for the dominant and universal (read: White) modern comedy of manners, which satirizes the norms, behaviors, and affectations of contemporary society and questions societal standards, yet without direct reference to Jewish identities, characters, or perspectives.

When Jewish producers and performers create Horrible White People shows, this self-deprecating catharsis sometimes becomes complicated by characters' middle- or upper-class comfort (apparent in wardrobe, set design, and locations) and their often openly acknowledged forms of cultural capital and racialized privilege. For example, *Broad City* is full of the witty and self-deprecating remarks about Jewish culture that Dauber describes (see especially "Jews on a Plane," S3E10). However, when Ilana buys a 1980s-style power suit in the color white and refers to it as her "white power suit" while she hires a rank of people of color—that is, subalterns with darker skin tones than her own—to act as her unpaid interns, she turns that self-aware, self-deprecating commentary on her privilege as a *White person*. That is, she puts herself in the position of the upper-class or authority figure exploiting the poor, and the self-critical strategies of Jewish humor that Dauber describes as preempting anti-Semitism are here turned to preempting critiques of White privilege. Demonstrating the mainstreaming of Jewish comedy, this strategy is found throughout Horrible White People shows, those created by Jewish and non-Jewish writers and performers alike.

A lot of Horrible White People shows focus on the satirical world of modern Jewish identity and anxiety, while also participating in a more general critique of contemporary society. Many of the shows we discuss in this chapter and throughout the book (*Broad City, Difficult People, Transparent, Crazy Ex-Girlfriend,* and *Girlfriends' Guide to Divorce,* for a few examples) are created, written, and performed by Jewish producers and actors. For some, the characters' Jewishness is a central part of the show's narrative. On *Transparent,* for example, even though the Pfefferman family describe themselves as secular, son Josh's most meaningful romantic relationship is with a rabbi; Jewish rituals and rites of passage like sitting shiva and covering mirrors (S1E10) to mark a family member's death or atoning and attending services for Yom Kippur (S2E7) punctuate the series; and the entire fourth season is premised on a family heritage trip to Israel. For others, Jewish culture is the backbone of jokes like the *Crazy Ex-Girlfriend* musical numbers "JAP Battle" (S1E13)[6] and "Remember That We Suffered" (S2E10) or the inspiration behind entire episodes of *Broad City,* like "Jews on a Plane" (S3E10), about a birthright trip to Israel, or "Knockoffs" (S2E4), about sitting shiva. In contrast to these explicit references, throughout the cycle, Jewish identity is also often either represented ambivalently by the text or absent altogether. We argue that American Jewishness is an identity that operates like the "otherwise privileged people of color" in Robin James's (2015) formulation of the limited and always-contingent inclusivity of White supremacy. Some of the programs we discuss, perhaps especially *Transparent,* use characters' Jewishness and this tradition of subaltern comedy to set their light-skinned characters outside the structures of White supremacy or to exculpate them from complicity with those structures. Yet, as we saw with the working-class ethnic sitcoms of the postwar period, Jewishness is a mode of difference that has largely been assimilated into Whiteness. That does not in any way deny the continued virulence of anti-Semitism. Yet, just as light-skinned privilege exists within communities of color, racial privilege can be contradictory. Jewish characters can be subject to the violence of anti-Semitism *and* benefit from the color of their skin *and* use self-deprecating humor to deflect from both—a combination that is in fact a prominent representational strategy in the HWP cycle. Another pertinent comparison is that of White women, who can be victims of misogyny *and* beneficiaries of White supremacy.

Transparent offers a particularly apt example of these racial tensions or contradictions when, in season 4, all the characters take a trip to Israel in order to escape their dysfunctional relationships in the United States. It is a search for meaning, heritage, and identity *and* a flight that enacts White fragility. The characters embark on a culturally specific trip, one that highlights their status as being part of a persecuted group but one that also simultaneously acknowledges their ethnic difference while imbricating them in the structures of White supremacy, when for example the younger daughter, Ali, meets a Palestinian woman and travels with her to Gaza, learning apparently for the first time about Israelis' persecution and violent suppression of their own neighbors. Like the Jewish story lines and characters of *Transparent*, those on a lot of Horrible White People shows are at times richly culturally specific, but the characters' pale skin and (for most of them) their middle- or upper-middle-class comfort grant them privileged access to the liberal Whiteness represented in Horrible White People shows, as well as the complicity of White fragility in shoring up the continued dynamics of White supremacy. It appears that now, for better and worse, as cultural and industrial factors are forcing TV to pay attention to difference, the industry turns to a (now but not previously) White ethnicity to help demonstrate its own inclusivity.

Alternative Families: Sex, Gender, and Rom-Coms

Seinfeld's alternative friend family and its mainstreaming of Yiddish critiques of contemporary norms of civility and the primacy of the nuclear family paved the way for the "friend family" sitcom that led to the success of shows like *Friends* (NBC, 1994–2004). *Friends* is another key antecedent to the Horrible White People cycle, with its challenges to the traditional sitcom's conservative focus on heteronormativity and patriarchy (San Martin 2003) and its centralization of alternative family structures that, like George and Susan's nonmarriage on *Seinfeld*, critique some of the conservative ideologies associated with the sitcom genre (Sandell 1998). *Friends*' pilot episode, of course, begins with Rachel fleeing the suburbs in her wedding gown to her high school best friend, Monica, in New York City after leaving her fiancé at the altar—a symbolic announcement that the series will be rejecting the utopian traditions of the sitcom's classic aspirational nuclear family. Nancy San Martin (2003) suggests that one of the structuring critiques of the show is of marriage and heteronormativity, as the characters repeatedly fail at marriage and conventional relationships, rejecting or substituting them with homoerotic friendships, casual flings, and playful sexual innuendo. Extending *Seinfeld*'s critique of civility, *Friends* presents a "laughably troubled heterosexuality" and "explores love and relationships in the contexts of lesbianism, homoeroticism, oral sex, non-genital erotic contact, voyeurism, pornography, multiple concurrent sex partners, public sex, group sex, masturbation, role-play and sexual fantasy" (San Martin 2003, 37). San Martin adds that the show continually criticizes biological families or families of origin by marginalizing them or representing them as troubled and dysfunctional, thus celebrating and rewriting norms of family, along the lines of the "post-modern gay social organization Kath Weston has termed 'families we choose'" (38). Yet the series' rewriting of families and questioning of heterosexual norms in the sitcom "occurs concomitantly with the presumption of whiteness as an unmarked category of racial identity" (40–41). Thus, however challenging *Friends* and its many copycat friend-family sitcoms were to classic aspirational norms of the sitcom's heterosexual nuclear family, they remained startlingly conservative regarding race.

The alternative family on *Friends*, Jillian Sandell (1998) argues, allows for sexual difference but uses that as a shield of sorts to avoid including other modes of difference, especially race. "Even though the show foregrounds and celebrates kinship networks which challenge the mythical nuclear heterosexual family, for example, the visibility of these 'alternative families' is made possible only by simultaneously rendering invisible other kinds of 'difference'" (143). She adds, "There is an underside to the fantasy of alternative families that *Friends* depicts, in other words, namely that this family is explicitly based on the exclusion of racial and ethnic others" (143). This critique can be extended to many Horrible White People shows, which use alternative families to despairingly wallow in the dissolution and instability of traditional family structures (often allegorized by unstable home ownership or living arrangements) but nonetheless contribute to the recentralization and validation of suffering Whiteness during the contemporary political turn toward the Right.

These alternative families are in part the result of HWP shows' relatively novel inclusion of romantic-comedy tropes into sitcom. Just as Ross and Rachel's exquisitely painful will-they-or-won't-they serial romance was one of *Friends'* generic innovations, characters on Horrible White People shows constantly fall in and out of both supportive and destructive relationships. They replay the romantic comedy over and over without ever providing the satisfying conservative ending in marital bliss. In fact, *Girlfriends' Guide to Divorce* and *Divorce* are about extricating oneself from marriage, and *Crazy Ex-Girlfriend* and *You're the Worst* end seasons with painful breakups of the central couples. Even though the series finale of *You're the Worst* ends with the central couple in a seemingly stable and fulfilling relationship, the flash-forward narrative structure framing the whole last season teases their impending breakup and indicates just how plausible that narrative conclusion could have been, not only for the show, but also for the whole cycle. This particular type of dystopic focus on sex and relationships also differentiates the shows in the Horrible White People cycle from several other precursors, as they often centralize female protagonists and infuse romantic-comedy conventions into the television-sitcom format. Rom-coms of course, are nothing new, but they have historically been understood as a cinematic rather than a televisual genre. *Sex and the City* (HBO, 1998–2004) changed that perception with its experimental form, mixing first documentary and eventually romantic-comedy conventions into the friend-family sitcom to celebrate platonic female friendships and to explore contemporary norms around sex and gender while promoting neoliberal postfeminist empowerment (Negra 2004).

Horrible White People shows make romantic pursuit and romantic conflict one of the central plotlines of half-hour TV comedies, marking a shift from the broad understanding of episodic TV comedy as consisting primarily of family, workplace-family, or friend-family sitcoms. While *Sex and the City* shares many characteristics with shows in this cycle, including more single-camera and high-production-value aesthetics and a structured unlikability of the female protagonists (Nussbaum 2013), the series predates the cycle and was invested in the historically and culturally specific presuppositions of postfeminism during the early 2000s. Chief among those presuppositions was the performance of consumerist femininity that the young women on Horrible White People shows reject in response to recession and emerging feminisms that we map in more detail in chapter 3. Horrible White People shows, through their characterizations and narrative concerns, explicitly critique many of the dominant ideological premises of the postfeminist sensibility (Gill 2007), through what Anne Helen Petersen (2015) calls the "postfeminist dystopia." They thus reflect contemporary mainstream media's messy and somewhat-uneasy incorporation of emerging feminism(s) and particularly the historical tensions around White feminism's inclusion of intersectional politics (see, for example, Crenshaw 1991; P. Collins 2012).

Yet, because of this inclusion of emerging feminisms and conventions of the romantic comedy, one of the defining features of Horrible White People shows is their setting within alternative families and active critiques of romance, biological families, and families of origin. On *Casual*, for example, a recently divorced mother and her teenage daughter have to move in with a brother recovering from a suicide attempt after cashing out of the tech industry. In just the pilot episode, the brother, Alex, dreams of his father's funeral, which is filled with the father's mistresses; he wakes up next to a one-night stand who is seen only as a silhouette in the bed; as he flees down the hall from their postcoital chat, he despondently watches through his home's glass rear wall as his teenage niece has sex in his hot tub; he cynically manipulates the algorithm of the dating app he invented to set up himself and his recently divorced sister, Valerie, with good-looking but terribly incompatible blind dates. Valerie flees that blind date and at a different bar meets Leon, whom she asks not to speak before they go home to have sex. The two then feel so uncomfortable with the casual sexual situation that they have created that they don't have sex and instead just lie awkwardly next to each other, awake all night. In between, Valerie has been to a meeting with her ex-husband, Drew, and their lawyers in which Drew is outraged that she has requested full custody of their daughter but does not want the house, which he sees as the symbol of the stable domestic family. The episode is a veritable festival of failed romance and alternative family constructions replacing dysfunctional and dystopian nuclear families.

Similar to *Friends*, as illustrated in both this chapter's opening narrative about *Transparent* and the pilot of *Casual*, most Horrible White People shows illustrate their dystopian views or ultimate rejection of the heterosexual nuclear family with the unremarked-on acceptance of sexual difference or experimentation—even when it is depicted as inappropriate or harmful. In season 1 of *Casual*, soon after the divorce of Laura's parents and after she and her mother move in with her uncle, Laura attempts to sleep with her high school teacher, leading to her eventual expulsion from school for sexual misconduct. After the public fallout from that, she develops a close sexual relationship with a peer dying of cancer, only to break up with him when his cancer is in remission, thus squelching her main attraction to him. She later develops an obsessive crush on her much-older boss at an environmental group for which she is interning, following her to Sacramento, only to be rebuffed upon arrival. More worrying is the *Transparent* story line in which it is revealed that as a fifteen-year-old, Josh regularly had sex with his adult babysitter and, in fact, still sees her, having casual, disturbing, subordinated sex with her (S1E1). When Racquel, briefly his fiancé, characterizes the relationship as abusive and tries to get him to seek therapy to make sense of it, he instead is forced to bring his abuser much more closely into his life when she reveals that she had a child as a result of their encounters when Josh himself was a child. In season 3, episode 1, of *Catastrophe*, Sharon is casually reminded by her friend Kate that she slept with a professor. She immediately responds that she did not sleep with him and that it was just a rumor. Her friend says, "Not *him*," prompting Sharon to remember a female professor she did in fact sleep with. Mickey, half of the central couple from *Love*, is a sex and love addict, a compulsion that is partially explained by the show's narrative as stemming from her dysfunctional relationship with her selfish, inattentive, alcoholic father (S2E8).

This list of examples could go on and on; in fact, almost every show in the HWP cycle includes characters who cheat on a partner or have sex with someone they know they shouldn't, because it is socially inappropriate, a distraction, or a stand-in for some other mental health struggle or emotional stress. On *Crazy Ex-Girlfriend*, for example, after Rebecca has alienated all her friends during the emotional fallout of being left at the altar and almost harming herself, she sleeps with her ex-boyfriend's father, a gesture she consciously describes as self-destructive in the musical numbers that frame the action. On *Casual*, when Valerie is feeling emotionally slighted by her brother and distanced from—or emotionally inept at dealing with—her charming and committed sex-addict boyfriend, she abandons them both at an engagement party, leaving to have sex with one of her acting classmates. This is her effort to purposefully self-sabotage her serious monogamous relationship and alert her brother that she still needs him for emotional support despite pushing him away in the previous episode. All of these examples and many more establish the cycle's willingness to challenge the sitcom's generic boundaries to explore the complicated and often taboo sexual relationships of the contemporary moment. Thus, they also explicitly criticize the hegemonic norms of heteropatriarchal family structures typically reinforced in the genre. These are not the liberatory critiques of *Modern Family* or *Will & Grace*, however. The total lack of judgment the texts place on sex with any gender is an important, progressive move in television representation, but all that sex is also often destructive, regardless of the gender or race of the sexual partner. These critiques are at best ambivalent and often, because almost all the characters are so unhappy, hint instead at a deep dissatisfaction with the loss of that norm and a nostalgic longing for a social order less complicated by, among other things, emergent feminisms.

Through these central explorations of sex and relationships, the shows in the HWP cycle are reflective of—or, in fact, a product of—the increased visibility of emerging feminisms at this historical conjuncture and particularly the changing expectations of sex, dating, marriage, and gender norms that have emerged as certain feminisms have become "popular" through a variety of discourses and practices circulated in popular and commercial media today (Banet-Weiser 2018). On the one hand, these representations illustrate progressive, important feminist issues and critiques of sex and gender issues that are typically absent from mainstream media discourses, earning them the liberal "quality" cachet that appeals to the upper-middle-class, educated, urban viewers the shows are targeting. *Broad City* especially but also *Crazy Ex-Girlfriend, Better Things, One Mississippi*, and *Girlfriends' Guide to Divorce*, among others in the cycle, are sex positive, normalizing a range of sexualities, sexual practices, and affective relationships far beyond the hegemonic heteronormative monogamy that leads to the eventual establishment of a utopian nuclear family that is typically represented in mainstream media, especially sitcoms. The loving, gentle way that Sam, on *Better Things*, accepts her daughter's shifting gender identity and potential

Figure 2.1. Sam consoles her child as they consider gender transition. (Still from *Better Things*; screenshot by the authors).

transition to identifying as a boy is one of the most uplifting versions of this challenge. The first season of *Better Things* ends with a montage featuring mother and child embracing in bed, intercut with a car trip along the beach in which the whole family sings along to Alice Cooper's "Only Women Bleed."

The primacy of nonhegemonic sex and gender dynamics in Horrible White People narratives are, nevertheless, also emblematic of what Sarah Benet-Weiser (2018) calls the common injury/capacity dynamic of popular feminism, in which the injury of gender inequality is recognized in a variety of media visibilities, but rather than collective, political, or structural change, popular media presents "individual capacity" as that which will suture the wound. Horrible White People shows incorporate emerging feminisms by tapping into a neoliberal notion of individual or familial capacity (for work, for confidence, for economic success) but position several key injuries as obstacles to realizing this capacity—sexism and racism but also at times multiculturalism and feminism itself. Like *The Cosby Show*'s individualized neoliberal representation of racial difference as ultimate sameness in the Reagan era, individual capacity in Banet-Weiser's observations of popular feminism implies that with enough gumption any girl or woman can overcome the "injury" of inequality. Parallel to magical postracial thinking, it implies individual solutions to structural inequality. Horrible White People shows tend to wallow in the "injury" of contemporary gender inequality, financial stresses, and intensified visibilities of racial inequality by centralizing the emotional distress, despair, and general ennui of their White female protagonists. So while Banet-Weiser describes the dominant mainstream-media answer to this newly visible injury as individual capacity of the neoliberal, entrepreneurial woman, Horrible White People shows—especially in contrast to some of the more utopian diverse-cast shows featuring successful, loving, capable women of color—focus, rather, on the White fragility, failure, and incapacity of their liberal, White, female protagonists.

Given this context, many of these representations of dysfunctional or inappropriate sex can be read as feminist-backlash narratives. Look at what happens, the cycle might say, when we give women equality and disrupt gender norms and expectations: it leads to young people not knowing how to have meaningful relationships or form happy families. This reading is especially apparent when HWP protagonists explicitly identify as feminist. Rachel Goldberg wears a T-shirt bearing the slogan "This Is What a Feminist Looks Like" in the first episode of *UnReal*. Yet despite being extremely capable professionally, Rachel is mentally ill and consistently forms self-destructive romantic relationships with inappropriate men: her superiors or subordinates at work, unavailable or even abusive men. What frames this character trait as a feminist-backlash narrative is that it is her romantic dysfunction and mental illness that make her so good at her job. In other words, were she to conform to more docile norms, she would be less good at her job but much more romantically palatable. The result of giving women access to high-powered careers, the backlash narrative might argue, is that they become ill and incapable of forming appropriate and meaningful relationships. The show makes this narrative text rather than subtext in season 3 when it casts a wildly successful thirty-something female CEO as the star of the dating-show-within-a-show. The suitress, as she is called, is told that she is dowdy, boring, too aggressive, too smart, and utterly unlikable to all twenty-five men *hired* to date her. Mirroring Rachel's (and her boss, Quinn's) romantic failures, the suitress's feminism is framed explicitly as the reason for her inability to achieve love and happiness.

This incorporation of discourses of emergent feminisms, and explicit endorsement of the postfeminist dystopian critique, is why we mark the beginning of the Horrible White People cycle with *Girls*. The series fits several of the main characteristics of the cycle and can even be credited with spearheading them, despite receiving sharp criticisms, especially from feminists of color (K. James 2012; Daniels 2014): it was positioned as "quality" television by its network paratexts, promotional discourses, and critical reviews, while also adhering to quality aesthetics that work to distinguish it from "ordinary television," as discussed in chapter 1. It centers on a fictionalized version of the auteur-creator Lena Dunham; it experiments with sitcom generic conventions; and most importantly it reflects the all-encompassing bleak affect of cynicism, melancholy, dread, and White fragility permeating comedies and satires across the television landscape at this historical conjuncture. The pilot of *Girls* also establishes the series as being critical of the nuclear-family structure and invested in reflecting certain discourses of emerging feminisms in its focus on a young millennial friend family. In the opening scene, Hannah's parents cut her off financially, disrupting the unconditional support of the idealized nuclear family as they admit to having interests and desires beyond child rearing or witnessing and supporting her eventual professional success. Over the course of the series, Hannah's family further disintegrates as her father comes out as gay and her mother disengages with Hannah to focus on her own hobbies, interests, and personal growth. Moreover, as Angela McRobbie observes, "One of the defining features of *Girls* is that it stands as a seemingly realist counter to the injunctions to young women in a post-feminist frame to strive for some western culture-bound notion of perfection, with a light-hearted endorsement of 'imperfection'" (2015, 13). This imperfection is often represented through Hannah's "nonnormative"[7] body type unabashedly on display throughout the series and the characters' many glibly narcissistic or inappropriate comments and actions.

Throughout the series, Hannah and her friends are actually utter failures at life, sabotaging professional and romantic opportunities alike, collapsing under the slightest bit of societal pressure, and deserting responsibilities at every turn. Gillian Silverman and Sarah Hagelin characterize this as the show's "feminist antiaspirationalism" (as opposed to postfeminist perfectionist striving), in which the characters' flaws and their rejection of the marriage plot and neoliberal success markers "detract from rather than reinforce [their] femininity, foiling audience expectations about young women" (2018, 879). The series' self-critical ethos is particularly apparent in a moment highlighted by Hunter Hargraves (forthcoming) when Shoshanna answers her friend Marnie's call for honesty among the girls and lets loose with a stinging indictment of each character, culminating in a collective condemnation that they are all "mentally ill and miserable" and thus reflect a millennial generation coddled by neoliberal entitlement and suffering postrecession ennui.

The miserable, struggling, alternative friend family on *Girls*, like many of the Horrible White People shows, thus further challenges the central ideology of the sitcom, one that remained strong even through previous challenging iterations. That is, the cycle explicitly critiques the utopian fantasy of recuperative collective solidarity offered by the family (whether nuclear or chosen) when faced with the disruptive realities of modern life, thus further centralizing the precarity of its floundering White protagonists. The darker lighting, isolating single-camera cinematography, grimmer aesthetics, and the varied on-location sets, departing from the habitual domestic studio sets of cynical White family sitcoms from *All in the Family* through *Seinfeld*, underscore their dystopian fantasies of failed domesticity, thus centralizing families that are unable to protect their members from the outside world. When Rebecca Bunch, the titular character of *Crazy Ex-Girlfriend*, is left at the altar, for example, she nearly harms herself, pushes her entire friend family away in a cruel diatribe, and relapses into serious mental illness; her emotional state is underscored by her fleeing her apartment's domestic comfort for a bland hostel and the blue low-key lighting that frames her as she walks away, making the comforting suburban tree-lined street look isolating (the light separates her from the location) and sad (figure 2.2, top). This colder aesthetic also structures the season 3 finale of *You're the Worst* when Jimmy abandons his girlfriend immediately after proposing marriage on top of a cliff overlooking Los Angeles at night. The dystopian last shot symbolically depicts them both in a split-screen composition of individual, isolated medium close-ups (figure 2.2, bottom), and the entire subsequent season chronicles Gretchen's embrace of drugs, alcohol, and inappropriate sex as she, now homeless, sleeps on the couch of her friend's tiny studio apartment, while Jimmy flees his architect-designed midcentury-modern house to an upstate trailer park for several months. The new trailer-park setting, with its dusty oranges and browns, glaring sun filtering through clouds of cigarette smoke, and cluttered set design, populated with outdated and obsolete technology, tattered 1970s-era furniture, and haphazardly hung Christmas lights, further underscores Jimmy's sense of emotional fragility, confusion, and dislocation. The clean lines, minimal furnishings, and cool-blue hues of his modernist house—symbolic of his professional success and class ascension—were representative of his controlling, pretentious, and self-aggrandizing personality. The show's abrupt departure from Jimmy's house as the primary setting in the season 4 premiere thus provides a layered underscoring of all the characters' sense of ennui and precarity, especially Jimmy's.

While a variety of aesthetic and narrative choices in Horrible White People shows underscore the dystopias of nuclear-family structure, the White fragility central to these shows seems to be particularly tied to threatened houses and the disruption of domestic spaces. The ending of *Transparent*'s "Letting Go" (S1E2) includes a telling match-cut that connects a shot of an elderly Maura to a much younger Mort as both look in on the family house from the outside, remembering the compulsory performance of happy nuclear family that she was forced to perform for most of her life as its patriarch, and in that moment, she officially decides to move and leave the house to daughter Sarah—the rejection of the house symbolizing her rejection of the role of patriarch and the false identity she enacted for so much of her life. For another example, during Sarah's extravagant wedding to Tammy (S2E1), which narratively reestablishes her in a new arrangement of domestic stability after imploding her previous marriage, she looks up into the sky during an anxiety attack at the altar to see a plane advertisement carrying a sign: "We buy ugly houses." The centrality of "ugly houses" at this moment links her anxiety to the impending domesticity represented by her wedding and connects her current sense of fragility to the postrecession housing crisis, one aspect of the historical conjuncture producing the Horrible White People cycle. Furthermore, the highly constructed, controlled aesthetic of the all-white wedding alludes to her failure or unwillingness to conform to a very particular form of fictionalized utopian domestic Whiteness.

Threatened houses and disrupted domestic spaces proliferate across the cycle as, in yet another example, a rug symbolizing the unlikely compatibility of *Love*'s central couple is ruined by a carelessly spilled glass

Figure 2.2. Rebecca flees; Jimmy abandons Gretchen. (Stills from *Crazy Ex-Girlfriend* and *You're the Worst*; screenshots by the authors).

of wine just at the moment the couple hits a rocky point in their relationship; or on *Casual* when teenage Laura sells her mother's expensive, custom-built dining-room table—one bought purposefully to symbolize her newfound independence after divorce and moving out of her brother's house—rejecting their new version of familial domesticity. Even beyond the symbolism of disrupted domestic settings, nuclear families of origin are often explicitly the target of critique. Season 4 of *You're the Worst* repeatedly enacts explicit and extreme critiques of those families. Lindsay and her sister, Becca, both come to the long-delayed realization that their narcissistic mother was actually neglectful and emotionally abusive (S4E10). They grew up believing that the kindest of their mother's boyfriends, a beloved father figure for them, had abandoned them; they discover, however, that their mother had kept him away. Their subsequent quest to find this man (Lou Diamond Philips, playing himself) is not, however, the catalyst for healing or maturation but instead a narrative of regression and accusation that finally ends with their estranged mother yelling at them, "You two are adults. You're goddamn baked. If your lives are a mess, you figure it out." Following the same theme, several episodes earlier (S4E7), the show broke its own ensemble format and focused on Gretchen's travel home for the birth of her niece. The episode begins with Gretchen stopping by her suburban family home alone. Upon entering the house, Gretchen is framed from an overhead angle, purposefully disorienting the typical establishing shot of the sitcom's communal space and ultimately abstracting Gretchen from the domestic environment—a feeling underscored by Gretchen's actions, as upon entering she quickly puts on the hood of her sweatshirt and pulls the strings tightly around her face as if protecting herself from the space around her and the family dynamics it represents. Retreating from the home's communal domestic spaces that are typically central to sitcom settings, she heads to her old bedroom, which has been converted into a welcoming shabby-chic guest room, perfectly staged for guests with crossed-stitched pillows and framed signs with the Wi-Fi password. Gretchen never turns the lights on, making the cold, low-key lighting render the space eerie and inhospitable, contrasting directly with typical sitcom lighting and atmosphere. Throughout the episode, Gretchen avoids the hospital where her family is gathered celebrating the ritual regeneration of the suburban family via the birth of the next generation. Instead she becomes obsessed with tracking down an old friend from high school, a digression that, like Becca and Lindsay's, provides no liberating understanding or growth. Rather, the episode ends with a teary, even more disillusioned Gretchen hiding behind a curtain, her face cast half in shadow, looking into the brightly lit hospital room where her parents, brother, and sister-in-law are gathered with the new baby. Gretchen makes eye contact and smiles at the baby but does not enter the room or speak to anyone else; no one knows she was ever there, and she simply walks away, in a move that represents her explicit rejection of or at least incapacity to fit into this romanticized cliché image of nuclear-family togetherness.

Throughout the cycle, programs also reject the idea that the patriarchal structure of the traditional nuclear family can offer solace and order, often by killing off or transforming the patriarch. *Transparent* features a transgender parent whose gender transition embodies the feminization of many HWP men who become obsessed with their homes, domesticity, and excessive emotions. *You're the Worst* and *Catastrophe* both feature story lines in which main characters' fathers die of natural causes. *Casual* and *Transparent* both euthanize ill fathers or father figures, killing mostly absent patriarchs in a rather overt metaphor for killing off, if not patriarchy, then an older social order that has become

Figures 2.3 and 2.4. Gretchen returns home and flees the hospital maternity ward. (Stills from *You're the Worst*; screenshots by the authors).

nonfunctional and burdensome. Yet in neither show does this serve as catharsis or the beginning of character growth or a metaphor or suggestion for any new order. Instead, the narrative simply continues, and characters return to their narcissism and ennui. So, while HWP shows lack the repetitive episodic structure of traditional sitcoms, their serialized story lines and other vignette or sketch structures never create or enable character development. The ideological dissolution of the self-sufficient neoliberal nuclear family is not replaced with anything. The changing economics of the recession and its impact on housing and the contemporary visibility of antiracist protest and emerging feminisms—for these affluent, liberal White characters—leads almost inevitably to sadness or even relapse into mental illness, a nostalgic yearning for a family past that turns out to be misremembered or no longer available.

These shows become dystopian, then, because, within them, all the social structures inherent to the dominant ideology of the American Dream—stable and loving hetero romance, family, work, home owner-ship, and even aspiration—are broken. Rather than being disrupted by a problem at the beginning of an episode and reassuringly repaired when the family (of whatever variety) comes together again at the end, the diverse narrative structures of this programming cycle never resolve or repair any of the characters' traumas. *Better Things'* vignette narrative structure is symbolic of the show's and cycle's disillusionment with the nuclear family and the White protagonists' general ennui, while resolv-ing neither. "Sick" (S2E4) opens with Sam's mother, Phil, illogically and uncharacteristically berating a young boy in a bookstore for wearing a fake mustache and then accidentally urinating on herself, signaling her emergent dementia. This incident is left unaddressed for the rest of the episode, and in the following scene, after the titles and commercial break, Sam returns home to find the family dog (typically a symbol of family love and unity) dead at the bottom of the stairs; the children each retreat to their own rooms, unwilling to process their grief together, leaving Sam to roll up the dog in the heavy carpet alone.

In a following scene, Sam, clearly upset, demands that her gay best friend, Rich, meet her at a bar. Yet instead of connecting either of the two earlier scenes, Sam stammers and stutters across from Rich, explain-ing not the emotional turmoil she just went through but rather why she wants to break up with her wonderful new boyfriend—the warm and optimistic feelings are so foreign and uncomfortable compared to her status quo of misery and ennui that she wants it to stop. Even though Rich convinces her to stay with him for the time being, the following episode, "Phil"—which traces Phil's further slippage into dementia and self-harm, along with a narrative arc of Sam successfully introducing her children to her new boyfriend—nevertheless concludes abruptly with Sam walking unexplained and seemingly unmotivated with a bottle of

Figure 2.5. A loving family vignette. (Still from *Better Things*; screenshot by the authors).

whiskey into the hotel room of another man, presumably to cheat on her new boyfriend and thus sabotage the relationship. But, like several narrative arcs and character actions in this series and the cycle overall, the series never returns to fully explore Sam's motivations or explain her feelings in more detail, leaving them unresolved.

"Sick" ends in a similarly abrupt fashion, thus also challenging the narrative and ideological closure of the classic sitcom. Sam witnesses an idealized vignette of nuclear-family domesticity when her ex-husband pays a surprise visit and stays for dinner. Composed in soft key lighting and symbolic blocking similar to classic Norman Rockwell paintings depicting romanticized 1950s American culture, the whole family is together in the living room: eldest daughter, Max, plays the antique baby-grand piano softly with her father, her head leaning comfortably on his shoulder; middle child, Frankie, feet tucked underneath her, reads under the warm side-table light; and youngest daughter, Duke, sitting casually on the living-room steps, head in hands, smiles to Sam as they lovingly take in the tranquil scene. The scene and episode conclude, though, not with father putting the kids quietly to bed, as Frankie requests and as the conventional sitcom might demand in order to reconstitute the nuclear family, but with Sam slamming the door on her ex-husband midsentence and turning nonchalantly back to her life as a single mother on a quick cut to the closing credits. The show's vignette structure, again, means it never returns to this scene, never addresses Sam's or her children's reactions to the evening and certainly does not follow up with a reconstitution of that former family.

As these examples illustrate, throughout the Horrible White People cycle aesthetic and narrative innovations challenge the classic conventions of the sitcom, resulting in parallel challenges to the genre's focus on idealized White nuclear families and domesticity. On the surface, then, Horrible White People shows use these challenges to the conventions and histories of the sitcom genre to appear progressive, self-critical, antiracist, inclusive, and feminist, but the ultimate effect of these challenges recentralizes White suffering under the seemingly protective guise of liberal social critique. The disillusion with family and lack of narrative closure in these shows leave the White protagonists suspended in a space of precarity, a space of injury, unable to fulfill their neoliberal capacity without the safety of family, jobs, or often even ambition.

Writing about a preceding shift of sitcoms toward a single-camera aesthetic in the early 2000s, Newman and Levine point out in relation to genre evolution, "Progress cannot be appreciated naively as steps forward, as improvements, moving us toward better and better forms and experiences. Formal changes are always to some extent responses to social, economic, and technological conditions" (2012, 78). Paralleling our argument in chapter 1, Newman and Levine see the aesthetic trend developing to serve particular niche audiences; but as we have laid out, genres also evolve to mirror and shape contemporaneous political, social, and cultural trends. The fact that this substantial cycle of sitcoms with similar aesthetic innovations and thematic concerns about dystopian nuclear families all emerged within a few short years needs to be understood as part of a dominant cultural ethos during the 2010s, reflecting and shaping the ideological tensions and anxieties of this historical conjuncture. Moreover, seen together with the contrasting, more conventional, utopian, diverse-cast sitcoms and other thematic consistencies mapped in the following chapters, these threatened families and floundering White protagonists work to ideologically insulate Whiteness from the threat of equality.

3

Emergent Feminisms and Racial Discourses of
Televisual Girlfriendship

UnReal's second season opens with the two female protagonists, Quinn
and Rachel, getting matching tattoos with the words "money. dick.
power." scribbled inside their pale, skinny wrists. The tattoo is copied
from a crumpled napkin where it has been scrawled in ballpoint pen,
presumably during a drunken party. The two friends, still drunk, clink
glasses, grunt as they bump fists, and pose for a photo, tattooed wrists
in the air, as Quinn proclaims, "We're going to be kings this year." Walking away from the tattooist's table, a tracking shot reveals that the two
are at work, striding through the mansion set of their reality show on
their way to a town car that will drive them to Las Vegas and a night of
sex, drugs, drinking, and carousing. This opening sequence celebrates
girls behaving "badly": drinking to excess, swearing, having casual sex,
wielding professional power with unbridled confidence, and occupying
televisual space—as we see with the long, uninterrupted tracking shot
that follows them through all the show's major sets—with the swagger
and aggressive sexuality usually reserved for straight White men. Most
importantly for this chapter, the moment also articulates the girls' intimacy and the power of their friendship.

Despite lying to, betraying, manipulating, and professionally sabotaging each other over and over throughout the show's four seasons, the
ultimately unconditional friendship between Rachel and Quinn is the
show's primary relationship. And because the genre of the dating-show-
within-a-show and *UnReal*'s own soapiness prioritize relationships, that
makes Rachel and Quinn's friendship the central narrative concern and
goal of the series. This is reinforced in the final moments of every season, which reconstitute the friendship, often as the women are shot from
overhead on poolside loungers on the set of their show. These shots pull
up, offering the two center frame, the calm focal point amid the excessive romantic trappings of the love mansion where they work. This is

true even at the end of season 2 when there are four side-by-side pool chairs and two male coconspirators lie in between Rachel and Quinn. Yet as the men lie flat, the women on either end are raised slightly, heads resting on matching red, patterned cushions that draw viewers' eyes to their faces (the men's cushions are darker, not matching shades, shoved down to be mostly hidden by head and shoulders). This small piece of set decoration links the two women visually, and their slightly raised positions mean that the camera can cut between them making eye contact over the men's heads. In this instance, the four are implicated in murder, but still, it is the connection between the two women that earns the season's last moments of emphasis.

That the series places Quinn and Rachel's tumultuous relationship at the center of the narrative and reinforces it with their reunification at key moments in the program's structure exemplifies Horrible White People shows' frequent focus on dynamic and complicated dimensions of (White) female sociality and particularly on the healing, supportive, and even feminist power of female friendship. If the Horrible White People programming cycle challenges the conservative ideologies of the sitcom by centering unlikable or horrible characters, leaving them without the typical support of the patriarchal family (see chapter 2), and narratively suspending them in their emotional suffering, girlfriends often step in to provide the unconditional love that is no longer offered by the promises of steady employment, middle-class contentment, and heteropatriarchal families. The central narrative tension of *UnReal*, like other HWP shows discussed in this chapter, is placed not on a romantic relationship but on the complex and multilayered interplay between female friends, which has historically been relatively rare in television representation, even in the friend-family sitcom from which this cycle evolves. But, perhaps not surprisingly given the centrality of Whiteness in the genre (see chapter 2), these friendships remain mostly racially segregated, typically featuring pairs of insulated White female friends or occasionally multiethnic friendship groups that surround and often support the White female protagonists—to show that these liberal White ladies have friends of all races and ethnicities, so they could not possibly be racist.

As the previous chapters illustrate, the shows in this cycle court quality audiences and critical praise in an era of "Peak TV" by deliberately challenging television's representational norms. The cycle's overwhelming focus on female friendship is one such challenge that allows for the integration of emerging feminist politics as well as a disruption of the postfeminist sensibility that focuses on individual achievement and often pits female "friends" against one another, signaling more multifaceted representations of girls and women. Opposed to the "fantasies of power" (Douglas 2010, 1–22) or the individualism, surveillance, and cruelties of "postfeminist sisterhood" (Winch 2013) that marked the postfeminist media environment of the first decade of the twenty-first century, the HWP cycle features intimate, loyal, female friends bonding while they flounder in postrecession insecurity. In a pushback against postfeminist "perfection" (McRobbie 2015), they love each other through abjection, failure, and horrible behavior in an assertion of female friendship as representative of emergent feminist solidarity. They are part of a trend that Rebecca Wanzo (2016) calls the "precarious-girl comedy" and Faye Woods (2019) calls "comedies of discomfort," in which endless alienation from social expectations is a source of humor. No longer aspirational as girlfriendships appeared in the postfeminist *Sex and the City* era, girlfriends in HWP shows "embrace the otherness found in the abjection of the self" (Wanzo 2016, 29). Julia Kristeva's concept of the abject describes those aspects of identity, the self, or the body that one might find repulsive but cannot be rid of, things like hunger, fat, blood, excrement, and need. Usually linked to filth, waste, or bodily fluids, the abject is also anything that is rejected by or disturbs the dominant understanding of social order (Kristeva 1982, 65). Thus, the abject is made up of aspects of identity that a person or a culture finds repulsive but are nonetheless an innate part of who they are. Female or nonbinary gender and non-White racial identities have both been theorized as abject (see especially J. Butler 1990; Kristeva 1982; Scott 2010). Horrible White People characters become abject when they fail to conform to middle-class norms like agreeable and passive femininity, stable employment, home ownership, and long-term hetero relationships. And while the forms of comedic abjection (narcissism, social awkwardness, blunt rudeness, bodily inappropriateness) in these shows tend to alienate the female protagonists from others (romantic interests, bosses, parents, and possibly even viewers), their abjection is typically supported, embraced, and echoed by their best friends. The best friends' shared abjection becomes a key aspect of the shows' critique of contemporary gender norms and expectations, offering nuanced complicated representations of women's intimacy and relationships with each other, thus earning the shows substantial critical praise (see especially Nussbaum 2017).

Yet the racial dynamics of these abject friendships are often left underexplored. In a published dialogue with Kyla Wazana Tompkins, pushing back against dominant progressive readings of a lot of Horrible White People shows like *Broad City*, Rebecca Wanzo articulates a discomfort she feels while watching the abjection of White girls. "Precariate chick TV," she argues, "seems to turn more than a bit on how incongruent it is for white girls to live demeaning lives" (Wanzo 2015). In response, Tompkins adds, "it's only if you experience poverty or abjection as a state that you are going to move through, or that doesn't adhere to your own body or your value in the world, that you can find comedy in that" (Wanzo 2015). Building on Wanzo and Tompkins's critique, we argue that the way girlfriends on these shows embrace or support each other's abjection structures the ways audiences are encouraged to cringe at, recoil from, identify with, or find comedy in that abjection. The cultural functions of these supportive friendships, especially their relationship to emerging feminisms and their racial dynamics within a cultural milieu of structural White supremacy, is the subject of this chapter. The intimate, supportive, sometimes even joyful female friendships and self-aware humor in Horrible White People shows often let White girls off the hook for participating in and benefiting from White supremacy through the way they center, excuse, and defend the White characters' abjection, liberal failure, and precarity.

A Brief Note about Vocabulary

In the title of this chapter and throughout the book, we refer to most of the female characters in this cycle—who range in age from teens (Laura on *Casual*) to late forties (Sam on *Better Things*)—as "girls" and their relationships with each other as "girlfriendships." We do this for specific rhetorical reasons. First, the experience of White precarity and abjection across the cycle features mostly female characters in quarter-life or midlife crises, with many of them clinging to a sense of youthful promise, identity, or "girlhood" that is just out of grasp or never experienced.

Lena Dunham, the creator and star of *Girls*, and the show's costume director, Jenn Rogien, for example, strategically conceived Hannah's wardrobe of lightweight rompers, skimpy crop tops, and juvenile hair barrettes to be ill fitting and inappropriate of her professional ambitions in order to reflect twenty-somethings clinging to a still-teenaged sense of style and self (Ferrier 2015). Similarly, Valerie on *Casual*, who is in her forties and had her child as a college student (thus missing out on some youthful rites of passage), buys motorcycle boots and skinny jeans to wear to her first acting class (S3E4), an outfit that contrasts drastically with her usual uniform of dowdy knee-length, A-line skirts and loose-fitting, often floral blouses. One of her classmates describes her new look as emblematic of her midlife crisis, "dressed like a quarterlifer crisis." Like Hannah and Valerie, many of the female Horrible White People characters reject or flee from the responsibilities of full-grown womanhood, clinging instead to a sense of girlhood in which vulnerability, play, irresponsibility, fun, and even narcissism are still acceptable. For a lot of Horrible White People protagonists, girlhood is a state of mind (and sometimes dress) that signals a rejection of the destination "woman" in favor of the constant process of female growth and evolution implied by "girl." The "girls" in the Horrible White People cycle, whatever their age, are still busy, as Hannah says in the *Girls* pilot, "trying to become who they are" or, like Valerie, reject who they have become.

Labeling adult women "girls" is also part of a larger cultural trend in this same historical conjuncture. This is reflected in a slew of literary representations of adult women, like *The Girl with the Dragon Tattoo* (2005), *Gone Girl* (2012), and *Girl on a Train* (2015) and televisual representations like *New Girl* (FOX, 2011–2018), *2 Broke Girls* (CBS, 2011–2017), *Good Girls Revolt* (Amazon, 2015), *Good Girls* (NBC, 2018–), and *Girlboss* (Netflix, 2018). In all these examples, the novels and TV shows in the girl-title trend, the word "girl" is decoupled from what is typically associated with girlhood—young age, innocence, naiveté, pigtails—as well as its derogatory roots, where it has historically been used to belittle women for performing their femininity or not being as emotionally or physically "strong" as men. Creators toy with the term's meaning, re-appropriating the traditionally more negative connotations of the term ("throw like a girl") to more powerful, sometimes less traditionally feminine connotations. In *The Girl with the Dragon Tattoo*, for example, the "girl" protagonist defies "girly" stereotypes as an antisocial, bisexual, punk computer hacker who seeks revenge on her abuser by raping him with a metallic dildo. But these girl texts also wrestle with the precarity of female identity itself during a historical conjuncture of social, economic, and political insecurity that has begun to smudge and demystify the once dominant neoliberal and postfeminist fantasies for women during prerecession times.

Discussing *Gone Girl* and *Girl on a Train*, novelists Sarah Weinman and Megan Abbott link their unreliable narrators, broken marriages, and women characters ambivalent about motherhood and relationships to the upheaval that many readers felt in the wake of the 2008 economic crash (NPR Staff 2016). The broken marriage based on lies, manipulation, and a false performance of idealized femininity in *Gone Girl* reflects the broken institutions of hetero marriage and family in the Horrible White People cycle that proliferated after the widespread economic, political, and romantic stagnation instigated by the crash. The term "girl" being attached to adult women, then, emerges to articulate a broad notion of cultural precarity and the questioning of normative roles, expectations, and gender identity during the historical circumstances outlined in the introduction to this book. The difference between these thriller novels and Horrible White People shows is that rather than facing these crises in isolation, the girlfriends on HWP shows bond over their shared experiences of precarity.

Choosing the moniker "girl" also becomes part of a feminist discursive project, challenging audiences to take seriously the typically derided or feminized concerns of contemporary women, young or old, who worry about romance, aging, motherhood and domestic labor, or balancing work and family. The novelist Robin Wasserman (2016), speaking again about *Gone Girl* and *Girl on a Train*, argues, "These books [and, we argue, Horrible White People shows] are grappling with an erasure of self by the identity of 'wife' and 'mother.' Their protagonists lead double lives, an ever-widening gap between the woman they present to the world and the girl hiding within. Despite being domestic thrillers about marriage and motherhood, the 'girl' books tend not to actually depict domestic life—instead, they track various escapes from it. These are women in flight or exile from the trappings of womanhood." Embracing the label "girl" then becomes a symbol of interrogating, and indeed breaking or escaping from, contemporary gender roles and expectations. Although the "girl" TV shows tend to be comedies, rather than thrillers like the books (a point we expand on later in this chapter), we see this flight, exile, or questioning of domesticity and adult womanhood in several Horrible White People shows: Valerie's neglect of her daughter on *Casual* as she searches for her own sense of identity; Lindsay's violent stabbing of her fiancé while cooking dinner on *You're the Worst* (described in the introduction); Sarah Pfefferman's nervous breakdown in the bathroom stall at her wedding reception in the second-season opener of *Transparent*; the active sabotaging of relationships with supportive and stable boyfriends by Fleabag and by Sam on *Better Things*. We could also include Rebecca's suicide attempt and return to her mother's home after being left at the altar on *Crazy Ex-Girlfriend* or Gretchen's retreat into drug abuse and agoraphobia after being abandoned by her boyfriend on *You're the Worst*; both adult women retreat from their professional and personal responsibilities after having failed to live up to romantic ideals, and they retreat either directly to the childhood comfort of their own mother, in Rebecca's case, or into Gretchen's complete rejection of the social world via agoraphobia and so many drugs that she often is not certain what day it is. Fleeing from the responsibilities of womanhood in these "girl texts" functions as a feminist critique of the lack of fulfillment offered by typical gender roles and heteropatriarchal narratives. Taking one step beyond their immediate predecessors, the "postfeminist dystopias" discussed in the introduction (Petersen 2015), these girls take advantage of discourses of emergent feminisms swirling in this historical conjuncture. In the context of the avowedly progressive characters, narrative and character complexity, and all the trappings of "quality" TV, the wielding of "girl" becomes an explicitly feminist act that situates the girls of HWP shows as feminist or progressive to attract "quality" audiences. "To be called 'just a girl' may be diminishment, but to call yourself 'still a girl,' can be empowerment, laying claim to the unencumbered liberties of youth" (Wasserman 2016). In this sense, "girl" has been used flexibly to describe women of all ages who aspire to a more youthful or even feminist lifestyle or sensibility.

But to call yourself "still a girl" or even a "girl" at all is a privilege often available only to White, upper-middle-class, straight, cis-gender young women. Sarah Projansky (2014), for example, traces a new "luminosity" or visibility of girls in the media but draws attention to the ways in which girls of color, like tennis superstars Venus and Serena Williams, who began their careers as teenagers, and Sakia Gunn, a fifteen-year-old African American lesbian murdered in a hate crime, are discursively and culturally excluded from being able to participate in an extended girl-hood, enact girlishness, or claim the label "girl." And while some women of color express this girly precarity in television shows with similar aes-thetic preoccupations, taste cultures, and thematic concerns as the HWP cycle—shows like *Insecure*, *Chewing Gum*, and *Dear White People*, on which we expand in chapter 4—these girls display a different, usually more resilient relationship to precarity and abjection than their White counterparts do, given the racialized hierarchies inherent in patriarchal White supremacy that use abject othering to justify inequalities.

Abject Girlfriendships

The HWP cycle features White girlfriends in arrested development, both economically and psychologically. They are socially awkward, inept, and display a vulnerability or weakness that has historically been avoided in liberal/progressive media representations so as not to rein-force long-standing gender stereotypes of women and girls being weaker and less capable than men. Like most girlfriendships in the Horrible White People cycle, the celebrated, close, intimate, and purportedly feminist girlfriendship between Abbi and Ilana on *Broad City* is intro-duced in the pilot episode through their shared abjection. Trying to scrape together the cash for Lil' Wayne concert tickets, the girls first attempt to return stolen office supplies for cash and eventually agree to clean a man's apartment in their underwear. Throughout the series, Abbi and Ilana video-chat while on the toilet and having sex and smoke excessive amounts of marijuana, sending them on surreal escapades around the city that often result in one or both of them losing their jobs, offending people, or experiencing some other economic or interper-sonal "failure." On *UnReal*, Quinn and Rachel solidify their friendship via their shared ability to manipulate contestants of their reality show in order to produce the spectacular interpersonal conflicts they and their audiences find entertaining. We enter the narrative of Gretchen and Lindsay's friendship on *You're the Worst* the morning after the wedding of "Fat Lindsay's" sister, when Lindsay drives hungover, driver-license-suspended Gretchen to work and the two reminisce about the good times, like when Lindsay gave four different men blow jobs at their five-year reunion. On *Crazy Ex-Girlfriend*, the titular protagonist, Rebecca, earns her "crazy" label through a series of abject behaviors, including the obsessive stalking of her ex-boyfriend Josh and meddling in his relationships, once sending him cupcakes made from her own poop. Yet rather than challenge Rebecca's desires and behavior, her new best friend, Paula, formerly contentedly conforming to her role as middle-class suburban wife, mother, and worker, is pulled into Rebecca's abjection, relishing their shared pleasures of the grossly socially unacceptable. Paula encourages Rebecca's stalking and manipulation when she tells Rebecca to befriend Josh's girlfriend; she hacks several people's phones and computers to gather intel for Rebecca; she even secretly implants tracking devices in friends' arms in order to have constant surveillance.

Throughout the cycle, girlfriends' shared sense of abjection and the comic escapades they experience are shown to be the result of their precarity. These girls are floundering, trying to make ends meet, and sharing in various forms of abjection that are "a principal sign of their precarity," which according to Wanzo (2016), "signifies what emotional and economic insecurity has wrought." Abbi puts up with her roommate's inconsiderate, freeloading, flatulent boyfriend because she can't afford rent on her own. On *UnReal*, Rachel and Quinn's friendship is built on the abject behaviors they feel are a necessary response to their differing, but nonetheless related, feelings of employment precarity: Rachel represents the precarious labor of the nonunionized reality-television industry, Quinn the precarious victim of institutional patriarchy that continually rewards straight White men while rendering the collaborative labor of women invisible or economically insignificant. Like Hannah, Marnie, and Shoshanna on *Girls*, who at the start of the series cannot secure paying jobs in the fields of writing, art, and fashion, respectively, *Broad City*'s Abbi and Ilana are financially insecure and unable to land the types of idealized postfeminist employment (often in creative industries) that they halfheartedly seek and think they deserve. Abbi, for example, wants to work as an artist or at least a physical trainer instead of a cleaner, and Ilana would prefer not to work but would rather be working for political causes instead of the group-sales e-commerce start-up she works for throughout most of the series. Thus, the girls' precarity is frequently depicted as an excuse for their abject behavior, and girlfriends support each other through socially unacceptable and downright inappropriate behavior because they empathize with that precarity.

In Kat George's (2014) praise of *Broad City*'s depiction of female friendship, she writes, "we got to watch two girls doing what girls do in their 20s—be total fucking dirt bags while loving the absolute shit out of one another. . . . They birth used condoms, clog toilets, fumble crushes, gobble drugs and discuss their bodies liberally with one another. Their adventures range from the completely feral to the surreal, their language is foul and they're blindly un-empathetic to the world around them in the most un-entitled way possible, which makes them, as disgusting and oblivious as they are, completely endearing." She argues that it is their unconditionally supportive friendship that makes them appealing and actually excuses their problematic behaviors. Most critics, like George, tend to see these abject girlfriendships as a welcome disruption that expands and diversifies televisual representations of women. As Elizabeth Alsop (2016) argues, "there is something radical in fostering empathy toward 'weak' female characters in the grips of powerfully negative emotions: anger, sadness, grief, self-doubt, shame." She suggests that these representations are a provocation, "challenging audiences to confront their own biases against historically less sanctioned forms of female behavior" and operating to "critique social expectations of women, rather than the women themselves."

Writing about the 1990s-era comedian and sitcom star Roseanne Barr, Kathleen Rowe (1995) described Barr's fatness and loudness and even the shrill tone of her voice and her working-class accent as "unruly" and therefore feminist behaviors that broke the rules of strict containment and decorum required of women in public. The unruly woman became, for decades, an effective way to theorize female characters behaving outside the bounds of antifeminist or even postfeminist strictures on clothing, body shape and size, behavior, and comportment. The emotionally distressed and abject girls on Horrible White People shows similarly give performances that demand attention. They are mostly slim and conform to postfeminist standards of dress and body shape, unlike Roseanne, but their despair and abjection offers them the opportunity to cry, scream, shout, act out, or even to lie silently on a bench staring into space for almost an entire episode, as Gretchen does on *You're the Worst* (S2E12). These performances are a welcome addition to the "strong female character," Hollywood's favorite mode of appealing to female audiences with characters who kick ass and win the day. Often the hallmark of film and television labeled feminist, this "strong female character" might be a gender-flipped superhero or detective and implies that feminist characters must be tough and resilient and shy away from the feminized emotions and signifiers of weakness—especially tears—of so-called women's genres.

In the early 2000s, there was a surge of female-centered "quality" television highlighting that precise conflict by focusing on the imbrication of work life (typically a setting for strength and emotional restraint) and home life (where feelings might be more freely expressed and women characters in particular might be nurturing and soft). Those female protagonists, women like Alicia Florrick on *The Good Wife*, Stella Gibson on *The Fall*, and Nessa Stein on *The Honourable Woman*, relied on intense restraint and fine-tuned facial performances that indicate the ways in which these often self-avowedly feminist female protagonists in their forties and fifties are *not* reacting emotionally (Lagerwey, Leyda, and Negra 2016). In contrast to abject Horrible White People protagonists, these more established, wealthier, older women exercise the emotional control of a generation accustomed to constant accusations of hysteria and characterizations of women as unfit for the high-powered professional positions they hold. Thus, we argue that the addition of completely unrestrained, failing, overemotional girls is a feminist addition to the "quality" TV landscape, offering women characters the opportunity to be something more multidimensional than a "strong female character." In fact, throughout the cycle, girlfriends take pride in abjection as a marker of liberal, progressive, or even radical critique of social expectations and gender norms. Rachel and Quinn's lying and contestant manipulation allows them to make what they deem "important television" that has the potential to "change the world." On *Crazy Ex-Girlfriend*, via the show's diverse musical styles, Rebecca masquerades as different versions of femininity, often using layers of irony to celebrate or wallow in the bodily abjection to which women subject themselves in pursuit of hetero romance and the markers of postfeminist success—especially a sexy body, a nuclear family, and career success (see McRobbie 2008).

Given these gender critiques, Horrible White People shows are frequently showered with praise and awards. And they are continually singled out for their compelling and nuanced representations of female friendships. In the *New York Times'* Watch List of "Convincing Female Friendships" (Watching Staff, n.d.), HWP shows make up almost half of the list, which includes films and television shows from as far back as the 1950s. *Fleabag, Broad City, Girls*, and *Crazy Ex-Girlfriend* are all highlighted for their celebrations of female intimacy and uncompromising depictions of female subjectivity. *Deadspin* calls *Broad City* "a fearless, priceless ode to female friendship" (Cills 2015). Tomi Obaro (2016) of *Buzzfeed* praises its centralization of female camaraderie, arguing that Abbi and Ilana's "friendship has #goals all over it." *TV Guide* similarly praises how *UnReal* "pushed the boundaries of female friendships on TV" (Gennis 2016), while the *Huffington Post* applauds Quinn and Rachel's complicated dynamic as the only "authentic relationship" on the show (Zarum 2016), and Anna Silman (2016) calls it "TV's most gloriously twisted female friendship." *Crazy Ex-Girlfriend* is particularly singled out for replacing the "marriage plot" with a "friendship plot," as Rebecca and Paula's unlikely friendship becomes "TV's best love story" (see Grady 2017; Leishman 2018; S. Allen 2016). This wave of praise points to the cultural impact these relatively niche shows have on broader discussions of emerging feminist discourses in the media. The girlfriendships on these shows—in which the girls support and even help each other into further abjection—offer explicit examples of a version of emergent feminism and model a type of female solidarity that disrupts and, in many ways, explicitly critiques gender norms and expectations, breaking drastically from the way the relationships between women are typically represented.

Girl Squads of Emerging Feminism(s)

The ubiquity of themes around girlhood and abject girlfriendship as feminism within this cycle reflects the current social, cultural, and media embrace of specific (albeit limited) feminist politics and feminist themes described as emergent feminism(s) (Keller and Ryan 2018). Sarah Banet-Weiser (2018) calls this phenomenon "popular feminism," in which spectacular, media-friendly expressions of girl power, gender-based inequalities, and feminist politics, such as celebrity feminism and corporate feminism, achieve more visibility, while feminist expressions that critique patriarchy and systems of racism and violence are obscured. This time of emergent feminism(s) is a departure from the postfeminist sensibility propagated in the first decade of the twenty-first century (Gill 2007), which wrongly but powerfully suggested that feminism was tired and outdated and had reached its goals of equality. The postfeminist sensibility presented feminism as no longer needed, because some White, upper-middle-class, cis-gender, conventionally beautiful young girls had attained some limited and individualized economic and cultural power. In contrast, the HWP cycle has proliferated during a cultural moment "in which feminism has seemingly moved from being a derided and repudiated identity among young women (Scharff 2013) to becoming a desirable, stylish, and decidedly fashionable one" (Gill 2016), represented, for example, by Rachel's "This Is What a Feminist Looks Like" T-shirt (*UnReal*, S1E1) and Abby and Barb's feminist lifestyle website, Ladyparts (*Girlfriends' Guide to Divorce*, S4).

The HWP cycle's girlfriendships reflect how a variety of feminist discourses, political activisms, and representations that were previously rare in, if not completely absent from, mainstream media can now be seen across different platforms, including magazines, commercials, films, social media, and television. Signaling some of these emergent or popular feminism(s), at the 2015 Super Bowl, for example, one of the most-watched television events in the United States, Always, one of the biggest makers of feminine-care products, debuted a sixty-second spot called "Like a Girl" that exposed the various ways boys and girls perceive the phrase "like a girl," finding that boys and even older girls frequently use it as an insult or to signal inferiority. The resultant campaign of corporate activism that reappropriated #likeagirl to signal strength and achievement, featuring the likes of Serena Williams, received widespread visibility and acclaim (Nudd 2015; Vagianos 2015). The Women's March on Washington and its sister marches around the world in protest of Donald Trump's presidential inauguration in January 2017 were another highly visible example of this mainstreaming of feminism, and women came together to draw attention to a variety of women's issues from abortion rights to domestic violence and sexual assault. Perhaps one of the most visible examples of the emergent mainstreaming of feminist activism was the Me Too movement, which was popularized in response to the sexual-abuse allegations against the now-former Hollywood producer Harvey Weinstein, which spread virally in October 2017, attempting to demonstrate the pervasiveness of sexual assault and harassment, especially in the workplace.[1] These campaigns and protests, in addition to the symbolism of Beyoncé's 2014 VMA performance in front of the word "feminist" (see Banet-Weiser 2015), seem to signal a new era of emergent feminist activism.

Along with these other examples, girl "squads" have become the pop-culture symbol of a potentially emergent feminism, in which a specific type of feminine-empowered collectivity has seemed to supplant the individualized, competitive, feminine consumer of the postfeminist era. Taylor Swift, for example, branded herself as a feminist through the prominent featuring of her (mostly White) celebrity girlfriend "squads" on Instagram (Affuso 2018); Beyoncé featured several women of color as part of her "Black girl magic" squad in the music video for "Formation" as well as its extensive promotional campaign; and throughout the oversaturated media visibility of the Kardashian family, they position themselves as an entrepreneurial "girl power" squad of neoliberal feminists. Throughout these examples and beyond, the girl squad represents a rejection of some postfeminist fantasies—particularly the heterosexual imperative and focus on romance. Instead, through the symbolism of the squad, these girls choose female-centered friendship, collective solidarity, and an appreciation of broader performative femininities in a renewed celebration of twenty-first-century "girl power."

Celebrity squads were also mobilized during Hillary Clinton's 2016 presidential campaign and seemed to model an explicit form of feminist political solidarity, as the hashtags #squad, #squadgoals, and #girlsquad were attached to high-profile examples of celebrity feminist activism. Lena Dunham, through her newsletter *Lenny*, gave actress Jennifer Lawrence the opportunity to discuss Hollywood's gendered pay gap. Director Ava DuVernay committed to an all-female directing squad for her TV series *Queen Sugar*. And Tina Fey and Amy Poehler highlighted their supportive squads of domestic and maternal labor in a *Saturday Night Live* spot, although it is a parody of Taylor Swift's squads. The girl squads of the early twenty-first century thus explicitly reimagined homosocial intimacy and became an important metaphor for feminist coalition building, encouraging affirmative bonds and forming communities among women and girls through affective ties.

For many philosophers and feminist scholars, friendship is vital to understanding oneself as a political agent. To Aristotle, friendship is central to our constitution as human beings as well as political animals. Friendship demands understanding and concordance with the perspectives and knowledge of others; it also emphasizes loyalty, negotiation, and forgiveness of mistakes and a sense of faith in and allegiance to others, which are all foundations of any notion of democratic collectivity. The contemporary popularization of the squad to describe friendship derives from militarized associations, where soldiers huddle around each other for protection and more powerful collective agency than fighting alone. The militant imagery and references to the Ferguson unrest in Beyoncé's "Formation" video, along with its lyrics "Okay, ladies, now let's get in formation," make the connection between squads and collective political activism explicit. Importantly, then, the metaphor of squads for early twenty-first-century friendship arises directly from the sometimes conflicting political entanglements of postrecessionary activist culture, emergent feminist activism, and the renewed visibility of civil rights protest in the era of Black Lives Matter, which together have illuminated the political, ideological, and identity foundations of friendship in explicit ways.

All of these "squads" nevertheless indicate that building close connections with fellow women is an immensely powerful feminist act. As Nigerian author Chimamanda Ngozi Adichie (2012) says, "We raise girls to see each other as competitors—not for jobs or accomplishments—but for the attention of men." She points out how insidiously, under patriarchy, women learn to scrutinize themselves, which often means scrutinizing other women to see how they compare. This competition and scrutinizing can lead women to distance themselves from other women, particularly from those who are different from them or who don't enact the same strictures of passive, agreeable, and conventional femininity. Therefore, female friendship and the idea of women communicating, laughing, accepting, and growing stronger with each other is a form of resistance; strengthening the bonds between women becomes a feminist act, particularly as patriarchy has sought to keep women apart (Weiss 2016). That is why, until recently, representations of female friendship have been relatively rare and why, in this context, cross-racial or multi-ethnic friendships and squads have the doubled potential to model not just feminist solidarity but urgently needed intersectionality. Unfortunately, TV's girlfriendships have historically been racially segregated, and when HWP shows do offer integrated friendship groups, they tend to undermine those goals by foregrounding the White main character and whatever suffering she is experiencing.

Women, Comedy, and Representations of Girlfriends Past

Among the various terrains of emergent feminism(s) proliferating in the second decade of the twenty-first century, "women's comedy has become a primary site in mainstream pop culture where feminism speaks, talks back, and is contested" (Mizejewski 2014, 6). For example, *Saturday Night Live* comedians Tina Fey and Amy Poehler's highly visible friendship centralized feminist themes in television comedy when they created and starred on *30 Rock* and *Parks and Recreation*, respectively, as well as hosting several televised awards shows together in which they purposefully and repeatedly highlighted gender inequality in Hollywood and championed other contemporary feminist political causes. Amy Schumer's satirical television sketches from her show *Inside Amy Schumer*, like "Last Fuckable Day" and "I'm Cool with It," spread across social media, making her one of the most visible icons of emergent feminism throughout 2015 and allowing her gender critiques to reach wide audiences (Nygaard 2018). Australian comedian Hannah Gadsby's revolutionary stand-up comedy special *Nanette* (Netflix, 2018), which deconstructs the painful nature of self-deprecating comedy for marginalized people, received surprisingly widespread acclaim and mainstream visibility throughout 2018. These are just a few examples that along with many HWP shows illustrate how the second decade of the twenty-first century saw an increasing number of women on television using "humor as a key political weapon" (Mizejewski and Sturtevant 2017).

Linda Mizejewski and Victoria Sturtevant (2017) point out that popular myths like "women aren't funny" and the "feminist killjoy" (Ahmed 2017) have historically curbed women using comedy for feminist political critique, but the sitcom has nevertheless been consistently associated with feminist heroines and with advocating a progressive politics of liberal feminism (Rabinovitz 1999, 145). From Lucille Ball's restless 1950s domestic housewife in *I Love Lucy* to the protofeminism of fantastic 1960s sitcoms like *Bewitched* and *I Dream of Jeannie, Mary Tyler Moore's* 1970s single working female protagonist, and *Murphy Brown's* 1980s brash, unmarried television journalist, the sitcom has reflected certain progressive discourses about representations of women. Bonnie Dow suggests that perhaps more than any other genre, feminist rhetoric has been absorbed, structured, and represented for public consumption through the sitcom. By looking at the history of the sitcom, Dow writes, we can trace "what we like about feminism, what we fear about feminism, and, perhaps most interesting, what aspects of feminism we simply refuse to represent in popular narrative" (1996, xxii).

In fact, outside of the sitcom, nuanced representations of female friendship have been historically relatively rare in the media. The trendy Bechdel test, which most popular films and television shows fail, asks (1) if there is more than one woman in a film or TV show, (2) if the women speak to one another, and (3) if they speak about something other than a man. The overwhelming industry failure to meet this rather simple requirement of female characters indicates just how subsidiary women's interests, desires, and fears are outside of their relationship to men. There have, of course, been exceptions to this dominant norm, including several celebrated '80s and '90s films about female friendship (see Hollinger 1998), like *Nine to Five* (1980), *Steel Magnolias* (1989), and *Thelma and Louise* (1991). Television soap operas also often feature a variety of complex female relationships, familial or platonic, and invite viewers to participate in that friendship via the intimacy of the close-up (see Brunsdon 2000; Modleski 1982). Furthermore, groundbreaking "textually negotiated" programs like *Cagney and Lacey* gender-reversed typically male-dominated genres like the buddy film and detective procedural to offer more diverse representations of female sociality (see D'Acci 1994; and Gledhill 1999). More often than not, however, these representations of female friendship trade in the tropes of melodrama or other "women's film" genres (Hollinger 1998), thus siloing them and distancing them from the mainstream comedic genres that Horrible White People shows draw from and from humor's potential political critique. Although girlfriendships have long been a part of television's representational tropes, however close and complex those friendships were, they were historically depicted as secondary to narratively central heterosexual couples' relationships.

In that history, then, *Mary Tyler Moore*'s foregrounding of Mary and Rhoda's friendship in an otherwise conventional workplace-family sitcom was an important representational shift. They were some of the first single-by-choice, career-focused female friends featured in the genre. Significantly, the series included almost-daily small gatherings at Mary's apartment with Rhoda and their friend Phyllis, where the women discussed a variety of issues in their lives, including but definitely not limited to romance and heterosexual coupling. After *Mary Tyler Moore*'s phenomenal critical and ratings success, the 1980s ushered in a series of sitcoms about female friendships that also addressed some feminist themes. *Laverne & Shirley* (1976–1983) was about polar-opposite best friends, roommates, and coworkers; *Kate and Allie* (1984–1989) featured two divorced women looking to each other for support; *Golden Girls* (1985–1992) famously put four mature women—Dorothy, Blanche, Rose, and Sophia—together in Miami to experience the joys and angst of their golden years; and *Designing Women* (1986–1993) saw four women running an interior-design firm in Atlanta. *Living Single* (1993–1998) provided a reprieve from the dominant Whiteness of these female friendships by following the lives of four single Black girlfriends living in a Brooklyn brownstone. Yet despite its popularity and its acknowledgment and celebration of Black culture, it became the exception that further normalized the racial segregation of female friendships that was still prevalent thirty years later in HWP shows. Nevertheless, by centralizing female solidarity and nuanced interpersonal relationships among women, all these sitcoms avoid advocating the submissive behavior that frequently characterizes women's relationships with men in other domestic family sitcoms and proved that girlfriendships could provide relationships with intensity and depth beyond those with the men in their lives. They thus laid the representational groundwork for explicitly feminist female friendships that are so prominent in the Horrible White People cycle.

In a comprehensive study of contemporary representations of "girlfriend culture," Allison Winch (2013) suggests that many television representations of female friendships are remediations—repeats and remixes, essentially—of *Sex and the City*, drawing attention to shows like *Lipstick Jungle* (2008–2009), *Cashmere Mafia* (2008), *Women's Murder Club* (2007–2008), *Girlfriends* (2000–2008), and *The Carrie Diaries* (2013–2014). Like *Sex and the City* before them, these representations of girlfriendships were aspirational, like the women's expensive designer clothing and idealized postfeminist careers. These shows are part of what Winch describes as the prominence of a "postfeminist sisterhood," in what she deems "Girlfriend media": "a porous term that illuminates instances across media platforms where (predominantly heterosexual) female sociality is used as representation and/or a marketing strategy, as well as an affective social relation" (2013, 4). Building on Lauren Berlant's (2008) observations about the affective and intimate spaces of women's culture, where the private intrudes into the public sphere, creating ambivalent political allegiances and consequences, Winch understands girlfriend culture as a niche within, or as an extension of, intimate publics. Using iconic representations of female friendship produced just prior to the rise of the Horrible White People cycle, like the film *Mean Girls* (2004), alongside television shows like *The Hills* (2006–2010) and *Cougar Town* (2009–2015), Winch notes how (White) postfeminist girlfriend culture encourages the regulation of normative femininities through the complex systems of surveillance and policing networks in exclusive homosocial groups, where women bond through their apparent control over the bodies of other women. "Girlfriend media," she writes, "reproduce these social pleasures of belonging to an intimate group, while also holding up the female body for analysis and scrutiny. They are sites that induce pleasure and belonging, while also enacting surveillance and cruelty" (9). These examples of early twenty-first-century girlfriend media, then, reject representing female solidarity in a way that could model collective feminist activism.

Reproducing some of girlfriend media's cruelty in the way they judge and hurl insults at each other for failing personally and professionally, Hannah, Marnie, Jessa, and Shoshanna of *Girls* were in some ways modeled after the foursome of *Sex and the City* (see Nygaard 2013). But, like *Pulling* (2006–2009), Sharon Horgan's first sitcom about a group of girlfriends trying to get laid, *Girls* started to challenge the aspirational friendship model and postfeminist sensibilities of *Sex and the City*, making it the beginning of the HWP cycle and shifting representations of girlfriendships to be more explicitly feminist and decidedly abject. The friends on *Girls* are narcissistic and so cruel to each other that they often make us question why they are friends in the first place. As we mentioned in chapter 2, *Sex and the City* and its echoes predate the HWP cycle and were invested in the historically and culturally specific presuppositions of postfeminism during the early 2000s, chief among them the performance of consumerist femininity that Horrible White People girls reject in response to recession and emerging feminisms. Horrible White People shows, through their characterizations and narrative concerns, particularly the focus on abject female friendships, explicitly critique many of the dominant ideological premises of the postfeminist sensibility that are most visibly represented by *Sex and the City* (Gill 2007). The girlfriendships of the HWP cycle present, in some ways, more nuanced but also more problematic representations than Winch's "sisterhoods" do.

HWP Shows' Intervention: "Complex" and Nuanced Female Friendships

The show most fêted for its celebration of female friendship and progressive representations of women on television is the webseries turned Comedy Central sitcom *Broad City*, created by and starring Ilana Glazer and Abbi Jacobson. It has solidified itself as one of contemporary television's feminist critical darlings (see Nussbaum 2016; Obaro 2016). Unlike the Whitewashed New York for which *Girls* was often criticized, the show has been praised for its diversity in the cast, where Abbi and Ilana's circle of friends and hookups include various people of color and sexual identities; and in the writer's room, where six out of its nine writers are women, two of them women of color. Like many shows in this cycle, *Broad City* wears its liberal politics on its sleeve, featuring episodes in which Abbi and Ilana volunteer for Hillary Clinton's campaign for president, advocate for Planned Parenthood, and frequently articulate progressive political discourses about economic inequality, immigration, and gun control. The whole fourth season features explicit anger at the election of Donald Trump, including an episode in which Ilana discovers that she can no longer orgasm because of her anxiety over Trump's policies and the season-long joke of bleeping out Trump's name as though it were a profanity.

Abbi and Ilana's open, unconditionally supportive friendship has also proven central to both the show's pleasurable appeal and its liberal feminist politics, as the girls see each other through job losses and transitions, medical emergencies, sexual firsts, and a slew of other life events. Through all of these crises or adventures, the show centralizes and celebrates platonic female relationships, "with great jokes, absurdist satire, striking moments of sentimentality, and actual real insights about love, sex, friendship, labor, New York City, money, race, drugs, and feminism" (Petersen 2014). One exemplary opening sequence, depicted in a split screen with Abbi's bathroom on the left and Ilana's on the right, reveals the often-hidden bodily truths of women's lives and experiences. Throughout the sequence, each in her own bathroom (although they appear together in each other's most intimate domestic space occasionally too), the girls repeat similar actions like reading Hillary Clinton's book and taking a pregnancy test. They enact a variety of sexualities across the spectrum and talk on the phone in various emotional states. They expose the rituals of feminine upkeep and performance (hair waxing and plucking) and desexualize the female body and its maintenance (defecating and performing breast self-examinations). The scene's montage of often-hidden feminine intimacies answers Adrienne Rich's (1980) call for an amplification of women's intimacies with each other that acknowledges women's experiences on the lesbian continuum, foretells a more woman-centered life for women, and lays the foundations for a collective feminist movement. *Broad City*, like several other shows in this cycle, thus highlights how building close connections with fellow women is an immensely powerful feminist act. Together, Abbi and Ilana, like so many of the female friendships in the Horrible White People cycle, have the support they need to vocally critique societal expectations of women and have the comfort they need to cope with those expectations until they change.

Like Abbi and Ilana, throughout the HWP cycle we see girlfriendships modeling new forms of feminist solidarity. The pilot episode of *Fleabag* addresses the type of surveillance and femininity policing that is a key aspect of postfeminist girlfriend culture (Winch 2013) but instead frames the two girls' failure to meet idealized expectations as a source of bonding and support. In one of the first flashbacks structuring the narrative arc of Fleabag's friendship with her deceased best friend, Boo, the girls try on clothes. When Fleabag emerges from the dressing room, Boo, who herself is wearing an ill-fitting sack of a red dress exposing her bra, authoritatively critiques Fleabag's dress: "No, definitely not; it does nothing for you. I hate that." Offended, Fleabag says, "These are my clothes, Boo. I've been wearing them all day." The girls embrace as Boo first tries to pass off her comments as joking and then apologizes profusely, telling Fleabag she is beautiful. Taking on patriarchy to the extent that the women might challenge the demand that women be sexy or wear clothes to highlight their shape and make them appear beautiful to men is still a step too far for commercial television. Nonetheless, these conversations do expand slightly the norms of feminine beauty and bodily containment. Much more importantly, though, they show female relationships full of love. These women might help each other survive the stresses of heteropatriarchy rather than burning it down, but they will support and love each other unconditionally.

In some ways, the friendships in these comedies directly replace the stability of the suburban nuclear family or hetero pair as the sitcom norm. That narrative act of placing female friend love on equal par with the overwhelmingly dominant heteropatriarchal family is, we argue, a powerful feminist act. This sort of support for women's physical appearance and abject behaviors, regardless of their ability to adhere to normative feminine ideals, is a key aspect of friendship-as-feminism in the cycle; for example, Ilana constantly tells Abbi how sexy and beautiful she is. In this cycle, girlfriendships are supportive, rather than (always) controlling or competitive in the ways Winch (2013) and Adichie (2012) lay out; they directly challenge the way film and television have represented female friends and offer instead a model in line with contemporary emergent feminist politics.

In addition to the unconditional love between peers that we see on *Broad City, Fleabag, Girlfriends' Guide to Divorce*, and others, Horrible White People shows also model intergenerational solidarity—surrogate mothers and daughters—that is rare in postfeminist media representations and further signals their participation in emergent feminisms. Kathleen Rowe Karlyn (2011) traces a generational divide in girls' media representations between empowered, seemingly materialistic and apolitical postfeminist girls redefining and embracing femininity and their idealized or demonized mothers embodying the ideals of second-wave feminism with their critiques of normative femininity and persistent gender inequality. This is true of contemporary female-centered quality drama as well, when older White women and their second-wave-rooted notions of feminism conflict with their younger coworkers' ideas either influenced by postfeminism or more deeply aware of intersectionality (see Lagerwey, Leyda, and Negra 2016). Although *UnReal's* Quinn and Rachel at times butt heads over their different generational embodiments of feminist activism—Quinn's individualized attempts for recognition and financial success in a male-dominated field (media production) versus Rachel's popular-feminist attempts to use their reality dating show as a platform to expose "really important issues" for increased feminist visibility (see Banet-Weiser 2018)—they remain supportive and understanding of each other's goals. The *Crazy Ex-Girlfriend* show runners insist, "the real love story of this show [is] a platonic one between two women of different generations" (S. Allen 2016). *Better Things* shows us literal mother-daughter relationships that are sympathetic and loving, as does *I'm Sorry*, and taken together, the cycle challenges the intergenerational conflicts that often plagued postfeminism and suggests more age-inclusive intimate female solidarity.

Another iteration of that intimate female solidarity celebrates the way these very close friendships do indeed sometimes shade into romantic or sexual relationships. Whereas homosexual desire is usually prohibited or marginalized in representations of postfeminist girlfriendships, HWP shows are more likely to reflect the "lesbian continuum" (Rich 1980) of women's lives with each other. On *Broad City* Ilana's physical attraction to Abbi is a frequent topic of conversation, and the promos for the fifth and final season play on their potential romantic coupling by teasing that the series will end not with the two friends marrying men but with Ilana dramatically interrupting Abbi's impending nuptials, professing her love, and the two running off together. Ali Pfefferman's relationship with her best friend, Syd Feldman, on *Transparent* also shows the range of female intimacies within girlfriendships that include or skirt homosexual desire, as the two first pursue and then agree to call off their sexual and romantic relationship, all in pursuit of being and remaining the closest friends they can be. On *You're the Worst*, when, out of politeness, Gretchen attempts to befriend her boyfriend's ex-wife, their drunken bonding eventually leads to almost accidental sex. Typically, lesbian relationships or even the possibility of sex and romance between women is so threatening to patriarchy and the norm of women's reliance on men that those relationships are not represented. Or if they are, it is often framed to appeal to the voyeuristic straight male viewer or to specifically cater to an LGBTQ demographic, and more often than not, queer women are narratively punished via death or violence. "Lesbianism, seen as non-reproductive," Julia Himberg notes, "is incompatible with patriarchal societies, where compulsory heterosexuality is built into the social structure" (2018, 196). Even when women on Horrible White People shows befriend men, the easy platonic heterosociality of those friendships on *Difficult People*, *Better Things*, and *I'm Sorry* also works to assert female identity outside of women's potential sexual appeal to men, even though many of those friendships still rely on the gay-man/straight-woman trope. But, for all of these new and progressive representations of intimacy between female friends that model types of feminist solidarity, most of the friendships remain racially segregated, contributing to the continued absence of racially diverse, culturally specific friendships on television. The central girlfriendships on *UnReal*, *Broad City*, *Crazy Ex-Girlfriend*, *Younger*, *Girls*, *You're the Worst*, *Casual*, *Divorce*, *Love*, and *Fleabag* are all among White women. Thus, rather than seeing these girlfriendships as an easy feminist progress narrative, where we have reached some idealized era of mainstream political engagement that universally protects the rights of women and girls while promoting intersectional equality, it is important to draw out their blind spots and limitations, particularly those concerning race and intersectionality, if we hope to see more progressive feminist representations on television.

Feminist scholars have been diligently mapping the complexities and ambivalences of feminist expression and activism in this conjuncture of emergent feminisms amid the lingering challenges and residual effects of postfeminist culture (see especially McRobbie 2015; Gill 2016; Keller and Ryan 2018; Banet-Weiser 2018). With the increased visibility of emergent or popular feminism also come new, insidious regimes of gendered discipline (McRobbie 2015); a parallel rise in popular misogyny (Banet-Weiser 2018); the persistent pull of postfeminist ideologies, particularly those connected to neoliberal, individualistic, entrepreneurial, or corporate empowerment of women and girls (Gill 2016); and a frequent evacuation of feminism's critique of capitalism and of other systems of (classed, racialized, and transnational) injustice (hooks 2013). In the place of critique is "hot feminism" (Vernon 2015), in which being a feminist is more akin to conforming to a trendy style than being committed to intersectional gender politics and structural change. Horrible White People television reproduces these ambivalences and complexities around feminist representational politics, especially in their centralization of abject White girlfriends.

Particularly through that focus on abject White women, their distress, and the type of feminist solidarity symbolized in their hierarchized or insular female friendships, the Horrible White People cycle forestalls representing or even imagining a more comprehensive, inclusive, or intersectional feminist politics. In particular, the multiethnic girlfriend groups on several Horrible White People shows represent lingering postfeminist and postracial dynamics that work to mask their centering of White precarity under the guise of racial inclusivity and also reflect the real-world lingering and always present possibility of a return to dominance of both postracial and postfeminist politics. On *Girlfriends' Guide to Divorce*, although Abby is the clear protagonist of the show—the title references *her* divorce and *her* line of self-help books or *Girlfriends' Guides*—like most HWP shows, the series centralizes the interactions of girlfriends, in this case a close group of diverse female friends, including Abby's eventual business partner, Barbara, who is Black; Abby's Latina childhood friend, Jo; Abby's Iranian American divorce attorney, Delia; and Phoebe, a White former model. On the one hand, friendship groups like these suggest an intersectional bridging across identity for girlfriends, but they also reflect what Kristen Warner (2015a) calls "colorblind casting," which was prominent during the era of "post-racial mystique" that flourished before the HWP cycle (Squires 2014). The girlfriends rarely, if ever, acknowledge the cultural specificity of their lived experiences, which might create real conflict and major challenges to the types of superficial female solidarity modeled in multiethnic friendship groups. *Girlfriends' Guide to Divorce* is particularly contradictory, with tensions arising from both postracial and postfeminist tropes operating in tandem with the emergent feminism of the show's premise, themes, and representations. All of the women, for example, adhere to the same extreme form of idealized, decidedly commercial White femininity: they frequently model designer fashions and fully made-up faces (regardless of the time of day or circumstance); wear large, expensive jewelry with perfectly coifed hair; and always don figure-flattering, often overtly sexy dresses. Any conflict within the group emerges from race-neutral interpersonal conflicts, like disapproving of Delia having an affair, worrying about Phoebe jumping into a new marriage too quickly, or Jo giving her alcoholic ex-husband too many second chances. Throughout the course of the series, the show alludes to the types of culturally specific conflict that might emerge within diverse friendship groups but defaults to postfeminist and postracial tropes of individualized critique.

In "Mind Your Side of the Plate" (S3E3), for example, Abby and Barbara go out for a "sexy night on the town." Their differing taste cultures and racialized and classed norms of femininity clash as Barbara, dressed in a flattering but simple top and jeans, chooses a casual sports bar for their evening out and Abby arrives in a tight cocktail dress and sky-high heels, ready for a posh club. Here Barb, a successful professional and a home owner—in other words, a woman with key markers of a secure middle-class identity—is represented as having much less money than Abby does. Class distinctions between middle and upper class are represented as simple taste differences and made palatable for White audiences by never overtly acknowledging the racial inflection of the insults that Abby eventually hurls at Barb. As the night evolves, Abby, who is clearly out of her element, orders a glass of wine and a plain, sad salad, looking on in shock and horror as Barbara orders a beer, fries, and jalapeño poppers. Later, when Barbara's sports knowledge attracts the attentions of Mike, a former professional baseball player and now aloof coach to Abby's son, Abby (presumably out of jealously) acts out passive-aggressively, critiquing Barbara's eating habits and all but explicitly calling her fat. Abby actively criticizes Barbara's refusal to uphold the strict disciplining of the thin, sexualized, female body that was normalized in postfeminist sisterhoods. The moment surfaces a clear disconnect between Black and White norms of femininity, and Barbara refuses to position herself as less sexy, beautiful, or powerful than Abby because she doesn't adhere to those norms. Instead, she retaliates by insisting that some men "like a real woman" and that Abby should not be the one judging others, as her own life is in shambles as she flounders for job security and romantic potential. As Barbara leaves Abby outside the bar, she hops in a cab, confidently asserting, "Deal with your own truth; and stay out of mine." Rather than follow Barbara to see how she is grappling with a racist insult about her body type or her inability to uphold the upper-middle-class White norms of femininity, the camera lingers with a dejected and wounded Abby alone on the street. The rest of the episode follows Abby as she comes to a self-realization that she is an emotional mess, experiencing a sense of failure and precarity unlike any other time in her life.[2] Like all of the multiethnic girlfriendships within the Horrible White People cycle, this scene centralizes the title character's precarious Whiteness, even while it seems to offer an example of intersectional female solidarity.

This scene could easily be read (by White viewers) as a purely interpersonal conflict resulting from Abby's high stress levels. In this reading, we get a welcome representation of complex female friendship in which women of different races and (slightly) different classes might argue but will ultimately come together and support each other in friendship. Yet the scene can also be read, as we have done, as an instance in which friendship ultimately emphasizes the well-being of precarious White women and enables them to read their own conflicts (as Abby does) as interpersonal, completely without racial inflection. In other words, Abby and other White women in these multiracial or multiethnic friendship groups are allowed to continue to inhabit a world in which their Whiteness is invisible to them. These kind of racist microaggressions (and sometimes much more overt aggressions) are framed most often not as painful experiences for the friend of color but as confronting emotional experiences for the White protagonists.

The diverse girlfriend group on *Crazy Ex-Girlfriend* operates similarly to the *Girlfriends' Guide to Divorce* friends, as the feelings of the Latina Valencia and the ethnically ambiguous[3] Heather are rarely the show's narrative focus, and they are often asked to call out Rebecca's self-centeredness or name her precarity, never fully engaging in a discussion of the cultural specificity of racialized precarity outside of the White woman's distress. Their roles remain "to make white lives better" (Winch 2013, 117–140), to visually reflect the White character's liberal "wokeness," and to remain the calm, rational, and successful foil to further underscore the White character's precarity. Multiethnic friends to White women are not denied style, romance, love, sex, or depth; nor are they yet more examples of the Best Black Friend Forever who sacrifices herself for the success and happiness of her White friend (Turner 2014). But the intersectional feminist solidarity on Horrible White People shows, seen through these friendships, lacks the cultural specificity and ultimately the narrative centrality of characters of color needed to model progressive collectivity. By focusing on individualism and allowing the White characters' privileges and Whiteness to remain unnamed, HWP girlfriends reinforce a postracial ideal.

An exception that seems to prove the representational norm of this multiethnic friendship dynamic can be seen between *Insecure*'s Black protagonist, Issa, and Frieda, her White friend from work. In chapter 4 we discuss *Insecure* as an example of a parallel cycle of what we call Diverse Quality Comedies that are similar to Horrible White People shows in their aesthetics, tone, and thematic concerns. In one telling narrative arc from season 2 of *Insecure*, Issa and Frieda test the limits of their friendship when they encounter a Black vice principal who is racist against the Latinx students at the school where they run an after-school tutoring program. Throughout the season, as the vice principal helps the two increase their enrollment, Issa is resistant to confronting his racism, and Frieda remains uncomfortable about the imbalance in demographics, urging Issa to do something and giving her the cold shoulder when Issa remains ambivalent about staging a confrontation. Through various conversations, they openly acknowledge the contradictions inherent when the "oppressed becomes the oppressor" and have a complex discussion about intersectional racism and the role and responsibility of cross-race allyship. By the end of the season, although Issa has finally confronted the vice principal—getting accused of being a race traitor and "coming at him with All Lives Matter"—her proposed answer to his racism, having a separate session for the Latinx students, is criticized by her White boss; and because Frieda was able to distance herself from the confrontation—by being White, she claimed it wasn't her place to call out the racism of a Black principal—Frieda eventually gets promoted. The narrative arc makes the complexities of racial inequality explicit, and unlike the multiethnic friendships in the HWP cycle, *Insecure* aligns viewers with Issa's frustrations when faced with an overt example of Frieda's White privilege and the double standards burdening Issa. The racial dynamics of this story line from *Insecure* are all but absent in the multiethnic girlfriendships of the Horrible White People cycle. While the insular female friendships between White girls in the cycle sometimes critique their privileged sense of abjection and narcissism through their comedy, the supportive, loving friendships in the center of their narratives structure an empathetic, rather than critical, reading of their precarity. As a result, Horrible White People girlfriendships emphasize the plight of self-aware, sometimes even self-critical, well-meaning, but ultimately ineffectual liberal White girls over the people of color they supposedly seek to help.

Quality Aesthetics: Centering White Precarity in Girlfriendships

As we have seen, situation comedy invites multiple identifications and polysemic readings. Some viewers might empathize with the well-meaning White women, while other viewers might read the same scenes as critiques of White privilege. As Brett Mills (2009) suggests, it is never entirely clear with whom laughter aligns itself—that is, if laughter is *with* or *at* the character or perspective of the joke. Moreover, because the cycle infuses the situation comedy with "quality" aesthetics—mixing high production values, the seriousness of social relevance, and complex characterizations with satire, wit, and the need for jokes—it makes identification, empathy, or critique of abject characters ambivalent. On *UnReal*, for example, Quinn often serves as the center of the show's satire. An exaggerated example of the heartless, money-hungry, racist, and misogynistic institution of network television, she embodies and frequently vocalizes the more insidious and less visible structural inequalities of the media industries. Her willingness to say the unspeakable, to curse, and to challenge norms of acceptable behavior for women in power make her an example of abject behavior serving as a form of social and political critique. Nevertheless, while positioning herself as witty, self-aware, and potentially working to change the system from within, Quinn nonetheless participates in and sometimes reinforces the racist and misogynistic discourses and institutions she is supposedly critiquing. When trying to forestall objections from the network president about casting a Black suitor, for example, Quinn describes Darius as "not that Black; he's, like, football Black." And, she contends, "the minute he lays Black hands on a White ass, Twitter will melt down, . . . [leading to] a ratings bonanza." Delivered in Constance Zimmer's dry, deep voice, always with a hint of insincerity or sarcasm, these are jokes meant to call out the racism of television studio heads who are reluctant to diversify TV representations as well as an American society still unwilling to accept interracial relationships. But the joke also runs the risk of viewers identifying with the quip, believing there are different levels of "Blackness" (just as, in chapter 2, we discussed the risk of viewers laughing at the content of racist jokes rather than along with their self-aware critique): some, like celebrity athletes and movie stars, who are acceptable to White culture because of their assimilation and achievement of heroic greatness—greatness often limited to entertainment fields—and others who are not because of the failure to meet those often-impossible demands. Quinn's quips are one of the show's main sources of humor, and she tends to relegate everyone to stereotypes in a way that could critique them as obvious constructions created and reinforced by the media industries—*or* could reinforce those narrow, dehumanizing views. We cringe at Quinn's comments because we don't know where to point our laughter; are we laughing with or at her assessments of American culture and media industries?

Identification with Quinn's satirical character is further complicated by the series' central relationship: the close, messy, but genuine friendship between her and Rachel. In a promotional image for season 2 (see figure 3.1), the Black suitor, Darius, is centered in the frame and in the text of the show-within-a-show, but it is really the two White women flanking him that audiences should be interested in. Rachel, in jeans on the left, stands slightly behind but also above the suitor with a walkie-talkie in one hand and the other resting possessively on the suitor's shoulder. Quinn, opposite in the black suit, leans casually against Darius's other shoulder. Its casualness makes the pose an eloquent gesture of power. The two women make eye contact with each other, further setting Darius apart and illustrating—for those who know the premise of the show—their control over his performance. Rachel and Quinn's eye contact also prioritizes the relationship between the two White female friends as the most important relationship on the show. This centralization of the female friends and their unconditional support of each other's abject and problematic behavior comes to a head in *UnReal*'s final-season narrative arc.

Throughout the series, both Quinn and Rachel can be manipulative and callous, but in season 4, Rachel takes her cruelty and coercion to an-

Figure 3.1. Promotional material for season 2 of *UnReal*. (Screenshot from eonline.com).

other level, testing Quinn's allegiance and the limits of their supportive "feminist" friendship. At the beginning of the season, *Everlasting* has assembled a cast of returning all-star contestants, supposedly to find love, but Rachel has handpicked two contestants to resurface and publicize a now timely, socially relevant conflict from a previous season: between a rapist, Roger, and his survivor, Maya. As the season finale of *Everlasting* approaches and because Maya has refused to play into the revenge or justice narrative that Rachel hoped would play out on national television, Rachel arranges the attempted rape of a Black female contestant with the hope of forcing Maya to intervene and thereby face her assaulter. Instead of the empowered "feminist" verbal confrontation that Rachel was supposedly expecting, Maya barges in to stop the attempted rape and, in a PTSD-induced psychotic break, nearly cuts off Roger's penis, as Rachel watches from the control room and prevents anyone from stepping in to help. When Quinn discovers Rachel's collusion in the assault, she at first says she is done with Rachel and the show, calling her a "bad person that does bad things." The series then teases an explicit critique of Rachel, as Quinn and Rachel hatch a plan for Rachel to take responsibility for her horrible behavior on live television. But instead of naming Rachel as the criminal manipulator that she is, Quinn names Rachel's smarmy fiancé and fellow producer, Tommy.

According to *UnReal*'s executive producer, Stacy Rukeyser, Quinn and Rachel were designed to represent the "primal" side of female friendships, suggesting they will always be there for each other, no matter how problematic their relationship is. "I'd like to think that [the show] celebrates female friendship," she says, "and the strength of friendship even when there is conflict, even when people lose their minds for a while and do terrible things" (Denniger 2018). As the show concludes, Quinn ultimately saves Rachel from having to deal with the consequences of her abject behavior, placing her fragility above everyone else's, and as viewers we are supposed to identify and empathize with that decision. The show concludes by foregrounding its melodramatic tone, not its comedy, thus centralizing White women, their needs, and especially their feelings of fragility, precarity, or mental distress over the needs—and frequently the violent victimization—of people color. Just as Quinn centralizes saving Rachel in the final season of *UnReal*, the cycle frequently centralizes White people's distress over the victimization of Black people rather than actually working toward more equitable social and political policies (see Lagerwey and Nygaard 2017).

These potentially problematic and ambivalent identifications reoccur throughout the cycle. Similar to Rachel in *UnReal*, many shows in this cycle tend to recenter Whiteness and foreground the failures and abjection of White girls more than those of people of color. This is glaringly true on *Broad City* when Abbi impersonates Ilana to fulfill Ilana's work quota at a food co-op. After a brief coaching session from Ilana, Abbi feebly attempts to mimic the hipster colorblind ideology that Ilana typically embodies. Abbi walks into the co-op throwing hand signs, hyping like a hip-hop singer, and shouting, "Rape culture sucks!" Later, when asked to clean the bathroom, she tries to get out of it by professing to the White manager, "We are two queens that shouldn't be sitting in the back of the bus cleaning up some White guy's dreadlocks, ja feel?" This impersonation of Black vernacular comes off as crude and offensive because Abbi fails to capture the same ease and warmth that Ilana embodies throughout the series. The humor of Abbi's impersonation is the cringe humor that comes from a White woman pretending to talk like a Black person. It could easily be read simply as racist appropriation of Black suffering and probably is read that way by some viewers. Yet it also has potential to be read as a critical mockery of White women like Ilana who embrace and perform their belief in postracial culture, particularly their equation of Black oppression (being forced by past legalized segregation and continuing structural inequality to clean the toilets) with White resentment (just really disliking cleaning toilets)—an equation that is a common device of colorblind ideology (Doane 2007).

We read Abbi's parody not as intended to be critical in either of those modes but rather as a loving homage to her BFF's quirky personality. Despite being painfully awkward to watch Abbi's exaggerated failure to embody Ilana, she nevertheless revels in impersonating Ilana's confidence and blunt self-assuredness as she flirts with her coworker. Overall, and given the context of the show as a whole, the audience seems to be asked to interpret Ilana's liberal colorblind ideology through Abbi's performative, friendship-based lens with admiration, love, and support rather than ridicule or critique. This complex, polysemic joke acknowledges and potentially even critiques White hipster racism. But in this scene, as more often than not throughout the show, Abbi and Ilana's unconditional love and support, their performative, feminist girlfriendship, are used to let White characters off the hook for problematic racial politics. The girls love each other no matter what, so audiences should too, the show and all its press plaudits seem to say.

This ambivalent identificatory dynamic—simultaneously loving and criticizing these feminist friendships—occurs throughout the cycle as White female friends continually support each other's abject behaviors, whether they seem parodic and critical or whether they are just plain horrible. A clear example of this ambivalence happens in the *You're the Worst's* episode (S4E6) in which Lindsay tries to make friends with her coworkers. Lindsay and Gretchen's girlfriendship is perhaps the most insular of all the friendships in the cycle, as they clearly embrace and even encourage each other's abjection while viewing and treating almost everyone else around them as the truly abject. In an exemplary scene from the episode, Gretchen sits across from Lindsay describing, but unable to name, the guilt she feels for sleeping with an older guy who she thinks is still married: "What is it . . . it's bad and involves other people?" Refusing to let Gretchen feel even the slightest bit guilty, Lindsay matter-of-factly and self-assuredly says, "If this hubster's cheating on a frumpus who masturbates with a children's vibrator, that's his problem. You do you." As this brief moment illustrates, like Quinn, Lindsay and Gretchen continually insult, lash out at, and objectify the people in their lives with creative and often-witty slurs. As the conversation continues, Lindsay admits that she is missing Gretchen since she has been spending all this time with the cheating "hubby." In an effort to be helpful, Gretchen mechanically suggests that Lindsay hang out with her coworkers, for whom she can't even muster a nicety or a banal compliment; instead she simply trails off, confused and smug, with her lips pursed, saying, "They seem . . ." Lindsay confesses that she doesn't feel like she can be herself around them, because at work, she feels like she needs to "keep her shit locked down." After Gretchen responds, "It sounds like work-Lindsay sucks," Lindsay decides to "be herself at work," which means opening the floodgates to her abject behaviors.

In the follow-up scene, Lindsay arrives at work, emerging from the elevator in a cloud of cigarette smoke, dressed in all black leather, reminiscent of sweetheart Sandy's rebellious cat-suited transformation in the iconic ending of *Grease*. The man coughing violently in the elevator behind her, however, marks Lindsay's behavior not as sexy and rebellious but as inappropriate and offensive. Throughout the scene, Lindsay admits to casual promiscuity while making an obscene mess in the break room: she fails to make coffee by taking the coffee grinds out of premade single-serve coffee cups. She then performs an awkward impromptu dance during a staff meeting that is revealed through a jump-cut montage of hilariously uncomfortable dance moves—punctuated by an abrupt cut to a medium close-up of an unamused coworker who ends the scene with a simple, "Are you done?" Lindsay tells a joke about a little boy and a pedophile and performs an off-screen Chris Rock impression. Given the embarrassingly abject performance, it is unsurprising when her coworkers politely decline Lindsay's drink request and go to a karaoke bar without her. Throughout her cringe-worthy hilarity, Lindsay remains an ambivalent character.

Like Ilana, Lindsay can be seen as an exaggerated performance of White millennial naiveté and narcissism that encourages self-awareness and critique, but she also runs the risk of reinforcing stereotypes of young women as vapid, vain, and irresponsible. Gretchen's unconditional support of Lindsay further complicates this ambivalence, often encouraging or justifying her bad behavior. In a later episode (S4E8), when Lindsay's coworkers have blown her off yet again, this time by not showing up to her divorce party, she discovers by stealing someone's phone what they think: "She's the worst person I've ever met, and I toured with Ted Nugent." On the one hand, this seems like an accurate reading of a parodic "horrible" character whom viewers are meant to critique, but the show's "quality" aesthetics, the nuanced dramatic acting by Kether Donohue, and the eventual support and reassurance from Gretchen actually encourage potential empathy with or sympathy for Lindsay's sense of isolation, suffering, and precarity. As Lindsay reads the insulting texts, she is slightly off-center in the frame, and the words pop up in large text bubbles on the left side of the image, overwhelming her (see figure 3.2). The scene's cool blue lighting and shallow focus obscure her surroundings, underscoring her sense of isolation; Donohue looks down, dejected. Her whole body loses its typically upright, almost aggressively confident posture, as the white light of the cellphone shines up, distorting her downcast features. She sits alone on the sofa in an elaborately sexy antiwedding dress, like a jilted millennial Miss Havisham with nothing to celebrate. More biting insults from her sister and her now-ex-husband appear to further kick Lindsay while she is down, leading her to retreat, broken and alone, to the balcony of Jimmy's house, where she sits confused and vulnerable in the darkness. When Gretchen comes to check on her, Lindsay asks with childlike innocence, Donohue pitching her voice even higher than usual and stuttering, "Is everything my fault because I don't do life good?" Gretchen, like a good friend, responds without pause, "No, of course not." Confused and on the verge of tears, Lindsay asks, "Whose fault is it then?" Deflecting, Gretchen tells Lindsay that she has learned in therapy that we are impacted by stuff that happened to us as kids and that, regardless, "I love you, dude." This inspires a narrative arc, common within the cycle, in which Lindsay explores her childhood in search of reasons to explain her current failures at life (described in chapter 2). As this emblematic Lindsay scene illustrates, the cycle's "quality" aesthetics support ambivalent, cringey, and polysemic identifications with its characters. But we argue that the loving, supportive, feminist representations of girlfriends, coupled with those same "quality" aesthetics, encourage an empathy and

Figure 3.2. Lindsay learns what people think of her. (Still from *You're the Worst*; screenshot by the authors).

identification with suffering White girls. That encouraged, or dominant (S. Hall 1993), reading lets liberal White viewers off the hook, simultaneously and via exactly the same methods as the insulated White girlfriends let each other off the hook. When (if) we identify with these loving, complex, novel, feminist friendships, we as liberal White viewers are enacting the flaws that are often read into White feminism—doing important cultural work but failing to see beyond Whiteness.

Demanding More

Given the incorporation of feminist representations, liberal discourses, and some nods to racism or racial dynamics, Horrible White People shows may appear to represent a different, more "woke" view of liberal Whiteness or the American racial order than other segments of the televisual landscape do. But similar to Sut Jhally and Justin Lewis's (1992) analysis of *The Cosby Show* before it, this cycle of programming tends to represent and legitimate a new, more enlightened—but no less insidious—form of racism that continues to not question the characters' White supremacy and that ultimately centralizes empathetic White precarity and abjection in its representations of race, thus supporting the contemporary racial order instead of imagining a way to transform it.

This is particularly frustrating because the Horrible White People cycle reflects a welcome contemporary rise of female-authored and female-centered comedies. While the shows in the HWP cycle are not exclusively produced by women, the cycle features series developed by established female producers like Marti Noxon (*UnReal* and *Girlfriends' Guide to Divorce*), Sharon Horgan (*Catastrophe* and *Divorce*), and Amy Poehler (*Difficult People, Broad City,* and *Unbreakable Kimmy Schmidt*), as well as several breakout first series from female writer/creator/stars like Lena Dunham (*Girls*), Phoebe Waller-Bridge (*Fleabag*), Pamela Adlon (*Better Things*), Maria Bamford (*Lady Dynamite*), Andrea Savage (*I'm Sorry*), and Tig Notaro (*One Mississippi*). The cycle also exemplifies good White male allyship to feminist media makers, as established male producers like Judd Apatow and Louis C.K. were key to helping several of these shows get made, coming on as executive producers in order to promote women creators and women-centered narratives.[4] Horrible White People programming represents a to-be-celebrated trend of female authorship in mainstream media within and beyond comedy.

Even with this slew of female creators, though, women still constituted only 27 percent of all creators, directors, writers, producers, executive producers, editors, and directors of photography working on broadcast network, cable, and streaming programs in 2017–2018, which is a decline of one percentage point from the already dismal 28 percent in 2016–2017 (Lauzen 2018). While almost a quarter of new series creators were women (22.6 percent), women and girls are still underrepresented on-screen across popular fictional content (less than 40 percent of characters); and when they are represented, they are more likely to be younger and sexualized and far less likely to be associated with a profession other than caretaker (Smith, Choueiti, and Pieper 2016; Lauzen 2018). This fact is comedically critiqued with the popular Twitter handle @femscriptintros, where the producer Ross Putman cites verbatim how women are introduced or described in scripts mostly by their attractiveness or sex appeal. Changing only the name to "Jane," some examples from the pool include, "Jane, 40, gorgeous blond, big breasted, great body, beautiful smile"; "Jane, 50s, still very attractive"; "Jane, 40s, beautiful but harsh"; "Jane, 23, . . . if she tried even a little, she could be pretty";

and "This is Jane, beautiful, complicated." With so many female creators and stars, the HWP cycle is thus a direct challenge to the industry norm's narrow focus on women's beauty, attractiveness, or relationships to men. The cycle celebrates the emotional depth, nuance, and complexity of women over forty and explores the interests and desires of women beyond heterosexual coupling or their appeal to and relationships with men. The swing of female writer/creators who are part of the HWP cycle are part of an important trend in developing more inclusive casting and hiring practices and fostering more inclusion in television storytelling. But, except for Issa Rae of *Insecure* and Mindy Kaling of *The Mindy Project*, all these comedic female auteurs are White. The lack of racial diversity within this rise of female creators in contemporary television comedy exacerbates the ambivalences tied to their representations of humorous, abject, or precarious girlfriends.

Nonetheless, we don't want to foreclose the possibilities for more contradictory or contingent readings of these shows and their ideological effects. They allow for varying and even contradictory interpretations. With *Broad City*, in particular, as a parody that moves between honest, loving homage and exaggerated critique, it is vital to note that Ilana's performances of postracial racism (see Nussbaum 2016; Herman 2017) and the girls' centralization of White precarity are open representations that allow for multiple pleasures and interpretations by audience members. Viewers may be able to see and actively critique the way Ilana makes problematic postracial comments and acknowledge that, as oblivious White women, the girls are exaggeratedly blind to the realities of race and racism around them in a way that is not dissimilar to many young White liberals. Thus, these shows can allow for a pleasurable space for audiences to deconstruct subtle forms of contemporary racism. Yet, because this cycle sits in the middle of celebratory discourses around Peak TV and its increasing diversification, liberalization, and politicization of television content, our goal is to outline the social, economic, institutional, and political forces that position audiences and texts as liberal and "quality," thereby structuring the shows and their ideological impacts in celebratory rather than critical ways.

4

Diverse Quality Comedies in an Era of White Precarity

Season 3 of the predominantly Black-cast HBO sitcom *Insecure* finds the protagonist, Issa Dee (played by writer/creator Issa Rae), in the same place as most protagonists of Horrible White People shows: struggling to pay rent and burned out at her low-paid nonprofit job, having coped with a wide range of race-based complications at work, from microaggressions from her mostly White colleagues and boss to being sidelined for promotion in favor of her work partner who, being White, was able to dodge accusations of racism by recusing herself from discussions of racial inequality (that incident is analyzed in detail in chapter 3). In that context, "Familiar-Like" (S3E2) opens in a nondescript conference room with the entire staff of We Got Y'all, the after-school education program where Issa works, sitting around a conference table, aiming bored gazes at an easel propping up the company's logo at the head of the room. Issa is the sole Black employee staring at the White company founder, who is defending the logo against accusations of racism. The logo is a simple outline of a hand, drawn in white, holding up three children, drawn in silhouette—in other words, a White hand lifting up Black children.

There are two things to draw out from the scene that follows. First, the boss represents the perfect encapsulation of what we have referred to throughout this book as a well-meaning White lady. She is perhaps fifty-ish, appears well educated, and would most certainly identify herself as a liberal who is actively antiracist. After all, she has devoted her professional life to founding and running a nonprofit organization—by definition a visibly unselfish gesture and of no real financial benefit to herself—with the goal of supporting underserved students with tutoring and after-school enrichment and educational activities. She "just happens" to be White, to have hired mostly White employees, and to be serving Black and brown children. When confronted with the possibility of advertising her company with an inadvertently racist logo, she reacts emotionally rather than pragmatically, with almost more hurt than indignation: "It wasn't racist when I made it. It's my hand. My hand is helping the community," she insists.

In the ensuing conversation, the condescension and cultural appropriation of using incorrect grammar to name a program targeting youth of color is pointed out alongside the White-savior narrative implied by the colors in the logo design. The well-meaning White lady boss is hurt by every comment, not understanding how a gesture she meant as kindness and service could contain racist dimensions beyond that generosity. Her inability to predict race-based criticism illustrates the persistence of the invisibility of Whiteness and White privilege for White people (Dyer 1997), even those who are consciously working to ameliorate structural racial inequality (such as that in the public education system, in this example). Her emotional reaction to criticism and unwillingness to hear or acknowledge the validity of that critique illustrates a prototypical reaction of White fragility and demonstrates White people's tendency to fight, flee, or cry defensively when confronted with conversations about race (DiAngelo 2018). She is an essential character despite having only a small role on the show because she is the figurehead of the Whiteness of the public and professional world that Issa has to navigate, which is a purposefully stark contrast to the Blackness of her private and personal lives, where almost the entire cast is Black. The contrast extends aesthetically into the lighting (here it is flat and fluorescent; more private parts of Issa's life have a broad range from bright, warm, natural sunlight to very dark, moody clubs or bedrooms) and music in particular (at work there is no diegetic music or score; Issa's private life is a rich tapestry of diegetic and nondiegetic hip hop and R&B). This separation of a public life that requires constant negotiation with powerful dominant Whiteness from a safer, richer, more culturally specific private space is repeated throughout the shows we discuss in this chapter and makes White supremacy visible from a much different perspective to that in Horrible White People shows.

The other dimension of this scene to highlight is how the staff treat Issa and the opinions Issa feels comfortable (or not) expressing in this environment of well-meaning, liberal White people. As comments come from around the table, Issa, who is always photographed alone in her own close-up, in contrast to the two-shots that frame the rest of the staff, subtly shakes her head and bites her lip or blows out her cheek. She is able to contain her speech but can't fully contain her frustrations. Finally, a colleague mutters, "Honestly, whatever Issa thinks is probably right." The camera cuts to Issa, centered in the frame and in medium close-up, as she exaggeratedly wags a finger and leans forward to shout, "So *now* y'all wanna be woke when a bitch has been an alarm clock since day one? Well, beep beep, motherfuckers, beep beep!!" The sound track lays heavy reverberation over the final "beep beep," indicating that something is different about this outburst, a moment of what Troy Patterson (2018) calls *Insecure*'s "eruptions of id." In the following cut, when Issa abruptly stills her body and changes tone to a quiet, moderated voice, saying, "Um, I think you've made some really great points. I agree with everything you've said, and I thank you for saying it," viewers realize that her moment of incredulously frustrated honesty was a fantasy. *Insecure* offers moments like this throughout its run, moments in which Issa carefully and consciously moderates her reactions, choice of words, and behavior for White audiences—audiences in the text like her colleagues in this scene but perhaps also viewing audiences at home. The way she visibly negotiates the Whiteness of her public spaces illustrates how the show as a whole, and the parallel programming cycle that it is part of, creates a dual text. One text operates within the television industry's established "quality" aesthetics, hailing "quality" demographics that bring with them historical presumptions of Whiteness and indeed of Whiteness's invisibility and supposed universality. The other text rebels against and resists those constraints.

Insecure is one example of what we call "Diverse Quality Comedies," a programming cycle running alongside Horrible White People shows and born from the same historical conjuncture of social, economic, and entertainment industrial change. Diverse Quality Comedies are generically, aesthetically, and narratively similar to HWP shows but have creators or auteurs and casts of color. We argue that the aesthetics of innovation, complexity, and "art" typically labeled "quality" television are in fact an aesthetics of Whiteness, a result of the racist historical understanding of desirably affluent audiences as White. Shows like *Insecure, Master of None, Atlanta, Chewing Gum,* and *Dear White People,* like Issa in this scene, constantly negotiate this aesthetics of Whiteness, performing it to often award-winning perfection while offering moments of rupture like Issa's outburst, as well as more consistent representations of cultural specificity made visible in aesthetic contexts like framing, musical choice, and set design, which can hail viewers of color while White audiences might not even be aware of them. The shows thus operate in multiple codes at once, in a program-scale performance of what Ralina Joseph (2018) calls "strategic ambiguity." The necessity of that performance, often directly cited by the shows' creators, illustrates the persistence of White supremacy and centralizing of Whiteness, even in the almost-always liberal, aesthetically innovative frame of "quality" television that we have been asserting throughout this book.

This chapter begins by defining Diverse Quality Comedies and examining how they function to make the industry look progressive and inclusive (a function they share with the liberal and progressive characters on Horrible White People shows) while instrumentally targeting underserved audiences of color who are perceived to have added value to a TV industry in flux. That is, having diversity on-screen and behind the camera serves the industry's financial needs of reaching relatively untapped audiences of color while simultaneously making the industry look good to itself and its existing liberal White consumers. The crux of the analysis in this chapter, then, picks apart the ways these shows confront and challenge and make visible structural White supremacy, as well as a wide range of racialized injustices, from online dating apps to potentially deadly violence. They do this by operating in multiple cultural codes simultaneously. They use "quality" aesthetics, thereby supporting the dominance of that aesthetics, which is in fact an aesthetics of Whiteness. Mobilizing that aesthetic mode, they contribute to the ethos of supposedly "universal" middle-class suffering that suffuses their Horrible White People show counterparts and, by sharing that suffering, contribute to the idea that it is general rather than culturally precise. Yet despite those not-inconsequential constraints, these shows reveal, with nuance, complexity, and specificity, some of the painful realities of living within White supremacy for non-White characters. We put them in conversation with Horrible White People shows to illuminate alternative programming that operates essentially within the definitions of HWP shows but, rather than recentering Whiteness, denaturalizes it by making it an often-central locus of conflict, rendering notoriously unrepresented structural White supremacy more visible for both these shows' viewers of color and their majority White audiences.

Diverse Quality Comedies: Defining a Parallel Cycle

Throughout this book, we have analyzed Horrible White People shows. We have defined them as a cycle of thirty-minute comedies or satires featuring suffering middle-class, self-proclaimed liberal White characters within generically and aesthetically innovative TV and sharing an overwhelmingly bleak tone. HWP programming is niche-targeted television aimed at predominantly White so-called quality audiences via streaming platforms, subscription channels, and networks with (or seeking) edgy or arty brand identities. But, of course, those Horrible White People shows are only a small percentage of the total transatlantic television production from 2012 to 2018, the period we investigate. In chapter 2, we discussed one counterpoint to Horrible White People shows, the family-of-color sitcoms like *Black-ish*, *Fresh Off the Boat*, and *One Day at a Time* that offer a more generically—and perhaps ideologically, with regard to family structures and domesticity—conservative inverse of the generic experimentation of HWP shows. We have also demonstrated White supremacy's limited inclusivity by highlighting the mobilization of multiethnic casts like that of *Friends from College* or *Girlfriends' Guide to Divorce* and well-drawn non-White characters like Edgar on *You're the Worst* or Lincoln on *Broad City*, who help demonstrate Horrible White People characters' liberalness and not-racist-ness. That inclusivity extends as well to HWP shows' tendency to focus on ethnic differences within Whiteness, particularly Jewish comedy and cultural specificity (again, see chapter 2), with the same goal of preempting critiques of Whiteness's obvious centrality by foregrounding its limited inclusivity.

But alongside the recentering of Whiteness, we have been demonstrating for the last three chapters that there is also more racial and ethnic diversity in television than ever, on both sides of the camera. In the introduction, we laid out the televisual landscape that produced Horrible White People shows and listed many of the contemporaneous shows directly addressing racial violence, historical racism, and persistent racial inequalities that helped mark the era as one in which racial inequality and racial violence became hypervisible. We also noted the surge in programming created by and starring people of color across genres. Shows like *Roots*, *Underground*, *Queen Sugar*, and *The People vs. O. J. Simpson* fit into that category. Programming built on the success of Shonda

Rhimes's empire gave us shows like *Empire*, *Power*, and *Being Mary Jane* in mass-market melodrama and *Black-ish*, its spin-offs *Grown-ish* and *Mixed-ish* (just beginning as we finish writing), *Fresh Off the Boat*, *The Mindy Project*, and *One Day at a Time* in the world of more generically traditional sitcoms, as well as *Jane the Virgin*, which straddles melodrama and sitcom with its telenovela satire. Among this surge of televisual voices from people of color, this chapter focuses on what we call Diverse Quality Comedies (DQCs).[1] These are the critically acclaimed, award-winning, aesthetically innovative, niche-market comedies with a grim outlook on the political, social, and economic world in which their characters live. Like their Horrible White People counterparts, it is the bleak tone (narratively and often aesthetically) and dark humor that are their most essential common trait. They are often linked with an auteur who creates, writes, and stars in the show. They target relatively affluent, educated, socially liberal viewers and feature self-proclaimed liberal characters who face precarity from recession, job loss, lack of access to housing, and failed hetero relationships. In brief, they share all the characteristics of Horrible White People shows without the White people and with less emphasis on central female characters.[2] Shows like *Insecure*, *Master of None*, *Atlanta*, *Chewing Gum*, and *Dear White People* are a parallel cycle created as a result of the same industrial factors that led to the HWP cycle, and like almost all of the Horrible White People cycle, many of them are coming to an end as we write in 2018 and 2019, further suggesting that they speak to the same cultural and economic entanglements of this historical conjuncture.

Not every comedy with a non-White star or cast falls into this category. *Friends from College*, for example, features the mixed-race comedian Keegan Michael-Key at the center of its ensemble, but as we noted in the introduction, we classify that program as a Horrible White People show because it demonstrates the inclusivity of White supremacy rather than culturally specific diversity. *The Mindy Project* is not on our list despite its Indian American auteur/star, Mindy Kaling, because its bright, bubble-gum color palette matches its peppy tone. Mindy is appallingly narcissistic, but the show's traditional sitcom structures emphasize punch lines, and the tone is never defeatist or grim. Kaling's character, Mindy Lahiri, also identifies herself as a gun-toting Republican, in direct contradiction to the appearance of social progressivism at the heart of our analysis. *Grown-ish* positions its female protagonist, Zoe, as a "terrible" person for, among other things, abandoning a sick friend at a party and later cheating on an exam. The show does display some of the quality aesthetics of Diverse Quality Comedies and explicitly engages with progressive critique. Yet as a spin-off of the more generically traditional sitcom *Black-ish*, it has been described as "goodhearted" (Poniewozik 2018) and "polite" (McDonald 2018), as opposed to grim and confrontational; and despite its self-centered protagonist, it reinforces the comfort of nuclear and friend families alike, which creates less despairing and precarious characters than those on DQCs. *Jane the Virgin* is left out of our definition because while it offers a complex, multivalent, multigenerational Latinx family, its self-reflexivity and creative aesthetics are aimed at melodrama (it is based on a Venezuelan telenovela) rather than sitcom. Furthermore, even when it addresses serious contemporary social issues like the undocumented status of Jane's grandmother, like *Mindy* and *Grown-ish*, it is a bright, happy show and revolves around a loving family—and an eventual green card. Even when Jane's romantic relationships break down, viewers know it is only a narrative pattern to render the payoff of reunion even sweeter. We don't exclude these shows lightly, but the very small size of the DQC cycle is part of our argument here, which contrasts the bulk of the HWP cycle and its sad, desperate White characters to the relatively tiny, albeit disproportionately celebrated, number of similarly "quality" shows with casts and auteurs of color.

Despite the similarities across these cycles, the protagonists on DQCs are not "horrible" in the same way as the HWP characters are. Issa, Dev (played by writer/creator Aziz Ansari) from *Master of None*, and Earn (played by writer/creator Donald Glover) on *Atlanta* are all rude, at times selfish, and emotionally immature, but they rarely shade into the pervasive criminality or excessive narcissism at the direct expense of their friends the way Gretchen and Jimmy act toward Edgar when they make fun of his PTSD on *You're the Worst* or when Rebecca, in a drug-induced haze, tries to hire a hit man to kill her ex-boyfriend's current girlfriend on *Crazy Ex-Girlfriend*. On Horrible White People shows, White people hurt others, and the suffering of people of color is rendered invisible or inconsequential compared to that of the White protagonis suffering ts. On *Transparent*, for example, after botching a conversation with Elizah, a young

Black transwoman who had called the suicide-prevention hotline she was monitoring, Maura (the titular trans parent) embarks on a panicked trip to South Los Angeles in an unsolicited attempt to rescue her (S3E1). Emblematic of the Horrible White People cycle, rather than providing support for Elizah, Maura's voluntary charity work becomes entirely about *Maura's* emotional needs. Throughout the episode, patrons and workers at the market she has tracked Elizah to push back against Maura's (invisible to her) microaggressions (like assuming that all transwomen of color know each other from "the streets") and challenge her White privilege by labeling it theft, rather than simply excusing an old lady with a lost purse, when she drinks a soda without paying for it. These confrontations result in an exaggerated example of White fragility, as Maura collapses from a panic attack, grabbing all narrative and aesthetic attention for herself as EMTs roll her away on a gurney. Indeed, she ends up demanding explicit emotional labor (hand-holding and pronoun defending) from the precise Black woman whom she meant to help.

In contrast to centering White fragility like this episode and others we have discussed throughout the book, on DQCs people of color suffer unambiguously because of structural inequalities, and their suffering is often represented as an intractable part of the racist governance of contemporary America. In *Atlanta*'s "Streets on Lock" (S1E2), for example, Earn is arrested for the first time in his life. Sitting beside his cousin, who is incredulous that Earn has not experienced the jail before, the eloquent framing conveys more than the dialogue. Earn and his cousin Alfred sit side by side on bolted-down chairs as they wait to be called. The scene cuts between a long shot in which the two are framed through a cutout in the reception desk, while the camera resides with the administrators processing arrests, and a closer shot. In the medium shot, Earn and Alfred occupy the lower-right quadrant of the frame, discussing how on the ride to the station the police tried to cajole them into confessing or turning each other in. The purpose of the shot's construction, however, resides in the upper-left quarter of the screen. Framed through the large glass window of a clearly locked, reinforced door, a Black man with a black eye is trapped within the borders of the window. Confined to that small portion of the screen and contained by the thick frame around the window, he does not have room to pace, so he sways, his gaze sweeping right and left. The posture, haunted look, bruise, and constricted fram-

Figure 4.1. Black men in jail on *Atlanta*. (Still from *Atlanta*; screenshot by the authors).

ing provide an expressive visual metaphor for the relationship of African American citizens to the judicial system, which Earn and Alfred discuss as Earn waits to be processed into it for the first time.

This chapter argues that because industry demands require DQCs to operate within a "quality" aesthetics of Whiteness, they negotiate the limits placed on them by the politics of respectability still active in a cultural environment where just a few valorized texts are deemed "quality." Thus, the complex framing of the *Atlanta* scene is written in a highbrow aesthetic mode that needs to be decoded, but the message to decode is resistant and challenging. That "quality" label is a relation to Whiteness—an adherence to White, middle-class ideals—and represents itself as a means of racial uplift in the same way as "respectable" texts from earlier TV eras (Gates 2018). As a result, DQC characters don't suffer, they brave; they don't wallow, they hustle; and they may be miserable, but they aren't horrible. This distinction is key to the way Diverse Quality Comedies offer plentiful examples of cultural specificity and overt engagement with racial politics—by encouraging both White and non-White audiences to sympathize and empathize with non-White characters who are not, because respectability politics do not permit them to be, as despicable as some of the White characters we have discussed so far. In stark contrast to their HWP counterparts, DQCs make visible and criticize structural

White supremacy and the well-meaning White liberals who benefit from it. We want to celebrate the ways these shows speak directly to structural racism and White supremacy, two forces that television struggles to represent, while acknowledging the labor-intensive negotiations they perform via aesthetics and representation in order to create so-called universal appeal, which most often means appealing to White audiences.

"We Solved It": The US TV Industry and Diversity

US television is indisputably casting more diverse actors and employing more diverse creators. This trend, as we discussed in chapter 1, is an effective public-relations tool for the industry to present itself as progressive and in particular to set itself in contrast to the Hollywood film industry, which is beleaguered by public critiques of its structural racism and sexism, including 2015's #oscarssowhite, and the Me Too and Time's Up movements in 2017 and 2018. It is a particularly important strategy for the streaming services branding themselves as innovative producers of "quality" entertainment in the highly competitive environment of Peak TV. But even from the superior marketing position of the US TV industry, it has hardly conquered inequality and its enormously high barriers to entry (see Smith, Choueiti, and Pieper 2016; Lauzen 2018). The opening number at the 2018 Emmy Awards show, "We Solved It," demonstrates a self-awareness and gentle self-critique of the industry's tendency toward self-congratulation, reminiscent of HWP shows' self-aware humor. The song's jokes offer multiple readings that range from meaningful criticism of the industry's persistent structural inequalities to an exonerating release valve for the tensions created by those inequalities.

This irony-laden song-and-dance number began with comedians Kate McKinnon and Kenan Thompson, a White woman and a Black man, welcoming the audience to the awards show and "celebrating the fact that this year's Emmy Awards has the most diverse group of nominees in Emmy history" (Television Academy 2018). Kenan Thompson says, to McKinnon's astonishment, "We solved it"—meaning they have solved Hollywood's problem with inequality—and the two *Saturday Night Live* alumni break into song, mocking the industry's answers or proposed "solutions" to Hollywood's historical lack of diversity. Best Actress nominee Korean Canadian Sandra Oh makes an appearance, solemnly intoning, "It's an honor just to be Asian," indicating with dry sarcasm how drastically underrepresented Asian Americans remain on television (Ramos 2017). McKinnon and Thompson are then joined on-stage by Kristen Bell and Tituss Burgess, followed by Sterling K. Brown, who notes, "Look at us. We're all different in the same way," indicating the stage, now occupied by two blond White women and three Black men. Straight, White, male comedian Andy Samberg descends from the ceiling to try to join in before being shooed away by McKinnon. Next, the early-2000s-era Puerto Rican heartthrob Ricky Martin turns up, says that the song style is far too White, and introduces a Latin beat. The "One of Each Dancers" take the stage to people the background with sparks of color: literally, with their brightly colored dresses, and thematically, with their purported representativeness. Black, gay, and extremely tall drag performer RuPaul next takes the stage, only to complain that he was cast for only one line. The song further sends up tokenistic casting with the line, "There was one, and now we're done." Finally, Black crooner John Legend takes the stage for a final chorus of "we solved it" before the camera cuts to applauding, laughing audience members—Black and White. The skit makes fun of its own tokenism and mocks the television industry's tendency to self-congratulate for its limited notions of diversity and inclusion (McKinnon and Thompson actually mime patting themselves on the back). The industry has not historically made it easy for creators and performers of color to access jobs or representation that would help challenge the overwhelming dominance of Whiteness. This skit's humor is emblematic of what we have argued throughout this book about Horrible White People shows' self-deprecating critique: it is meant to position the characters, or in this case the entire US television industry, as liberal and "woke" (as the song says, the people at the Emmy Awards range "from Democrat to liberal Democrat") while allowing comedy to release the tension by acknowledging the industry's flaws and to stand in for, substitute, or even excuse further action.

Despite that potential release, however, the self-congratulation and cultivated move away from White and male voices on- and off-screen that the song parodies nonetheless indicates a real shift in the industry. The early twenty-first century reflects a periodic and calculated move to find underserved audiences to shore up the industry in the face of technological and economic crisis. There are strong parallels to be made between the 2010s proliferation of diverse-cast programming and the brief abundance of Black-cast sitcoms in the mid-1980s to early 1990s, for example. As Herman Gray (1995) notes, the prevalence of Black-cast sitcoms in that historical moment coincided with a sharp decrease in broadcast-network viewership. More diverse programming (at that time, specifically Black programming) was a tactic of a TV industry in transition and under the strain of competition brought by new technologies, pressures similar to those that fostered the Horrible White People cycle and this linked cycle of Diverse Quality Comedies. Gray writes of that earlier era, "The recognition and engagement with Blackness were not for a moment driven by sudden cultural interest in Black matters or some noble aesthetic goals on the part of executives in all phases of the industry. In large part they were driven, as most things are in network television, by economics" (1995, 68). So, while Horrible White People shows have proliferated, TV-industry economic imperatives to capture as many elements of the fragmented audience as possible have also notably challenged—or added complexity to—the postracial Blackness of (for just one example) producer Shonda Rhimes's empire (*Grey's Anatomy, Private Practice, Scandal,* and *How to Get Away with Murder*) and overtly tackled American racism in numerous genres including the historical epic *Roots*; the family melodramas *Empire, Power,* and *Queen Sugar*; the romantic melodrama *Being Mary Jane*; and comedies like *Atlanta* and *Insecure*. Nonetheless, as we traced in chapter 1, most studio heads tend to echo Gray, claiming that these more diverse representations are the result of economic pressures to attract underserved audiences in an environment of increased competition, even though they are, of course, also responding to cultural pressures.

In later work, Gray amended his argument about the economic motives of diverse programming to say that the "periodic crisis in television over racial representation is less about the network's loss of markets and audience shares than about governance and order" (2005, 89). These occasional drives for inclusion, he argues, are about "managing difference" (89), a task made more urgent in eras like the one this book analyzes when racialized injustice and even violence are hypervisible. This governance comes with representational limits that value quantity over complexity and allow innovation and cultural specificity only within certain bounds. The well-developed secondary characters of color on

HWP shows are an example of this governance within limits (see the introduction and chapter 3). Brandy Monk-Payton argues that "in the current period of Black Lives Matter, the television industry strives to compensate for an inability to coherently register threats of material violence to African Americans by repairing psychic wounds through representation" (2017, 12). In other words, the precarity of simply living as a Black person in America (Monk-Payton is writing only about US television) is, apparently, unrepresentable. Because moments in DQCs like the *Atlanta* and *Insecure* scenes described earlier do seem to effectively represent that precarity also helps explain why so few of those scenes and programs exist. It further explains why those moments might be constructed as interruptions or structures requiring "reading" the image and are therefore easy to miss or ignore. So quantity of representation, on both sides of the camera, is what the industry is willing to offer as a form of what Monk-Payton calls "televisual reparations." "The industry," she writes, defining the contemporary version of Gray's governance, "maintains a tenuous commitment to provide opportunities for African American producers, writers, directors, and actors to the degree that such practice continues to be helpful to the reputation of the medium as well as profitable" (2017, 12).

The Emmys' "We Solved It" skit makes the relationship between diverse representation and the medium's reputation explicit. It further acknowledges, at least ironically, the limited scope of opportunity that it is willing to offer when Sterling K. Brown sings about all the creators of color granted access, "but mostly Shonda Rhimes." Rhimes's outsized success with mass-market genres on broadcast network ABC has become a prime exemplar of the representational limits the mainstream industry offers Black creators. Writing about the major hit medical soap opera *Grey's Anatomy* (ABC, 2005–), Kristen Warner describes Rhimes's "post-Civil Rights, post-feminist" "blindcasting" practices (2015b, 631) that put a broad array of visible difference on-screen but don't develop long-running characters with any cultural specificity. Warner quotes Rhimes discussing Christina Yang and Preston Burke's relationship: "It's not about the fact that she's Asian and he's Black. It's about the fact that she's a slob and he's a neat freak" (2015b, 632). Warner argues that "Rhimes's blindcasting works to acknowledge difference in ways that will cause the least amount of discomfort to White audiences while providing an illusion that under liberal individualism, the marketplace will do right by historically marginalized individuals" (2015b, 645). Another common way Hollywood does this, Warner (2017) argues, is via "plastic representation," "a combination of synthetic elements put together and shaped to look like meaningful imagery, but which can only approximate depth and substance because ultimately it is hollow and cannot survive close scrutiny." For Warner, the best examples of plastic representation appear in remakes of classic White- or male-centered texts that simply replace lead roles with women and people of color. Films like *Ocean's 8* (2018), *Ghostbusters* (2016), or *Annie* (2014), she argues, rely on "the wonder that comes from seeing characters on screen who serve as visual identifiers for specific demographics in order to flatten the expectation to desire anything more" (2017). This instrumentalization of visible difference is the common thread among Gray's, Monk-Payton's, and Warner's analyses of how the US television industry mobilizes race, especially in moments like the late 1980s–early 1990s and the 2012–2018 period we study, when there is an unmistakable push toward inclusivity on-screen.

Rhimes's notion of diversity works well within television's, and particularly broadcast network television's, propensity toward conservative or at least unchallenging representations, in contrast to the niche-market "quality" programming we analyze. Rhimes's overture laid the groundwork for what can be seen as a move to more cultural specificity in racial diversity on television (seen in the progression, in her own work, from *Grey's Anatomy* to *How to Get Away with Murder*). But the negotiations required for, and limits placed on, televisual representations of difference that her shows reflected still operate. The contemporary ideological and economic consequences of the management and governance of televisual difference that Gray has noted came to a head, for example, in early 2018 when "creative differences" between ABC network executives and *Black-ish* (and *Grown-ish* and *Mixed-ish*) creator, Kenya Barris, led to a decision not to air an episode of *Black-ish* that Barris wrote and directed, titled "Please, Baby, Please." The episode reportedly touched on then-current events, including controversy over professional athletes kneeling during performances of the national anthem. According to an official statement, "neither ABC nor [Barris] were happy with the direction of the episode and mutually agreed not to air it" (Goldberg

2018). This book's conclusion expands on how the NFL's anthem controversy illuminates, for mass audiences, similar tensions around White supremacy and precarity as the HWP cycle does for niche audiences. But the "creative differences" between Barris and ABC are indicative of the persistent governance of difference on "legacy television" (Christian 2018)[3] that many people postulate led Barris to break from his first-look contract with ABC and sign a three-year overall deal with Netflix, where he will develop and produce series exclusively for the streaming service (Holloway 2018; Goldberg 2018). Barris follows Rhimes and Ryan Murphy as part of a trend of extremely successful television producers fleeing the constraints of network and even cable for streaming platforms that are consciously marketing diversity for global audiences (see Lobato 2019; Petruska and Woods 2018; and chapter 1 of this book).

Like HBO before it, Netflix has positioned itself as a destination for creative freedom, supposedly allowing auteurs to tell their stories without the close governance or "management of difference" associated with traditional broadcast and cable television. Aymar Jean Christian notes that "because of limited distribution through broadcast, legacy control in series development historically has limited storytelling possibilities, with networks copying existing hits and working with established producers" (2018, 18). This copying and relying on existing products and creators (another iteration of Avi Santo's [2008] "paratelevision," discussed in chapter 1) extends throughout television's history. It is a straightforward example of structural White supremacy. If the industry begins as predominantly White, its successes will be predominantly White. Therefore, when it relies on repetition, it rehires White creators and reproduces their cultural perspectives. In yet another era of temporarily increased visibility for people of color on television (though not behind the camera), in the 1970s, CBS spun off *The Jeffersons*, which became one of the longest-running US television series with a primarily African American cast. From White superproducer Norman Lear, *The Jeffersons* was only possible because the characters had been established on Lear's White-cast sitcom *All in the Family*. In the same way, one hit Shonda Rhimes show leads to three more, and the success of *Girls* and *Louie* pave the way for the entire Horrible White People cycle. In dramatic contrast to this pattern of what Christian calls "legacy television's" habitual recycling of rather limited diversity, he posits "open

TV," the online, user-generated platforms that characterize a twenty-first-century alternative to broadcast and even to big streaming platforms. Open TV, he argues, is more innovative, particularly in its ability to tell stories "about those marginalized by race, gender and sexuality, and class in politics and culture" because they "create stories for communities perceived 'too niche'—of too little value for television and theatrical distribution" (2018, 108–109). But despite being online distributors, Netflix and other streaming platforms where both HWP programming and Diverse Quality Comedies thrive don't reflect the open TV that Christian describes. Rather than being independently produced, distributed, and promoted by creators and the communities they seek to represent, portals like Netflix include the same layers of executive gatekeepers that ultimately pick and choose which shows to green-light or distribute as traditional TV outlets, and thus they adhere to some of the same conservatism around racial diversity in representation (for more, see Christian 2019). When Issa Rae's hit webseries, an example of open TV, was noticed by HBO, for example, she needed an established male producer, Larry Wilmore, to come on board before the network would offer a contract and cede control to her. Rae's experience parallels Lena Dunham's development of *Girls*, as Judd Apatow needed to come on board as an executive producer in order for HBO to take a risk green-lighting her series. These are yet more examples of how legacy television allows for innovation and cultural specificity only within certain bounds; in these cases, representations of gender are accepted into the "masculinist" discourses of quality TV (see Newman and Levine 2012; Nygaard and Lagerwey 2016), as long as they have a male producer's seal of approval or a masculine influence.

In particular, streaming platforms and cable networks operate according to what Katherine Sender (2007) calls "dualcasting" or what Julia Himberg (2014) updates to "multicasting," in which networks favor programming that attempts to corral Peak TV's increasingly fragmented audiences by actively courting multiple distinct demographics at once through strategic branding and textual characteristics. When the creator of *Orange Is the New Black*, Jenji Kohan, described the thought process behind her pitch for Netflix's flagship original series, for example, she called the show's upper-middle-class White protagonist, Piper Chapman, a "Trojan Horse":

You're not going to go into a network and sell a show on really fascinating tales of black women, and Latina women, and old women and criminals. But if you take this white girl, this sort of fish out of water, and you follow her in, you can then expand your world and tell all of those other stories. But it's a hard sell to just go in and try to sell those stories initially. The girl next door, the cool blonde, is a very easy access point, and it's relatable for a lot of audiences and a lot of networks looking for a certain demographic. It's useful. (Gross 2013)

Kohan's statement reveals the negotiations that creators of color who want to tell stories about non-White characters make to skirt limitations imposed on them by networks concerned with "managing of difference" and appealing to traditional "quality" White audiences (what Kohan calls "a certain demographic") by pursuing programming that encourages, above all else, "an identification with the fictions of whiteness" (Lipsitz 1998, 99). Jason Demers (2017) suggests that "one has to recognize a type of structural analysis at the heart of Kohan's political, tactical move: not only is Piper being used to sell a show to network executives, but the character is also being used to open up a subject position—a structural position within the field of filmic [or televisual] representation." What Demers and Kohan are explaining is that the show, because of the structures of the television industry, *must* assume a White audience member first. The alternative, according to Kohan, is not being selected for production. So she uses the White character strategically. The strategic use of White characters, aesthetics of Whiteness, and established "quality" modes of storytelling are essential tactics mobilized and structured throughout the cycle of Diverse Quality Comedies in order to achieve a version of multicasting in which they speak to White audiences while subtly acknowledging other viewers. Ralina Joseph calls these "strategic performances of ambiguity, carefully created constructions designed to wink at certain audiences and smile blandly in the face of others. Strategic ambiguity provides space to resist both facets of postracialism: the myth that racism doesn't exist, and racism itself" (2018, 29). This dual-coded address is central to how DQCs function as comforting or even pedagogical for White audiences, while offering other audiences meaningful recognition. Joseph R. Winters evokes W. E. B. DuBois's double-consciousness that stems from Black

Americans judging themselves through the lens of White supremacy and the simultaneous "desire to be recognized, the desire to see oneself and be seen as an equal among those who have historically stigmatized Black life" (2016, 137). While we don't include *Orange Is the New Black* in the Diverse Quality Comedy cycle because it predates the cycle's peak and straddles both groups, with a clear Horrible White Person protagonist in Piper as well as a creator of color and the cultural specificity of Diverse Quality Comedies, Kohan's explicit acknowledgment that the show essentially tricked White executives and White viewers into watching exemplifies the labor-intensive negotiations of dualcasting and strategic ambiguity emblematic of Diverse Quality Comedies. The Diverse Quality Comedies don't have White female protagonists (although *Dear White People* makes excellent strategic use of a "woke" White boyfriend, and *Insecure*'s astute White coworker fulfills a similar role) but employ, as we discuss shortly, other negotiated textual strategies in the same way in order to appeal to White audiences and satisfy the mostly White executives of the networks and portals on which they appear.

Significantly, DQCs, like their Horrible White People show counterparts, may have small or difficult-to-measure audiences (because they are distributed on streaming platforms that don't allow access to their viewership data). But the little information available suggests that they make up for smaller audiences through a combination of crossover appeal (like Kohan's use of the Piper character) and critical praise that gives their networks or portals prestige. *Variety* reported that "nearly all of the series nominated for best drama or comedy at the upcoming 69th [2017] Primetime Emmy Awards have been watched by fewer than half of all potential viewers. . . . *Master of None*, *The Handmaid's Tale*, and *Atlanta* tied at 5% each for the least-watched of all nominees—although *Master of None* exceeded all nominees in 'never heard of' responses" (Holloway 2017). Within these tiny audiences, according to figures from Nielsen (the primary TV ratings pollster in the United States) published in August 2017, 61 percent of US viewers of *Insecure* and 50 percent of *Atlanta*'s audience were nonblack. That same Nielsen analysis indicated that several programs with a predominantly Black cast or a main story line focusing on a Black character are drawing substantial nonblack viewership (Nielsen 2017). So, while the audiences for DQCs may be small, they don't fall victim to Christian's "too niche" discourse because of their substantial, calculated, cross-race appeal. So for example, when Dev dates on *Master of None*, viewers of any race or ethnicity might identify with the struggles of appified dating, while viewers of color will further identify with the racism that Dev and his dates encounter on the app. Similarly, while most viewers could identify with slightly awkward family dinners or being continually pestered to provide tech support for their parents, a smaller subset of viewers might further identify with the specificity of immigrant parents and navigating multiple cultures when Dev and his Taiwanese American friend Brian take their families to dinner (S1E2).

Along with this crossover audience appeal, Diverse Quality Comedies have the same outsized cultural impact as Horrible White People shows, as measured by awards and hyperbolic critical praise, making them important to study despite the scale of the "never heard of it" response. *Master of None*, *Atlanta*, and *Insecure* have all been nominated for awards for their acting and writing, as well as in aesthetic categories like cinematography, editing, and sound design. Michaela Coel won a BAFTA for Best Female Performance in a Comedy for her cringe-inducing, sex-crazed performance as the protagonist on *Chewing Gum*, which we include as a DQC, despite it being the only British production discussed in this chapter, because it shares so many textual characteristics with the other DQCs and speaks to the argument made in chapter 1 about the transatlantic circulation of our key concepts and texts. Furthermore, the *New York Times* called *Master of None* "the year's best comedy straight out of the gate" (Poniewozak 2015b), and the *Hollywood Reporter* called *Insecure* "HBO's sharpest comedy" (Bahr 2018). *Atlanta* won the Golden Globe for Best Comedy in 2017 and was nominated for twenty-two Emmys between 2017 and 2019, winning in Best Actor (for creator and star Donald Glover, 2017) and Best Director (Glover, 2017) categories, among others. One reviewer rhapsodized, "*Atlanta* isn't a show, it's a state of mind. . . . Its stellar first season married seductive surrealism with a lovely, oblique portrait of Black creative aspiration in the South" (Saraiya 2018). In 2018 alone, it appeared on top-ten lists from the *Guardian*, *Rolling Stone*, and the *Washington Post*, among others (Bakare 2018; Sepinwall 2018; B. Butler 2018). The *Atlantic*'s best of 2018 catalogue put *Atlanta* in the category of "Weird TV" for its surrealism and disconcerting flights of fantasy but noted that those aesthetic choices all "captured a sense of the systemic anxieties that accompany being black in America" (Gilbert 2018). That sense of systemic anxiety, not just for Black Americans but for all Americans of color and to transatlantic circulations of those images and audiences as well, is central to DQCs' bleak outlook and grim tone.

Whereas HWP shows wallow in despair because rights to jobs, housing, and relationships that middle-class White characters felt were their due have been denied them, DQC characters' despair comes from those deprivations *plus* the constant onslaught of getting "strapped with having to prove our [black Americans'] humanity inside and outside of the workplace and classroom, often by circumspectly navigating the tears of white women. It's doubly (triply?) exhausting" (Clark 2019). Tiana Clark's emphasis, in that *Buzzfeed* column, on the tears of White women is reflected again in the resilience of the Black characters on Diverse Quality Comedies in contrast to the more prominently female-centric HWP shows, where most women characters wallow in emotional distress, addiction, or even mental illness (*Love, You're the Worst, Crazy Ex-Girlfriend, UnReal, Fleabag, Transparent, Girlfriends' Guide to Divorce*). Speaking to the distinctions we made earlier between *horrible* White people and *miserable* people of color in DQCs, we see this racialized representation of affect when we compare Issa's reaction to losing her home to Gretchen's loss of her home on *You're the Worst*. For both women, it is the dissolution of a long-term hetero romance that had been (or had been fantasized to be) leading to marriage that leads to their not being able to afford (financially or emotionally) to stay in the home they had shared with their partner. Whereas Gretchen responds with complete collapse, Issa responds with hustle. Gretchen moves into her best friend's studio apartment, where they take turns sleeping in the bed. She does copious amounts of drugs, stops going to work (although inexplicably does not lose her job), and develops agoraphobia. Gretchen is barely functional; she rarely bathes; she wallows in abjection. Describing that "abjection aesthetic," Rebecca Wanzo writes, "There may be freedom in a middle-class white 'girl' associating herself with sexual abjection, dirt, and feces, given traditional representations of pure white womanhood, but perhaps unsurprisingly, a black girl may resist or play with Western constructions of abjection" (2016, 30). In contrast to Gretchen's wallowing, Issa allows herself a moment of sadness—a

gorgeous, heart-wrenching, melodic flash-forward fantasy of reconcilia-
tion, marriage, sex, baby, and happiness, all bathed in a warming golden
filter—as she says a final good-bye to her boyfriend and her apartment.
The moment of self-indulgence and melancholy ends with an uncer-
emoniously shut apartment door and a cut to the season-ending credits.
When Issa returns the following season, she is living on a different ex-
boyfriend's couch, unemployed, single, and broke. She is flailing, but
she does not approach Gretchen's abjection and crippling despair. She
applies for multiple jobs, attempts to organize a music festival for her
community, dates, sees friends, gets advice, drives for the ride-sharing
company Lyft at all hours of the day, and works hard. She doesn't necessarily find success. Neoliberal individualism works no more easily or
effectively for her than for Gretchen. The difference in emotional register of the two women's reactions, however, is key to the racialized trend
we are trying to understand. If HWP shows are about the specificity of
White fragility, DQCs are about the specificity of people of color's resilience. DQCs must negotiate and be strategic about appeals to Whiteness but can offer, if not a respite, a specific expression of the exhaustion
that Clark describes.

Negotiating an Aesthetics of Whiteness

Before offering that expression of cultural specificity, however, Diverse
Quality Comedies must overcome the industry's barriers to entry, in
particular the historical legacies of structural White supremacy built
into TV's development process and presumptions about lucrative audiences and the aesthetics that appeal to those audiences. DQCs do this
the same way their Horrible White People show counterparts do, via
generic innovation of the sitcom. Their structural and aesthetic novelty
may even exceed HWP shows', as evinced by their frequent nominations in categories like cinematography and editing, which also speaks
to the creative labor of creating multicoded aesthetics. This innovation
aligns them with understandings of "quality" TV that we have been
using throughout the book. We have used the discourse of "quality" to
help categorize and define the cycle of Horrible White People shows.
And, if it has been implied so far, we want to be explicit here that "quality" aesthetics are *White* aesthetics. As Alfred L. Martin (2018) writes,

"When discussing quality television and its value proposition, one thing is clear: quality television (and its demographic) is white." This is what Aymar Jean Christian implies when he argues that the place for people of color to create authentic and specific representations of themselves is *entirely outside* the structures of the existing industry in the realm of open TV; and it is what Timothy Havens (2018) means when he writes that the aesthetics of Black-cast prestige dramas, like Showtime's *The Chi*, exist in a lineage of "film schools and art house cinemas." Havens put this in contrast to "the Afrofuturist aesthetics of a film like *Black Panther* [which foregrounds] a populism that transcends class-based African American taste cultures. . . . *The Chi*'s aesthetics appeal to a decidedly middle-class, liberal subscriber, regardless of race." Havens's phrase "regardless of race" emphasizes class identity as a more important indicator of whether a viewer would be hailed by or recognize the pleasures of a particular show. This parallels our argument in chapter 1 that class (and racial) identity trump national identity for the aesthetics and audience address of programming that is marketed transatlantically or even globally for streaming platforms.

Furthermore, Racquel Gates argues, in her recuperation of "negative images" of Blackness in television genres typically described as the antithesis of quality, such as reality television, that "respectability often comes with the consequence of [racial] muteness. Or, to be more specific, the burden of respectability places limitations on the forms that certain types of discussions can take" (2018, 6). Extending her argument, then, "quality" operates in the same burdensome way as respectability, forcing "certain types of discussions" to happen within aesthetic codes, as we will discuss later. All these authors speak to the notion that valued, awarded, "respectable," "universal," or "artistic" aesthetics are an aesthetics of Whiteness. DQCs thus operate within this aesthetics of Whiteness in the mode that Joseph (2018) calls "strategic ambiguity," with its "bland smile" at White audiences and its "wink" of recognition toward audiences of color. Just as postfeminism doesn't disappear but exists within and alongside emergent feminisms, so heightened visibility of difference, racial and cultural specificity, and racial violence exist within and alongside lingering and possibly resurgent postracialism. Like Issa's White boss, who claims that her own White hand in We Got Y'all's logo carries no racial meaning or significance, DQCs must fit into a TV industry and a culture of White supremacy that still value assimilationist representations that make difference palatable to dominant perceptions of desirable audiences, who remain White. So the cultural specificity that Warner (2017) argues is the antidote to plastic representation battles with a supposed universalism that networks attempt to impose in order to reach that half or more of the viewership that Nielson (2017) reports is White.

One of the main ways Diverse Quality Comedies garner their "quality" label is through their innovative disruptions of the generic conventions of sitcom and romantic comedy, just like HWP shows. Both cycles explore modern dating and romance and challenge the sitcom's narrative and aesthetic characteristics, which as a result allows both cycles to contest hegemonic representations of gender, family, and relationships typical of the genre and to speak to the same trends around emerging feminisms and culturally shifting norms around sex and gender that we discussed in chapter 2. DQCs are similarly littered with alternative families, relationships, and living arrangements. *Atlanta*, for example, begins with Earn sharing an apartment with the mother of his child, while they both casually date other people; the series' first few seasons follow a will-they-or-won't-they narrative of them getting back together, a potentiality that is finally shut down in the middle of season 2 when Van calls it off, realizing that Earn is not invested in them moving toward monogamy and stability. *Insecure*'s first season introduces us to Issa questioning her stagnant relationship with her longtime, underemployed boyfriend, a stable relationship that she actively sabotages through an immediately regretted fling with a childhood crush. This active sabotaging of stable hetero relationships is shared by several Horrible White People protagonists, including Rebecca on *Crazy Ex-Girlfriend*, Mickey on *Love*, Michelle Pierson on *Togetherness*, and almost every Horrible White Person, a pattern that works to expose the "postfeminist dystopia" (Petersen 2015) or lack of fulfillment offered from traditional heterosexual coupling and monogamy in this era of emerging feminisms.

In the same vein, *Chewing Gum* offers another challenge to conservative representations of sex and coupling typical of sitcoms as it follows the hysterically awkward exploits of a twenty-four-year-old shop assistant, Tracey Gordon (played by the show's writer/creator, Michaela Coel). A religious virgin living under her mother's highly restrictive rules, Tracy wants to have sex and learn more about the world outside her public-housing community. In addition to her class status, which marks a significant departure from both cycles (but aligns the show with traditions of working-class sitcoms in Britain), Tracey reveals her inner, often-carnal, thoughts and erotic fantasies through the stylistic flourish of direct address to the audience (like its HWP counterpart *Fleabag*), reflecting what *Rolling Stone* calls its "radical candor" about female sexual desire (Kaplan 2017). In yet another example of this kind of generic innovation challenging representations of idealized heterosexual relationships, *Master of None* beautifully critiques typical romantic-comedy happy endings. After building a courtship between Rachel and Dev over the season's first eight episodes, "Mornings" (S1E9) condenses into a half hour months of the central couple's relationship as their passion cools into routine and doubt. Those often-banal domestic conflicts would be the fodder for multiple seasons of a traditional sitcom. Thus, through textual characteristics similar to Horrible White People shows, like direct address and anthology-like episode structures, among others, Diverse Quality Comedies disrupt the aesthetic and ideological conventions of the sitcom and offer a similarly dystopian picture of hetero relationships and patriarchal families compared to the happy families of color described in chapter 2.

There are further thematic parallels between the two cycles as well, reflecting the ways they react in tandem to the events of this historical conjuncture. Facing similar threats to home ownership after recession as Horrible White People characters, the protagonists of Diverse Quality Comedies also confront housing insecurities. When Issa breaks up with her boyfriend, she has to move out of the apartment they shared, as we noted earlier, and she sleeps on another ex-boyfriend's couch, eventually becoming an apartment manager in order to lower her rent; Tracey lives in a homeless shelter after being kicked out of her family's apartment; and Earn secretly lives in a storage garage when he is not staying with Van. DQCs also share the Horrible White People cycle's focus on a lack of access to stable, fulfilling employment. In addition to Issa's frustrations with her nonprofit job, her boyfriend, Lawrence, starts the series severely underemployed, working at an electronics superstore after his app pitch fails to secure funding, and her best friend, Molly, feels overworked and underappreciated at her predominantly white law firm. In the pilot of *Atlanta*, Earn, a Princeton University dropout, is pushing credit-card sign-ups at the airport for $5.15 an hour, only to later struggle to pay his bills or provide for his child while managing his cousin's up-and-coming rap career.

All of these thematic similarities across the cycles point to the universal suffering that Lauren Berlant calls "cruel optimism," in which the frayed fantasies of "upward mobility, job security, political and social equality, and lively, durable intimacy" accumulate into the twenty-first century's bleak prevailing affect, felt and experienced by everyone (2011, 3). That the universality of suffering is represented through similar themes and aesthetic disruptions across the two cycles operates as a type of assimilationist representation, or assimilationist aesthetics, akin to Gray's description of assimilationist Black-cast programs in the 1980s. Gray defines shows as "assimilationist to the extent that the worlds they construct are distinguished by the complete elimination or, at best, marginalization of social and cultural difference in the interest of shared and universal similarity" (1995, 85). Diverse Quality Comedies most definitely do not completely eliminate social and cultural diversity. Yet aesthetically, they foreground a "quality" look and feel that has been honed for its appeal to "universal," or White, audiences. This aesthetic similarity suggests that the people of color featured in Diverse Quality Comedies experience the same precarity as White people, *in the same way*. While this aesthetics of Whiteness might advocate the idea of "universality," narrative moments (and historical realities) like Issa's loss of promotion to a White coworker or casting agents' insistence that Dev audition with an Indian accent challenge it. This performance of "universal" White culture is presented as necessary for entrée into the award-winning, critically adored pantheon of "quality" TV. DQCs then weave challenges to and negotiations with that institutionalized Whiteness into their texts via interruptions like Issa's "beep beep, motherfuckers," and subtler aesthetic cues that often appear in the form of musical choice, set design, or casting.

While *Atlanta*, *Insecure*, *Chewing Gum*, and *Master of None* don't have the "Trojan Horse" middle-class, liberal, White lady character that Jenji Kohan referred to, they hail that "certain demographic" via thematic consistencies, art-house references, and "quality" aesthetics, sliding in moments of racialized specificity but often through a winking register (as Ralina Joseph [2018] suggests) that requires close reading of the show's aesthetics, like the example of complex framing in *Atlanta* described earlier. *Master of None* is particularly overt in these art-house "quality" references. One entire episode (S2E1) is an homage to the Italian neorealist classic *Ladri di biciclette* (*Bicycle Thieves*; De Sica, 1948), and another episode, "New York, I Love You" (S2E6), mimics the anthology structure of the 2008 film of the same name that collated short films about the city made by ten different directors. This episode serves as a particularly apt example because it references this somewhat obscure art-house film, but just as the film is made up of episodes by directors of varied nations, races, ethnicities, and genders, so the episode's vignette structure follows incidental background characters as they navigate racially inflected interactions in the city. Eddie, a Latino doorman, copes with an elderly White tenant's racist comments about how he should stop eating mangos on the job, even though he has never done so; and a Cameroonian taxi driver wonders why "White girls are so obsessed with grain bowls" on his way home to the apartment he shares with three other African immigrants (each has the flag of his home nation hanging above his bed). Despite the visible diversity in this episode (and throughout the show), which might hail multiple audiences, similar to Havens's (2018) discussion of *The Chi*, its aesthetic references to art-house cinema and its complex, not-really-narrative structure center the middle- or upper-middle-class target audience it shares with the films it references, an audience historically understood as White.

Atlanta offers a consistently subtler, more continuous negotiation of the tension between White "quality" aesthetics and culturally specific critiques of structural racial inequality. The episode "Helen" (S2E4) offers a good example, when Earn and Van's relationship finally ends at an out-of-town German festival called Fastnacht in a predominantly White part of Georgia that Van frequented as a child. Positioning the series in conversation with other texts of the "new Black Gothic," Sherie-Marie Harrison (2018) places this White, Germanic otherworld in direct conversation with the haunting "sunken place" in Jordan Peele's film *Get Out*, where Black consciousness is imprisoned so that the Black bodies it once inhabited can be used by White people. Operating in this haunted, Gothic mode, Fastnacht is no ordinary cliched stereotype of a beer-swilling, polka-dancing German American festival. Yes, it includes the social rules, rituals, and traditions of any in-group that are illegible to a visitor, exemplified when Earn accidentally triumphs in a bizarre ball-passing game of which neither he nor the viewer understands any of the rules. But the festival also has heavily surreal elements like masks and costumes—and White people in blackface—including a towering goat man who haunts the festivities and must be found somewhere in the surrounding village, after dark, in order to win the festival. It is a bizarre, disturbing episode shot in dull gray light that seems to convey Earn's lack of enthusiasm and with sometimes-frantic cutting (as in the mysterious ball game) that creates an off-balance spinning effect to align the viewer with Earn's dislocation. In these respects, the episode participates in the heightened aesthetics of "quality" TV. Van, however, functions in this episode somewhat like what Jane Naomi Iwamura (2017) calls a "bridge figure." Bridge figures are liminal, often multiracial, characters who, by simultaneously inhabiting two cultures, work to translate or encapsulate the "othered" culture (often inflected with an element of the mystical) for the dominant one. The dynamic in this instance is slightly more complex, as Van, who is biracial, brings Earn along but doesn't attempt to help him understand the festival; but it is also the normally dominant culture—Whiteness, in this case ethnically marked—rendered aberrant and in need of translation.

It is this aberrance made visible in a norm that invokes the new Black Gothic. Van participates in this surreal event with a visibly uncomfortable Earn, whose discomfort clashes with her unbridled enthusiasm; their clash, her comfort and excitement about this ritualistic White space, in contrast to Earn's palpable distaste and discomfort with it, seems to encapsulate the tensions of her biracial identity and Earn's apparent sudden rejection of it. The episode ends with Van concluding, "We can be good together, but only when we really have to be. And I'm slowly figuring out that maybe we don't have to." Reflecting the show's "universal" concerns about modern relationships, the narrative foregrounds Van being robbed of her expectations of a functioning, long-term, adult relationship with Earn, but it could also be read as bleak commentary of biracial displacement in an American culture still operating according to a deeply embedded racial inequality tied to clearer binaries of Black and White. It could further be read as a frustrated roar back against the need for Black auteurs and artists to work within established White "quality" parameters. *Atlanta* thus uses surreal aesthetics that tie it to industry discourses of quality but mobilizes them to make Whiteness weird while illuminating culturally specific Black experiences—in this case of being "the only one" in a ritualized White space.

As *Atlanta* illustrates, in DQCs' strategic negotiations of the "quality" aesthetics that disrupt the generic conventions of the sitcom, they also often challenge the genre's overwhelming Whiteness far beyond the actors' more diverse racial visibility. The genius of these shows is that they create multiple texts, one that uses the codes of an aesthetics of Whiteness and a second that quotes an alternative non-White aesthetic tradition—using lighting techniques, wardrobe, music, set design, and visual and aural references to the work of non-White auteurs like Spike Lee. In chapter 2, we discussed Horrible White People shows' low-key lighting, single-camera cinematography, and on-location shooting, which threaten the stable, brightly lit comfort of sitcom's reliable domestic spaces. Diverse Quality Comedies similarly disrupt the representational norms of the genre, as we have seen, but offer a more intersectional challenge to the sitcom's hegemonic ideologies.

Cinematographer Ava Berkofsky, for example, established a signature look for *Insecure* by focusing on lighting and making "black faces not only legible but striking" (Harding 2017). Reciting the "discourses of distinction" (Polan 2007) common to all the series creators as part of HBO's network branding, Berkofsky said the secret to making television resemble film (presumed to be a move toward prestige; we could replace her use of "film" with "quality" aesthetics and arrive at the same point) is providing different levels of light to the scene. "[In sitcoms], everything is the same level of brightness. That's what I'm trying to avoid," she said. "The trick is keeping [light] off the walls. If you keep it off the walls, you can expose for the faces and it still has a cinematic look" (Harding 2017). Avoiding the saturated, overly bright, blanket intensity of light common in traditional multicamera sitcoms, Berkofsky built on the innovations of Spike Lee's go-to cinematographer, Ernest Dickerson, to focus on the reflection of light. She uses moisturizer, shiny reflective makeup, and custom lightboards with little LED lights inside to help bounce indirect light off Black skin and give gradations and depth usually reserved for White skin. Since color film was developed and adjusted against "Shirley Cards," named after the White model and Kodak employee Shirley

Page, film stock has been inherently racist (Smith 2013; Del Barco 2014; Dyer 1997). The light range was so narrow that "if you exposed film for a white kid, the black kid sitting next to him would be rendered invisible except for the whites of his eyes and teeth" (Smith 2013). Berkofsky, then, worked to create a culturally specific "quality" visual aesthetics that pushes back against some of the dominant aesthetic norms or universalities of Whiteness that are taken for granted in mainstream film and television, especially the sitcom.

Similarly, *Dear White People*, discussed in detail shortly, threads African American cultural references through its music, set design, wardrobe, and character discussions about Black hair and skin care, creating a distinct divide between culturally White public space and culturally Black private space (a divide that *Atlanta* exaggerated to excess in the episode described earlier and that *Insecure* makes clear between Issa's work space and home space). It also brilliantly reveals normally invisible White cultural specificity (in a more quotidian mode than Fastnacht) when the all-Black dorm is integrated by university decree and White students suddenly populate the background of the main cast's frames in a delightful reversal of the normalized sprinkling of faces of color in the background of White-cast programming. The opening episode of season 2 contains close-ups of herds of White feet in flip flops, two White extras strumming acoustic guitars, and Coco, the queen-bee character, leading a flock of White acolytes through the dorm while giving a lecture on understanding black slang. Here, the series disrupts the "universality" of Whiteness by denaturalizing its cultural specificity using stereotypes and tokenism as Whiteness disrupts the comforting Blackness of the dorm. Diverse Quality Comedies thus suggest that challenging the sitcom genre's stylistic conventions creates the space or even the necessity to challenge its representational conventions as well.

Aesthetic innovations like those from Berkofsky, coupled with culturally specific characters and subject matter, have led many critics, like the *Guardian*'s Hannah Davies, to praise DQCs for speaking directly to Black and other non-White audiences. She writes that "*Insecure* is a show that embodies the concept of 'for us, by us'—that is, art and culture made for, and by, the black American community. It's an antidote to excruciating portrayals of blackness crafted by undiverse TV execs" (Davies 2018). Davies highlights the way "current race politics often permeate [*Insecure's*] world." These permeations are like those outlined in the conference-room scene described earlier as well as in instances like Molly's discovery of her law firm's major gender and racial pay disparity when she accidently opens her White male colleague's paycheck; the drastic discrepancy inspires her eventual move to an all-Black firm (where she unexpectedly discovers the gender dynamics to be just as complex and unequal as in her White firm). Davies also emphasizes *Insecure's* culturally specific soundtrack (curated by Solange and the R&B producer Raphael Saadiq, featuring everyone from Junglepussy to SZA and Kendrick Lamar), which emphasizes how, as Brandi Monk-Payton suggests, "the terrain of the sonic becomes crucial to channelling Blackness in contemporary television" (2017, 18). The series introduces us to the world of *Insecure* with sweeping overhead shots of Los Angeles underscored by Kendrick Lamar's Black Lives Matter civil rights anthem "Alright." The track opens with lines from Alice Walker's *The Color Purple*, "Alls my life, I had to fight," and the bleakness of the rap's lyrics detailing contemporary Black struggles like police discrimination and poverty contrast with hopeful optimism of the hook's chorus, "We gon' be alright!"—a contrast that then structures the tensions underwriting Issa's life, especially as the song transitions us into an introduction to Issa. She is pitching her tutoring services in hopes of making a difference in the lives of young kids of color, only to be verbally assaulted by those same students for her inability to perform an authentic Blackness: "Why you talk like a White girl?"

These nuances and character complexities, made more legible through the soundtrack, lead critics to celebrate the way DQCs' casting and characterizations push back against and complicate prominent television stereotypes. Michaela Coel, the creator of *Chewing Gum*, for example, wants people to think differently about why working-class Black characters like her show's protagonist are not seen in TV and the movies more often: "In terms of women of color, especially in British TV, there's not often a dark-skinned character who is vulnerable, who has a naiveté about her, who is lovable—and is not just a sexual vixen, a crackhead or a criminal" (Kaplan 2017). *Master of None* explicitly addresses the stereotyping and lack of complexity offered non-White characters that Coel refers to in its episode "Indians on TV" (S1E4). Throughout the episode, Dev tackles the anxieties of navigating stereotypical performances in Hollywood, an industry that still relies on tokenistic diversity casting and operates on casual prejudice and exclusion (as the Emmy's song and dance described earlier poked fun at). Beginning with a brief montage of stereotypical Indian caricatures across the history of pop culture, the episode follows Dev and his actor friend Ravi, who both go out for the part of "Unnamed Cab Driver" on a TV crime show and end up discussing their feelings about stereotypical casting, especially adopting an Indian accent for auditions. The episode is refreshing as it offers a variety of perspectives and a range of complicit agents who end up supporting Hollywood's systemic racism, whether intentionally or not. Thus, it disrupts and challenges the typical individualism of most televisual depictions of race relations.

This episode illustrates why, out of all Diverse Quality Comedies, *Master of None* has received the most accolades for its culturally specific narratives. In another important example of the show's innovative representations of diversity, *Master of None* writer and supporting actress Lena Waithe made history as the first Black woman to win an Emmy for best comedy-series writing for the episode "Thanksgiving" (S2E8), which follows Dev and Waithe's character, Denise, over a series of flashbacks to Thanksgiving holidays from childhood to college. The episode, loosely based on Waithe's own life, shows Denise's struggle to come out to her mother. Describing how Ansari convinced her to write the episode, Waithe told *Variety*, "Aziz was like, 'No. I can't be that specific. That's your world. It's very niche'" (Pham 2017). Ansari's unwillingness to write Waithe's story for her and insistence that it be told acknowledges his sensitivity to the specificity of intersectional experience, leading Vikram Murthi (2015) to call *Master of None* a "racially-diverse, culturally-enlightened series" that "doesn't shy away from the inherent thorniness of representation, . . . refusing to offer neat answers to difficult questions in favor of opening up a legitimate dialogue about the issue." *Master of None*'s refusal to "offer neat answers" about racial identity and belonging is directly tied to its narrative and aesthetic innovations of the typical sitcom. As these examples suggest, Diverse Quality Comedies' generic disruptions often extend their critique of the genre's conventions to include its prevailing Whiteness in a way that Horrible White People shows don't.

A comparison between *Master of None*'s and *Casual*'s handling of technologized modern dating further reveals a significant difference between the way the two cycles embed cultural specificity. *Master of None* creates a dense, multilayered text that combines unexpected editing with potentially confrontational (for White viewers) dialogue, negotiating the Whiteness of "quality" aesthetics by offering an overtly racialized take on a supposedly universal experience. *Casual*, in contrast, offers a creative story but a more conventional aesthetic that sits comfortably with its presumption of universality. Dev and Alex both experience frustrations and failures that speak to the universal lack of "lively, durable intimacy" that Berlant describes under cruel optimism. Both reflect power imbalances embedded in the technology of contemporary dating, but perhaps unsurprisingly, those inequalities are discussed openly by the Black and Asian characters on *Master of None* and left silent, to be read only by audiences actively looking for them, in the Horrible White People show. On *Master of None*'s "First Date" (S2E4), Dev goes on nine awkward, fun, and disorienting first dates, which he arranges via a gamified, Tinder-like swiping app. On his date with Diana, an African American actress he knew slightly from auditions, the couple discuss dating apps and how she gets far fewer matches than her White friends do, and, as she says, "I rarely match with guys outside of my race." Dev echoes her experience, explaining, "A lot of my matches are Indian women." Diana ends the conversation saying sarcastically, "Well, it's great White people finally have an advantage somewhere." The sequence reflects research in Ansari's own book, cowritten with the sociologist Eric Klinenberg, about "modern romance" (Ansari 2015) and work on the racial bias built into search algorithms often written by White coders (Noble 2018). By the end of the episode, Dev has had one very boring second date with Indian American Priya and has had sex with a White woman who turned out to have a racist Aunt Jemima cookie jar filled with condoms beside her bed. The confrontation he has with the latter is cringe-worthy for everyone, as she predictably reacts badly to being called racist and he has to admit that he slept with her even after noticing the racism. The episode's narrative paints a grim but astute and insightful picture of technologized dating for people of color.

Casual's narrative offers an equally grim picture but one that requires interpretation—that is, the racialized power dynamics, unlike Dev's date conversations, are implicit and easy to ignore if you are not looking for them. In the series pilot (S1E1), it is established that Alex wrote the algorithm for a successful dating app, which he now manipulates into setting him up with attractive but incompatible dates for him to have one-night stands with. He and his sister each go out on one such disastrous date that he has arranged for them and end up leaving to hang out with each other instead. Then, in the final season (S4E3), which is set several years in the future, Alex tries a new dating technology, the virtual-reality bar. In the virtual reality, which is occupied entirely by White people, he chats up a beautiful woman who turns out to be a phishing scam, prizing his security questions, signature, and credit-card information out of him by flirting and encouraging in-app purchases. The clever predictions about imminent technological developments (his home is mostly controlled by an egg-shaped, female-voiced listening device called Ova) characterize the season and reflect the sophisticated, knowing Horrible White People taste culture we have established. But the season is also characterized by a dystopian dissatisfaction with the separation between connections made in physical space and those mediated by technologies. Alex cannot manipulate the virtual-reality dating world the way he could completely control the dating app he created, leaving him bereft and fragile (or enacting White fragility). Being the victim of a scam that was immediately spotted by the first woman he told about his experience—that is, it was obvious, and his superior technical knowledge should have alerted him to it but didn't—illustrates his lost power and lack of control. He is devastated by the interaction because it means he no longer has complete power over the dating and emotional interactions he has; the experience sparks an intense emotional breakdown that leads him to eventually flee his life in Los Angeles. Although race, let alone Alex's Whiteness, is never acknowledged in the text, the virtual dating world seems to literalize the threats to the privileges of patriarchal White supremacy— particularly the "advantage" that Diana explicitly mocks in the parallel *Master of None* episode. The intense vulnerability that Alex feels after being victimized on the virtual-reality dating app is an explicit example of the way the cycle encourages viewers to empathize with White male fragility, presented unquestioningly as universal.

Significantly, *Casual's* virtual-reality story line is also told in an aesthetically simpler fashion than Dev's series of first dates is. Ads and text appear on-screen as buttons for the characters to push; but techniques like text messages or computer interfaces appearing on-screen are no longer unique, and the story otherwise unfolds linearly from start to finish. *Master of None*'s dating episode mimics the actual experience of swiping by intercutting a series of essentially interchangeable dates throughout the episode. Dev uses the same initial chat-up line on everyone, as he reluctantly shows one date. He brings them all to the same restaurant, followed by the same bar, followed by a cab ride home during which he attempts to kiss them and sees what will unfold after that. The repetition of location and cuts that appear to initiate a shot/reverse-shot conversation but cut unexpectedly to a different woman in the same seat in the same restaurant on essentially the same date creates an artificiality and an awareness of mediation that actually exceeds that of the arguably much more mediated virtual world created on *Casual*. Dev's interactions all seem to happen outside of reality—despite his best efforts, they feel forced, robotic, inauthentic—and thus the episode's complex aesthetics speak even more to the artificiality of experience for people of color when dating while using "algorithms of oppression" (Noble 2018), an experience that is doubly or triply (to use Clark's terminology) more exhausting than Alex's experience—a White tech bro by and for whom these sites were originally designed. These two episodes reflect the obvious thematic parallels between both cycles but also significantly highlight the more nuanced, aesthetically complex representations of cultural specificity portrayed in *Master of None*. The comparison points to the way DQCs can operate in multiple codes at once, offering strategic representations that actively decenter Whiteness through their negotiations with and rebellions against "quality" aesthetics and notions of universality, while also illustrating the way HWP programs often frame their culturally specific Whiteness as universal.

Conclusions: *Dear White People*, Hope, and the New Black Gothic

Yet despite DQCs' commitment to cultural specificity in characters, stories, and style, it is clear from interviews in industry trade presses that creators of color feel obligated to work hard to negotiate their appeals to White and non-White audiences. For example, the creator of *Dear White People*, Justin Simien, speaks to the way his show operates within multiple codes at once:

I think the key to the show is making you care about the characters first, because it's not a thesis. And if we tell the truth about what they're going through, then maybe you'll care and think about it. I think the show has two goals. One is to allow people who don't necessarily look like us to see themselves in characters they don't expect to, so that the next time they see a black guy at Starbucks, they won't feel the need to call the cops on him. And the other thing is to make people who've actually gone through these experiences go: "Oh my God, totally. I'm so glad someone finally put it that way." I think both of those things allow black folks to feel more human in society. (Ugwu 2018)

Kristen Warner (2016) echoes this sentiment in her analysis of *Insecure* in relation to HBO's branding: "At every level of *Insecure*'s construction, the series makes sure to speak to two audiences simultaneously. . . . This type of bilingual audience address is not a new phenomenon for Black-centered productions. To the contrary, this act of bifurcating messages of universality and cultural specificity between two audiences is a long-held survival tactic in an industry that does not often allow marginalized groups access or entry." Like Kohan's "Trojan Horse," Simien's "care about the characters first," or Ralina Joseph's (2018) conversations with creators and executives of color reporting their use of strategic ambiguity, Diverse Quality Comedies, unlike their Horrible White People show counterparts, are in a constant process of negotiation: of representing authentic experiences for viewers of color, making Whiteness visible and acknowledging subtle (to White people) structural White supremacy, often alongside more overt or even violent eruptions of racism; of operating within an industry-approved "quality" aesthetics of Whiteness, while representing culturally specific histories of non-White representational aesthetics. While all DQCs operate in this mode, we want to end the chapter with close readings of *Dear White People*, a show that makes its strategies of aesthetic and racial negotiation explicit and thus, by contrast, throws the relative race muteness of Horrible White People shows into relief.

The show's title, of course, makes our choice obvious. Created by a Black author, Justin Simien, based on his 2014 film of the same name, with a predominantly Black cast, its setting in a predominantly White, fictional Ivy League university and its direct address to White people make its dual- or multicasting strategy clear. Significantly, *Dear White People* has not received the extensive critical praise of the other DQCs we discuss. Also intriguing is its lack of mainstream nominations. Its accolades come in the form of NAACP Image Award and GLAAD Award nominations. Its Gotham Independent Film Awards nomination echoes the film version's Sundance special jury award. These more niche awards gifted by organizations intending to highlight minority representations of all kinds or, more specifically, the show's relative lack of mainstream recognition indicate its confrontational stance toward the aesthetic and representational negotiations that other DQCs undertake.

Every narrative conflict on the first two seasons of *Dear White People* is an explicitly racialized conflict—even its romantic entanglements. The series is structured around the biracial Samantha White's titular radio show, which narrativizes and explains the varying forms of discrimination that she and her fellow Black students experience, from small microaggressions to cultural appropriation and even overt racial violence. Its anthologized episodes—following one character's point of view of the overarching entwined narrative—often begin or end with the featured character confronting viewers in an intimate Brechtian direct address, interrupting narrative immersion and implicating the viewer in the characters' emotional turmoil. This is especially apparent when Coco debates having an abortion (S2E4). After a brief romantic fantasy flash-forward bathed in warm, soft lighting, featuring Coco, now a successful lawyer, taking her hypothetical daughter to orientation at her alma mater, the episode ends abruptly on a cut to a tracking medium close-up of Coco in the cold, harsh lighting of the women's clinic, where she strides angrily, almost defiantly, down a hallway to have the procedure. Her direct eye contact with the camera challenges the audience to consider how improbable that romanticized future is for women of color who drop out of college and face layers of systemic oppression. Although the show paints beautiful portraits of its characters that provide both depth and nuance to their emotionality and experience that anyone could potentially identify with, *Dear White People*'s explicit provocations and discussions of race and racism are often less strategically negotiated or couched in "universal" highbrow aesthetics than in other DQCs. While the White fragility of Issa's boss is visible for those who are paying attention, as are racial dynamics we have noted in *Atlanta, Master of*

None, and *Chewing Gum*, Sam and by extension *Dear White People* continuously name major and minor racial assaults directly and explicitly, seeming to purposely trigger uncomfortable responses of White fragility in the show's audiences. The show's relative lack of awards recognition reflects this dynamic.

The governing bodies and voters at awarding institutions like the US Television Academy's Emmy Awards and the Academy of Motion Picture Arts and Science's Oscars still tend to be predominantly White, meaning that they historically honor films and television shows that are less racially confrontational or that adhere to postracial narratives. The Emmys and Oscars tend to award historical texts in which racism is depicted in the past, signaling a comforting (for White audiences) progress narrative; easily digestible tales of individualized racism eventually overcome; or heroic or anthropologic stories of White saviors or White protagonists who navigate and thus explain the minority experience or culture to White audiences. This racist tradition extends throughout film and television history but is best exemplified by *Driving Miss Daisy*—the story of a kindly but racist White woman befriended by a Black man in a service position who, through the force of his individual personality, overcomes her bigotry—winning the Best Picture Oscar in 1989 over the not-even-nominated *Do the Right Thing*, Spike Lee's complex, sometimes belligerent, operatic examination of racial conflict and alliance on one city block in Brooklyn. The pattern persists despite the Academy's attempts to improve the process with new members and a larger slate of nominees. In fact, the 2019 awards ceremony essentially repeated 1989's when *Green Book*—basically the *Driving Miss Daisy* story in reverse: a White driver's racism overcome by the individual charisma of his Black passenger—won Best Picture over *BlacKkKlansman*, another Spike Lee feature, and *Black Panther*, Marvel's enormously successful superhero picture. *Dear White People*'s lack of mainstream awards, even in comparison to other highly awarded DQCs that make their racialized conflicts that much harder to read or easier to overlook, continues this tradition.

Yet, like all DQCs, *Dear White People* uses humor to soften its political critique. Humor is central to the way the show creates a visually and aurally layered aesthetic, one punctuated with quick, witty dialogue, self-aware voice-over narration, and carefully constructed framings that invite close readings and multiple viewings. In particular, Sheri-Marie

Harrison's concept of the new Black Gothic (which she applies to *Atlanta*) helps unpack the multiple texts and racist hauntings that suffuse the texture of *Dear White People*. The show visualizes the legacies of institutional and historical racism in its elite university setting through flashbacks in the style of midcentury anthropological or historical documentaries (incidentally also a technique used by Spike Lee in *BlacKkKlansman* and *Bamboozled*). The intercut snippets feature extradiegetic voice-over by Giancarlo Esposito, who introduces himself in the pilot as "an ethnic but not threatening voice." These, along with the show's other historical references, particularly in season 2, to the Underground Railroad tunnels that run under the campus and that housed the secret society begun by formerly enslaved students and locals, create the haunting historical echoes that help define the new Black Gothic. Harrison (2018) argues that the new Black Gothic is "defined partially by its black humor—forms of black danger and violence that lurk in the most mundane circumstances—where humor functions as sort of a tension release. . . . Daily black life can suddenly descend into horror. This shit is not supposed to be funny, but we laugh uncomfortably anyway." This uncomfortable laughter parallels the "cringe" aesthetic of Horrible White People shows, produced by the tensions between comedy and drama, particularly their differing relationships to political critique (Havas and Sulimma 2018). Whereas throughout this book we have talked about how the "cringe" of Horrible White People is the result of not knowing where to point our laughter—*at* or *with* the Horrible White People and their emotions or actions—the bleak, dark humor of Diverse Quality Comedies tells us there is nothing funny here. Rather, jokes are the way they address the systematic oppression of structural White supremacy, negotiating a political and social critique aimed at the very demographic that makes up half their viewership—and gets us to keep watching.

This bleak humor and *Dear White People*'s quick, layered address and densely packed visuals are introduced in the pilot when Sam and her best friend, Joelle, have a conversation during Sam's radio show, in which she is raging against a recent blackface party held by White students. After Joelle admits that she has not been paying attention because she is on Instagram learning how to lose weight while still being able to eat a McDonald's McRib sandwich, Sam riffs, "I'm pretty sure the McRib was created by the Republicans in the '80s to destroy Black communities,

along with crack and Jerry Springer." Sam's comment links the popularity of the McRib with disproportionately high obesity and health problems in the Black community and other historical initiatives explicitly
intended to undermine Black communities (see, for example, the 2016
documentary *13th*; or Michelle Alexander 2012). In this quick joke, the
violent and destructive effects of the War on Drugs and other Reagan-
era political policies for people of color are softened by their association
with a trivial, if delicious, food commodity. Sam and Joelle's continuing,
quickly paced conversation is depicted with an almost choreographed
rhythm, underscored by the low diegetic hip hop beat curated by the
radio station; their almost overlapping back-and-forth of mutually understood slang, inside jokes, and Black vernacular reflects their intimate
girlfriendship but makes cultural references and political critiques appear fleeting, easy for some audiences or viewers to miss or choose to
ignore. This is exacerbated by the rather fast editing, ping-ponging in
a shot/reverse-shot pattern, and the fact that both actors look at their
phones and graphics of their text messages pop up on-screen, all while
Sam seamlessly transitions to speaking to her radio listeners and back
to Joelle, never missing a beat or a quip. The voice-over of Sam's interactions with White callers criticizing her show as "offensive and divisive"
masks the scene transition as we follow Joelle and Sam outside. Sam's
voice-over is intercut with the girls' ensuing conversation, which reflects
another example of the series' gallows humor. Picking up on a comment
from the earlier conversation, Joelle tries to explain her "secret shame"
of binge-watching *The Cosby Show* at the moment of peak visibility of
Bill Cosby's sexual-assault allegations. She says, "The man can take an
episode about Rudy getting a B-minus and turn it into a half hour of comedic gold." To which Sam responds dryly, "God, I pray he didn't stretch
little Ruby out in any other way." Almost spitting her coffee out, Joelle
intones, "Bitch, you goin' to Hell." One of the reasons Harrison suggests
there has been a contemporary rise in the new Black Gothic is that black
comedy makes threats of racial violence and discrimination legible but
not debilitating, thus strengthening the morale of the oppressed while
undermining that of the oppressors. According to Wylie Sypher, "to be
able to laugh at evil and error means we have surmounted them" (Zhou
2006, 132). *Dear White People*'s quick moments of gallows humor—in
the *Cosby* example suggesting that the youngest actor on the show might

have been one of Bill Cosby's rape victims—help create the rich, layered fabric of the show's political critique. Similar to the self-deprecating critique of Jewish humor that we discussed in chapter 2, black or dark humor can be an empowering tool when speaking truth to power and, as Harrison and Sypher argue, to relieve some of the traumatic pain of oppression.

Yet it is important to note that the almost chaotic or frenzied nature of a scene like this one in *Dear White People* also illustrates how the show operates in multiple codes at once. While obviously carefully constructed, the dense texture created by the pacing, passing cultural references, sonic layers of diegetic and nondiegetic music with voiceover, and detailed production design layered with extradiegetic graphics can be difficult to process. The show's visual landscape, for example, is divided between public and private spaces that each have their own distinct address to both characters and viewers. The public spaces are beige and hung with a phalanx of portraits of the college's White founders and luminaries, while the private spaces of the Black students' dorm rooms offer an alternative history and reading of popular culture in which their taste, culture, and history are made visible, unerased. In the final episode of season 2, for example, Sam waits for a text message from her White boyfriend as she leans against the wall in the dorm's public corridor, just beneath and beside a White plaster bust of Benjamin Franklin (one of America's White "founding fathers") and opposite a portrait of some White man in an early twentieth-century suit. In contrast, in Sam's dorm room, a portrait of Fredrick Douglass (a prominent abolitionist who was formerly enslaved) has the intimate position on the wall just above her bedside table, an example of the historical haunting that characterizes the show's version of the new Black Gothic. The set design offers this kind of racialized distinction of spaces frequently. The campus radio station, which feels like an extension of Sam's own private space, features a prominent piece of art shouting "RESIST" in capital letters, making it feel like an assault for Sam and Joelle when they arrive at the station to find an alt-right panel show taking up space in the recording booth where we have only ever seen Sam speak before this moment (S1E2).

The camera works with the set design to halt the action and highlight the violation of a formerly safe space by White racists. Sam and Joelle's conversation halts, as does the camera that had been tracking them into

Figure 4.2. Sam and Joelle watch White racists take over their radio booth. (Still from *Dear White People*; screenshot by the authors).

the station. The camera cuts to their perspective, and Sam's and Joelle's heads frame a shot of the window (another frame isolating the White actors from the radio-station space and highlighting their intrusion) into the recording studio. The camera cuts back to a medium two-shot of Sam and Joelle and begins a slow zoom backward. The two, managing to look stone-faced and heartbroken at the same time, demonstrating the resilience demanded of characters of color throughout the cycle, recede in the frame and thus in narrative significance as the camera pulls back through the window and ends by residing with the White students but gazing back through the studio window at Sam and Joelle, now blurry, in long shot, isolated, on the wrong side of the sound-proof barrier, silenced and shrunken. It is a powerful shot and sequence that exemplify the show's manipulation of "quality" aesthetics in order to highlight the racialization and the power structures those aesthetics reflect.

Earlier in the same episode, Joelle sits on her own bed in the room she now shares with Sam, where her *Poetic Justice* (Singleton, 1993) poster has pride of place, taking up nearly half the frame. The framing puts Joelle in the bottom left quarter of the image, while Janet Jackson, on the poster, mirrors her hairstyle, screen direction, and forthright attitude. Jackson stands, arms crossed, in full profile, looking rightward out of frame. Joelle strikes the same pose on her bed. So much of the frame is given to the poster and the mirrored poses of the two actresses that

Figure 4.3. Looking back at Sam and Joelle from inside the booth. (Still from *Dear White People*; screenshot by the authors).

the affinity is unmistakable (figure 4.4). While this is quite an obvious moment, the visual (and aural) texture of the show is filled with things meant to hail Black audiences while being missable to White audiences. That dual address parallels the show's subtle distinctions between public, White spaces requiring negotiation and private, safe, Black spaces where characters express their own personality and illustrate cultural affinity with culture makers and history makers who look like them—a division echoed, as we noted earlier, in the divide between Issa's work and home spaces. This sort of cultural Easter egg becomes part of *Dear White People*'s narrative drive in season 2 as budding journalist Lionel and documentarian Sam look for clues to a Black secret society. They have to read clues and markers and calls for their attention so small that they escape anyone else's notice—in an echo of the way Black viewers are often required to actively search mainstream White texts for their own cultural histories and experiences.

Harrison (2018) adds that "another unifying feature of the new black Gothic then, along with humor that is not comedic and a preoccupation with the domestic legacies of the War on Drugs, is a sense of inescapability and the eschewal of hope for the future. These contemporary black Gothic texts bring into sharp focus the near-constant vulnerability of black life." This, ultimately, is the key distinction between Horrible White People shows and Diverse Quality Comedies. In *Dear White*

People, campus cops pull a gun on Reggie at a college party; in *Chewing Gum*, Tracy becomes homeless when her devoutly Christian mother kicks her out for having abandoned the church by having sex with her deadbeat boyfriend; in *Atlanta*, Earn is arrested in one episode and almost caught with a weapon at the airport in another episode; in *Insecure*, Lawrence is needlessly pulled over by police. Black lives and the safety of Black homes are endangered, sometimes almost casually or incidentally as a matter of course, on Diverse Quality Comedies. Their HWP counterparts, as we have seen in earlier comparisons between *Insecure* and *You're the Worst*, for example, have a sense of security, of the temporariness of their abjection, of the framing of their fragility as primarily emotional and not deadly regardless of inhabiting similar narrative circumstances as the Black characters on DQCs.

Joseph R. Winters argues that a satisfying and comforting progress narrative too often "conflates hope with optimism, a process that cultivates expectations of a better future by marginalizing or downplaying dissonant memories and attachments" (2016, 6). For us, DQCs, along with the much larger proliferation of non-White characters on-screen and the somewhat smaller but still significant uptick in non-White creators off-screen, fight back against that marginalization. Hope is evident not at all via optimism but rather by haunting and critique. Optimism might result in jokes at which all audiences can laugh. Optimism might

Figure 4.4. Joelle and Janet Jackson. (Still from *Dear White People*; screenshot by the authors).

be more evident in the Oscar-winning *Green Book* than in *Atlanta*. But in creating comfort, optimistic texts approach a "universal" address that is in fact a White address. Diverse Quality Comedies instead negotiate, strategize, and operate in multiple codes simultaneously. Their gallows humor might create laughter but in an unsettled, uncomfortable register. Hope, if it is present here, comes from the beginnings of making structures of White supremacy more visible to White audiences. Hope, if it is present here, comes from the visibility of critique. It is a hope embedded in the shows' textual characteristics and one that is needed to combat the nihilistic threat to Black America (West 2006), a threat structured and maintained by the continued invisibility of Whiteness and White supremacy in all forms of cultural production, even in "quality" liberal programming like Horrible White People shows.

Conclusion

NFL Protests and White Supremacy in the Mass Market

The final season of *Casual*, a Horrible White People show, jumps forward five years from where the previous season left off, updating viewers on characters who are almost all still flailing. The flash-forward creates a hypothetical near future cynically peppered with new technologies further isolating these Horrible White People characters from each other, exacerbating their sense of emotional fragility and precarity. This imagined future includes snarky, unreliable, self-driving cars and snarky, controlling, smart home devices, as well as incredibly realistic virtual-reality dating environments where dream partners actually butter people up to steal their identity. In this imagined future, the US Supreme Court has also sided with arguments from the Players Association and ruled the insatiably profitable National Football League (NFL) too dangerous to continue. Thus, Alex and his reluctant best friend, Leon, throw a "Last Super Bowl" party, celebrating—or waking—the final championship competition before the league disbands (S4E5). As the most-watched television event of the year in the United States, the overwhelming mass-market appeal of this football game's broadcast is essentially the televisual opposite of the niche taste culture of Horrible White People shows like *Casual* and the liberal/progressive, hyper-trend-conscious snobbery typically spouted by characters like Alex (see chapter 1). Like other HWP characters, Alex prides himself on his hip, elitist, liberal, tech-savvy, antiestablishment, upper-middle-class (read: White) taste. And, while he tries to defend his logic for throwing a Super Bowl party by claiming that his "hatred for the NFL is deep-rooted and real" and that he is "celebrating the end of a barbaric tradition," his niece and other party guests "poke holes in his paper-thin logic," by pointing out that "being antifootball is basically on trend at this point." If he was really anti-NFL, they point out, he would not watch the game or even the NCAA (college football) in order to deprive both corrupt, exploitative institutions of the profits generated from high television ratings.

Ignoring their criticisms, Alex proceeds with the party—that is until his Wi-Fi TV signal cuts out for the third time, right before kickoff, and a room full of disgruntled party guests threatens to flee. Deflated, Alex stumbles through an impromptu speech; feigning exaggerated liberal outrage at the NFL, he pleads for people to stay. He stutters, "This, this is a protest. OK? By not watching, we are turning our backs on the NFL. Just like they turned their backs on Colin Kaepernick and, and, Mike Webster, and all the other players fighting for progress and equality and social just—" His line is cut off by an abrupt cut to a dark, claustrophobic shot of his sister, Valerie, and her self-centered new boyfriend sitting silently in a self-driving ride-share car in search of another place to watch the game. That Alex's posturing is obviously just that—a trendy liberal outrage at the NFL—and that it is narratively discarded with a hard midsentence cut, worsened by the fact that Valerie and her boyfriend go out of their way to watch the game anyway, offers a jokey microcosm of the limited and ultimately ineffectual liberal rhetoric that unconsciously recenters White people's fragility over others' more material suffering that pervades the Horrible White People cycle. This self-critical moment's focus on the NFL, the most popular televisual product in the United States (as well as an increasingly global commodity), also highlights the vast separation between Horrible White People shows and the mass market. This is only a small moment in the cycle, but Alex neatly represents these shows' narcissistic White central characters. The fact that he also watches the NFL overtly connects the discourses of White precarity and the very specific politicized, classed, and racialized address of the Horrible White People cycle to parallel economic and racialized discourses made hypervisible by protests and counterprotests in and around mass-market sports programming during precisely the same historical conjuncture that created Horrible White People shows.

Throughout this book, we have shown that White precarity dominates representations of liberal elites in female-centered niche comedy programming and that it is often masked or even excused by the progress narratives of Peak TV and emergent feminisms. Here, we analyze the same cultural dynamics but in mass-market, explicitly conservative, male-centered programming—programming more associated with reactionary conservativism than liberal elitism—to show how to-gether these opposing "mediated taste communities" (Banet-Weiser and Ouelette 2018) support an overarching cultural ethos of White precar-ity. In the contemporary political climate, in which consciously sow-ing openly affective ideological division is an effective path to power, it seems that denying the continued cultural impact of television—easy to do if you have read this book and thought, "I've never heard of any of these shows"—is an effective way to dismiss a formidable mass-cultural forum that is still in operation.

While it is a dramatic departure from our focus on television comedy, the NFL offers an analogous microcosm of historical, political, social, cultural, and TV industrial tensions to those expressed through Hor-rible White People characters and their representations of precarity. In the 1980s, Herman Gray (1989) contextualized fictional representations of Black middle-class successes within the entire televisual landscape. He put fictional families like *The Cosby Show*'s Huxtables in conversa-tion with nonfictional representations of Black urban poverty. In doing so, he argued that both sets of representations operated intertextually to produce a broader ideological field, to borrow John Fiske's (2011) term. It is the entire ideological field that, in this example, displaced social and structural factors in order to shift focus to individualized rationales for Black success and failure. Conceptualizing television as a mass me-dium that produces ideological fields created by conversations and in-teractions among all different kinds of television watched by all different kinds of viewers creates a much stronger argument for TV's impact and for the relevance and importance of studying a group of shows operating within a niche market. The rest of this conclusion, then, places Horrible White People shows' discourses of White fragility in the same ideologi-cal field as the 2016 NFL national anthem protests. In this ideological field, the relationships among representations of structural inequalities of race, class, and gender are constantly negotiated relationships that refer to and influence each other over and over, all the while reflecting the circumstances of their contemporary historical conjuncture. White fragility and White precarity are rendered visible very differently in the HWP cycle and the NFL anthem protests, but their overlap reveals the ways that White supremacy continues to structure *all* of television and especially the way Whiteness maintains its powerful invisibility.

NFL Anthem Protests and White Fragility

Spearheaded by former San Francisco 49ers quarterback Colin Kaepernick in August 2016, NFL players began kneeling during the pregame playing of the national anthem in order to draw attention to the Black Lives Matter movement and broader racial inequality and violence. Kneeling because they did not feel the United States' ideals of liberty and justice for all applied to *all* Americans, they intended to draw attention to racial injustice including systemic oppression against people of color, police brutality, and massive inequality in the criminal justice system (Reid 2017). Their protest was especially urgent in the wake of the highly publicized deaths of several unarmed Black men at the hands of White police officers who were never held accountable. Despite consulting Nate Boyer, a retired Green Beret and former NFL player who advised them that kneeling was a respectful way to protest, the actions of Kaepernick and his teammate Eric Reid were quickly framed by predominantly White critics inside and outside the sports arena as disrespectful to the country, flag, and military personnel who fight and die for their country. Eric Reid (2017) responded to the criticism in a *New York Times* op-ed, "It should go without saying that I love my country and I'm proud to be an American. But, to quote James Baldwin, 'exactly for this reason, I insist on the right to criticize her perpetually.'" Despite his rational and well-researched explanations and justifications, drawing on his First Amendment rights to free speech and protest (usually a conservative favorite), in a clear example of the defensive posturing that Robin DiAngelo (2018) calls "White Fragility," White critics reacted emotionally, refusing to engage in a discussion of racial inequality and instead forcibly reframing the issue as one of nation and the universality of the anthem. There are "better ways to protest," they argued; they insisted that sports is not a politicized arena, that sport is about unity and community and should not divide or polarize (see, for example, Marty O Radio Show 2016; *Sports Illustrated* 2017).

Yet despite sports being idealized as apolitical, US President Donald Trump, in a clear display of White fragility despite great power, explicitly engaged with the NFL and individual players via Twitter condemning the protests as unpatriotic. The politics were personal when the once highly praised Kaepernick was blackballed by the league but became undeniable when he was featured in a high-profile, extremely polarizing Nike ad. Discourses of White fragility and feelings of White precarity further became explicit when conservative fans burned their Nike shoes and cut labels out of clothing in a form of protest against the company. A variety of sports figures, from the Black National Basketball Association (NBA) superstars Lebron James and Kobe Bryant to celebrated White coaches (and "woke bros") like Gregg Popovich and Steve Kerr, among many others, all weighed in on the protests, explicitly discussing structural racial inequality and its overt expressions in the world of high-profile sport. The NFL anthem protests thus spread across sports broadcasts, newscasts (both sport and mainstream), social media, and popular culture (as illustrated by turning up on *Casual*), becoming a significant element of television's ideological field as well as a "media event." Media events "are processes which construct not only our sense of a social 'center,' but also the media's privileged relation to that 'center.' Media events, then, are privileged moments, not because they reveal society's underlying solidarity, but because they reveal the mythical construction of the mediated center at is most intense" (Couldry 2003, 56). The NFL protests, as a media event, sparked intertwined discourses about television ratings, consumer activism, patriotism, civil rights, and especially the powerful yet tenuously, often reluctantly acknowledged relationship between television, sport, and politics.

Just as the Horrible White People cycle disrupts the generic conventions and comforting hegemonic ideologies of the sitcom, thus contributing to the cycle's centering of White precarity, the NFL national anthem protests signaled moments of political rupture in a highly constructed escapist consumerist fantasy, which then triggered defensive posturings of White fragility. Just as White people tend to live in segregated spaces of racial comfort that afford them the privilege of not confronting racial inequality or race in general (DiAngelo 2018), sport is positioned as a "safe" space to celebrate apolitical and inspiring expressions of human physical exceptionalism. Sport reinforces comforting myths of meritocracy, equality, and idealized neoliberal success stories (Serazio 2019). Despite the obvious fictions of those myths, they remain deeply rooted in sport's cultural fandom. The NFL anthem protests' explicit engagement with racial politics challenged those mythologies and generated a microcosm of the current historical conjuncture's ideological tensions—feelings of White precarity, hypervisible racial inequality and violence, and emerging feminisms.

In *The Power of Sports*, Michael Serazio traces how sports culture has become the "definitive 'civil' or 'folk' faith of our time," filling "the vacuum created by the decline of traditional religion" (2019, 20). Sport is a dominant ideological force that structures hegemonic meanings about nationhood, community, and identity, while providing moral guidance. Sport's dominant story lines function similarly, ideologically, to generic structures in fictional TV. So, as we argued that sitcom idealizes heteropatriarchal families and encourages identification with Whiteness (see chapter 2), the NFL idealizes an imagined unified United States and the romantic ideal of meritocracy. For Serazio, the league is especially adept at propagating cleverly concealed conservative ideologies that rationalize corrosive political issues like income inequality and military intervention, all the more effectively and invisibly for its apolitical posture. Sport culture, he argues, replaces the diminishing public trust in all manner of social institutions, offering a form of escapism, unity instead of division, and relative simplicity and objectivity in contrast to complicated sociopolitical realities. In its celebration of success as opposed to failures, "sport remains a beacon for hope and the scaffolding for such belief in progress" (Serazio 2019, 24), offering "the 'glue of collective consciousness' that the acid of modern life has otherwise dissolved" (26). Serazio postulates that the symbolic power of sport in people's lives, then, leads them to act and react emotionally rather than rationally (just as White people react to racial confrontation) in relation to sport culture, particularly when the myths and ideologies tied to it are threatened.

Like the wallowing grief and despair that HWP characters demonstrated in the wake of the Great Recession that threatened their jobs and homes, the romanticism of the NFL's "American Dream" success stories were severely undermined by a variety of factors that, like the HWP cycle, enact Lauren Berlant's (2011) paradoxical "cruel optimism." In particular, the football league's celebration of the symbolic power of the virile male body was threatened in the 2010s by an increased fan awareness of the link between playing football and chronic traumatic encephalopathy (CTE), a neurodegenerative disease caused by repeated head injuries that leads to permanent damage, significantly affecting mood, decision-making, judgment, and cognition and eventually leading to dementia. Described as the NFL's ongoing "concussion crisis" (*Frontline* 2013; Laskas 2015), the increased awareness has led professional players to weigh early retirements and parents to grapple with whether to allow their young sons to take up the sport. It has contributed to a decade-long decline in high school football participation (Cook 2019) that could eventually threaten the league's viability, as *Casual*'s flash-forward predicts. Notably, the way NFL athletes' newfound precarity is most visible corresponds to the centralization of White characters on Horrible White People shows, even when surrounded by friends of color. While over 70 percent of NFL players are non-White, the predominantly White quarterbacks (the central White character to a team's diverse cast) became symbols of the newly precarious male body, with a slate of new tackling rules implemented to protect them from head trauma more than others, while equally dangerous positions were left vulnerable. CTE's newfound visibility has also led to "the White flight from football," a growing racial divide between White kids (and their parents) who choose not to play football and Black kids (and their parents) who still flock to the sport as one of the only extracurricular activities for mentorship and support in their communities. "This divergence paints a troubling picture of how economic opportunity—or a lack thereof—governs which boys are incentivized to put their body and brain at risk to play. Depending on where families live, and what other options are available to them, they see either a game that is too violent to consider or one that is necessary and important, if risky" (Semuels 2019). Similar to the White protagonists on Horrible White People shows, White quarterbacks and White children are frequently centralized in the discourse of football's increasingly visible physical danger, even though Black players and children are disproportionately more vulnerable.

The NFL's Increased Visibility of Racial Inequality

In addition to potential violent injury on the field, the NFL's postracial mystique of pure meritocracy is fraying off the field as well, just like the broader cultural postracial mystique discussed in the introduction. Plagued by accusations of racism, the league has been called a modern plantation system, "home of 40 million-dollar slaves" (R. Hall 2018). The 2007 documentary *Two Days in April*, which follows four NFL prospects through the process of preparing for and participating in the 2006 player draft, made the analogy plainly visible when, during a day of intense training and testing, the predominantly Black players walked across a stage bare chested to be weighed and measured in front of the predominantly White owners and coaches in a striking visual analogy to nineteenth-century slave auctions. Basketball legend LeBron James repeated the analogy on his HBO talk show when discussing the anthem protests and players' contracted rights: "In the NFL they got a bunch of old White men on teams, and they've got that slave mentality. This is my team, and you do what the fuck I tell you all to do, or we get rid of y'all." In contrast, James applauded NBA commissioner Adam Silver for giving athletes more autonomy (James and his teammates had been involved in Black Lives Matter protests a few years earlier) and urged the NFL to do the same for players kneeling during the national anthem (Welk 2018).

The divergence that James highlights between the NFL and the NBA parallels the distinction we have made throughout between Horrible White People shows' seemingly liberal address while nonetheless centralizing stories and feelings of White precarity, in contrast to their Diverse Quality Comedy counterparts, which offer more explicit critiques of structural White supremacy. Some NFL ownership and coaching staffs initially locked arms in solidarity with players kneeling, but because they were predominantly White and politically right-leaning conservatives, the gesture neither lasted nor rang true (see Moore and Levitt 2018; Serazio 2019, especially 276–281). After President Trump suggested teams fire any protesting players and—an essential fact of the timeline—after the protests proved to hurt their financial bottom line (see Serazio 2019, 270–271), the owners ultimately suppressed players' political engagement by ratifying a new policy that required players either to stand or to remain (invisible to television cameras) in the locker room during the anthem (Maske 2018). The NBA, on the other hand, leads the men's sports industry in race- and gender-equitable hiring practices and has been explicitly supportive of players using their platforms to voice their political opinions (see Lapchick 2018). At the 2017 San Antonio Spurs media day, celebrated White coach Gregg Popovich explicitly criticized Donald Trump, eloquently acknowledged White supremacy and White privilege in the United States, and openly discussed the vital intersection of sports and politics, while supporting his players in voicing their own opinions (for excerpts, see Gus P. 2017). Golden State Warriors coach Steve Kerr and star player Stephen Curry were also explicitly embroiled in the clash of politics and sports as the openly liberal team debated whether to attend the traditional White House celebration of their 2017 championship win. President Trump petulantly rescinded their invitation before they even made a decision, but Kerr nonetheless used his platform to condemn the president's rhetoric and policies: "How about the irony of, 'Free speech is fine if you're a neo-Nazi chanting hate slogans, but free speech is not allowed to kneel in protest?'" Kerr said. "No matter how many times a football player says, 'I honor our military, but I'm protesting police brutality and racial inequality,' it doesn't matter. Nationalists are saying, 'You're disrespecting our flag.' Well, you know what else is disrespectful to our flag? Racism. And one's way worse than the other" (Shelburne 2017). Kerr's comments call out and critique the hypocrisy and White fragility evident in the president's and others' emotional reactions to the protests in the same way Diverse Quality Comedies often criticize their characters' White fragility (see the opening example from *Insecure* in chapter 4). The two professional sports leagues, the NBA and the NFL, then, further contribute to the broad ideological field underlying this book by offering highly visible, distinct responses to the intersections of sport, race, economics, and politics. The NBA's explicit engagement with racial politics and open acknowledgment, even celebration, of the league's cultural influence and power underlines the NFL's contrasting conservativism and race muteness; it disrupts the football league's postracial, apolitical mythologies and highlights the team owners' and league management's emotional responses—White fragility—when confronted with realities about race and the indelible relationship between sports and politics.

The NFL's Faltering Negotiations of Emergent Feminism(s)

In conversation with hypervisible racial conflict, emergent feminisms are a key feature of the historical conjuncture underlying this book. Horrible White People shows most often feature complex, albeit emotionally fragile, female characters and their supportive, feminist girlfriends. Despite the NFL's hypermasculine posturing, the league also consciously engaged with emergent feminisms during the 2010s, but as one might expect from a conservative-leaning mass-market product, that relationship was fraught with ideological tensions. Sports culture and the sports industry have historically been male dominated, with men being much more likely to participate in sports and women often being actively discouraged from doing so with rhetoric of their supposed physiological inferiority and entrenched gender roles that position women as passive and docile and men as active and aggressive and therefore more athletic. As a result, men's professional sports leagues have longer histories, are larger and more elite, and generate millions, if not billions, more dollars than women's leagues do. Female sports fans of men's and women's sports have been similarly marginalized in a sports culture understood as a masculine domain. Title IX of the Education Amendments, which bans discrimination based on sex within public education and other programs that receive government assistance, was designed as a radical challenge to this binary in the 1970s United States. The law raised girls' participation in high school sports and eased social acceptance of future generations of female sports fans. Women now make up an estimated 45 percent of the NFL's more than 150 million American fans and represent the league's biggest opportunity for growth, essentially forcing the league to engage with contemporary discourses of popular feminism. Tapping into this underserved demographic, one already highly sought after by advertisers, became one of the NFL's chief goals in the 2010s. The league funded research, expanded merchandising, and sponsored spreads in women's magazines (Harwell 2014b). In the initiative most visible on TV broadcasts, players wear pink, and the league devotes a small percentage of merchandise sales to cancer research during Breast Cancer Awareness Month each year.

For the NFL to grow its television ratings, it has to court women. Nielsen data show that women have grown to represent more than a third of the league's average viewership, with *Sunday Night Football* ranked as the most watched program among women aged eighteen to forty-nine for the first time ever in 2013. "No matter how you measure it, female viewership has grown much faster than male viewership in the past several years. There's still potential to convert more women into full-time fans, and that's where the league's revenue growth must come from" (Chemi 2014). The league's appeal to female fans was complicated, however, by the plague of domestic-violence accusations against players throughout the 2010s, which left fans questioning the sport's blind celebration of aggressive masculinity. On February 15, 2014, for example, Baltimore Ravens running back Ray Rice was arrested and charged with assault of his then fiancée (now wife), Janay Palmer, after a physical altercation. The celebrity news website TMZ posted a video of Rice dragging Palmer out of an elevator unconscious, after he punched her in the head. ESPN's Keith Olbermann said the images of Rice's assault were "symbolically knocking out every woman football fan in this country" (Harwell 2014b). In March of that year, a grand jury indicted Rice on third-degree aggravated assault, with a possible jail sentence of three to five years and a fine of up to $15,000. Yet the NFL only suspended Rice for the first two games of the 2014 season; later, after significant public outcry over the league's leniency, Rice was released by the Ravens and retired from football. Thereafter, in a news conference announcing longer suspensions for future domestic-violence incidents, NFL Commissioner Roger Goodell said that he "didn't get it right" with Rice's punishment. Nonetheless, the league continues to fumble its response to the problem. In 2018, Reuben Foster was released by the San Francisco 49ers after multiple domestic-violence arrests, only to later be picked up by the Washington Redskins (a team name that itself speaks to the durability of structural White supremacy and has also been the subject of protest). Similarly, the Kansas City Chiefs released Kareem Hunt after video emerged of him kicking a nineteen-year-old woman, but he was later signed by the Cleveland Browns. In all, seventy-seven players across twenty-seven of the league's thirty-two teams have been arrested since 2000 on charges of domestic violence, according to a USA Today NFL arrests database (Harwell 2014b). Domestic-violence awareness organizations have blasted the league's ineffective handling of violence against women, suggesting that its minor punishments are doing nothing about the sport's culture of violence and celebration of aggressive masculinity that justify and even encourage these behaviors in its players. As the Me Too movement gained increased visibility and political traction during the 2010s, the NFL has also been under increased pressure to respond to this much-grimmer element of emergent feminisms as consciously as its marketing machine has responded to female fans. But the league's powers-that-be appear paralyzed on this front. Compounded by the concussion crisis, the anthem protests, and the public debates they sparked, the domestic- and sexual-violence epidemic signaled "a league in perpetual crisis" (Maske and Kilgore 2018).

This "perpetual crisis" is the result of the broader breakdown of the league's mythologizing of virile masculinity and postracial meritocracy, a collapse instigated partially by the NFL's uneasy incorporation of the politics of emergent feminism to court female viewers. The sense of loss or uncertainty that accompanies the demythologization of sports culture's "folk faith" contributes to the feelings of White precarity that we have discussed throughout the book. Challenging the treasured national institution of the NFL to be more gender inclusive and racially just triggers emotional responses much like the "rural resentment" credited in part with sweeping Donald Trump into office (Cramer 2016). If broadcast sport is a genre like any other on TV, its rocky attempts to shift generic conventions toward political engagement and gender inclusivity parallel the way Horrible White People shows and Diverse Quality Comedies court prestige by disrupting sitcom's aesthetic and narrative structures to critique the genre's traditional ideological comforts: heteropatriarchal romance and families. The significance of these parallels should not be discounted or overlooked. They reflect a broad cultural ethos—or ideological field—that links these disparate cultural products and underscores a shared affect of despair among opposing political demographics.

The NFL's "perpetual crisis" is also linked to its loss of lucrative ad revenue due to the falling ratings created by all its controversies. The intertextuality of economic and ideological threat was rendered visible in 2017 and 2018 when rebellious and outspoken female sportscasters Jemele Hill and Michelle Beadle disrupted cable sports juggernaut ESPN's supposedly apolitical order by explicitly engaging with the discourses of precarity circling the NFL, its anthem protests, and problems with domestic violence. Just as networks and online streaming portals incorporated female characters, themes of emergent feminism, and self-aware jokes about White privilege and structural racism to innovate the sitcom and disrupt its apolitical frame, so the sports industry, especially ESPN, hired vocal, overtly feminist, female sportscasters to innovate its programming and disrupt its own apolitical frame. In February 2017, Hill and Michael Smith became cohosts of *SC6*, the six p.m. edition of ESPN's flagship *SportsCenter*. The new show was expected to focus on "the duo's developed chemistry, and bold personalities instead of the traditional *SportsCenter* which mostly stuck to highlights of the day's events" (Saponara 2017). Beadle was similarly brought on in April 2018 to cohost ESPN's newly conceived morning talk show *Get Up!* with Mike Greenberg and Jalen Rose, featuring more colorful coverage of sports news, opinion, and analysis from the hosts and guests.

Both established journalists, Hill and Beadle were brought on to help revitalize ESPN in the wake of a 13 percent drop in subscriptions over the previous six years, down from about one hundred million in 2011 to eighty-seven million in 2017. The decline was primarily caused by cable cord-cutting and increased competition from the internet as people turned away from linear television to follow sports, including live events, on Hulu, Amazon, YouTube, and Facebook Live (Berg 2017a). Fans no longer have to wait for ESPN's highlight reels or news programming to catch up on their favorite teams, so Hill and Beadle were brought on as the "added value" to lure back viewers with opinion and analysis. Facing the same challenges as the fictional TV industry, ESPN's hiring and programming strategy parallels Horrible White People programming's explicit engagement with contemporary social issues in an effort to stand out in an era of Peak TV. In the case of television sports programming, its generic innovations with chat and opinion programs like *SC6* and *Get Up!*, alongside its move to feature female sportscasters, hope to appeal to the severely underserved and often ignored demographic of female sports fans (Harwell 2014a; S. Ryan 2016; Berri 2017; Gillette 2017).

But these innovative strategies seemed to backfire on ESPN in September 2017 when Hill responded to President Trump's impromptu comments urging NFL owners to fire players who knelt during the national anthem and encouraging fans to walk out because the players' protest is "a total disrespect of our heritage" (CBS News 2017). In a series of tweets, Hill described President Trump as "ignorant" and "offensive" and suggested that his popularity was directly related to a rise in White supremacy. Trump, of course, responded to Hill by criticizing her and ESPN, suggesting the network had a liberal bias and was therefore easily discredited. White House press secretary Sarah Huckabee Sanders called Hill's comments a "fireable offense" and demanded an apology (Serazio 2019, 272). In a clear display of Trump's own defensive White fragility, he linked ESPN's political engagement with its falling ratings: "With Jemele Hill at the mike, it is no wonder ESPN ratings have 'tanked,' in fact, tanked so badly it is the talk of the industry!" Trump tweeted (Berg 2017a). Inadvertently or not, Trump identified the financial stakes, the potential economic precarity, for White liberals (ESPN, in this instance, playing the liberal foil to more conservative rhetoric coming from the NFL itself via its ineffectual responses to domestic violence, for example) willing to challenge the cherished invisibility of politics in mass popular culture. Following this Twitter exchange, Hill was suspended from the network for two weeks and forced to differentiate her views from those of ESPN. She was eventually fired after tweeting again, this time in response to Dallas Cowboys owner Jerry Jones's hardline stance that he would bench any protesting players. "If you strongly reject what Jerry Jones said, the key is his advertisers. Don't place the burden squarely on the players," Hill tweeted, alluding to a potential boycott of the team, thereby "violating ESPN's social media policy" (Berg 2017a). As Serazio (2019, 272) notes, it was the commercial consequence, particularly Hill's threat to sports broadcast ratings and ad revenue, that crossed the line for ESPN and got her fired.

Similarly, Michelle Beadle left *Get Up!* in August 2018 after announcing her personal boycott of the NFL and NCAA, suggesting they don't care about women. Beadle made her comments about not watching football in light of the tone-deafness from suspended Ohio State University head football coach Urban Meyer, who mishandled a 2015 felonious domestic assault involving one of his assistant coaches, former wide receiver Zach Smith and his now ex-wife, Courtney. Covering Meyer's press conference on *Get Up!*, Beadle was visibly disgusted by Meyer's performance, in which he failed to even mention Courtney Smith's name and robotically and apathetically denied having any knowledge of the assault (even though Meyer's wife, Shelley, and Courtney Smith had texted extensively about it). When Beadle was given her chance to comment, she flatly called Meyer a "liar" on air and said (despite being a co-host of a talk show devoted to all sports) that she would no longer watch football because it so completely "marginalized women." Consequently, and perhaps reflecting Beadle's White privilege compared to Hill (who is Black), she was not fired but rather moved to a basketball-specific hosting position. Both instances of women crossing the line in their political engagement with sports culture reveal the continued importance of live sports to the traditional ad-supported television model and underscore that the most dangerous discourses of precarity are those concerning the NFL's and the entire sports industrial complex's economic bottom line. Furthermore, they reveal television's continued presumption that lucrative audiences are White audiences, as both ESPN and the NFL acquiesced to the emotional reactions of predominantly White fans to the explicit politicization of sports. We argue that the network's and the league's responses to these various critiques of the patriarchal and post-racial myths at the heart of American football are examples of the White fragility we have discussed throughout this book.

A Precarious Industry and the Limits of Innovation

In chapter 1, we outlined the era of Peak TV as an era of transformation, innovation, and increased artistic output but also one of increasing precarity as the television industry faces a great deal of uncertainty about what its future will look like with the fragmentation of audiences, increased competition from streaming platforms, and altered business models based less on advertiser-supported ratings and more on proprietary algorithmic audience targeting and strategic content development. The characterizations of sometimes-satirical but ultimately empathetic White precarity in the Horrible White People cycle represents Peak TV's insatiable demand for ever-diminishing and harder-to-reach audiences of White, upper-middle-class, tech-savvy, educated, urban viewers. Those viewers' inflated importance to the still-dominant cultural force of television and its incredibly lucrative industry is thus a cultural structure that helps maintain and support White supremacy. ESPN's firing of Hill and movement of Beadle and the NFL's new anthem policies requiring players to stand offer a mass-market counterpoint to the same forces in action, with the same ultimate result of operating as a cultural structure that supports White supremacy.

With the large and diverse audiences of live sports, rights to them have long been the economic foundation of broadcast network programming. In fact, the Fox broadcast network was successfully launched in the late 1980s on the back of its then-perceived overpayment for rights to live NFL games—which then served as the immensely successful launchpad for its original fictional shows *The Simpsons* and *Married with Children* (Siino 2018). In addition to propping up the ratings of subsequent programs by attracting reliably large audiences, sports programming has traditionally accounted for a disproportionate level of ad revenues. Nearly 40 percent of broadcast television revenue in 2015 was tied to sports programming (Crupi 2015), and "ESPN is, by far, the 'worldwide leader' in cable revenues, pulling in nearly $8 per household in monthly subscriber fees" (Serazio 2019, 7). Former Disney (ESPN's parent company) CEO Michael Eisner even joked about the outsized financial impact of ESPN's sports programming, saying, "[Disney] would not exist without ESPN. The protection of Mickey Mouse is ESPN" (quoted in Serazio 2019, 7). Yet, over the past twenty years, the $74 billion US television industry (Watson 2018) has transformed in reaction to threats from new technologies and increased competition, which have given viewers the freedom to record and time-shift, skip over commercials, and cut their cable subscriptions altogether in favor of Netflix, Hulu, and Amazon Prime Video accounts. In particular, in the Peak TV era, it is no longer normal for fictional television shows to gather a large and diverse mass audience (Lotz 2018), which remains most attractive to advertisers. So the broadcasting of live sports is key to keeping legacy television afloat. "And *live* is the key word. The rise of on-demand video has thinned out ratings and partially severed the tendon between live-viewing and lucrative advertising. But, in a time-delayed video world, the biggest games still drive dependable live audiences, making sports rights the most valuable resource in the whole TV ecosystem" (D. Thompson 2013). Thus, when the anthem protests, and Trump's public reactions to them, inspired viewers to boycott the NFL and its television broadcasts, the league and networks took a massive financial hit. The broadcast networks experienced "double-digit ratings erosion" over the two years following Kaepernick's protests, "with nearly half of NFL fans naming the protests as the main reason they were watching fewer NFL games; more illuminating still, negativity toward the NFL tripled among Trump supporters over just several weeks of his offensive, making it one of the 10 most polarizing brands in America" (Serazio 2019, 271). Since the survival of traditional television networks relies on the retention and flourishing of live sports, the protests threatened a complete disruption of their already-struggling business model.

In May 2018, to address the backlash and stop the ratings bleed, the NFL released its new national anthem policy requiring players to stand or stay in the locker room for the song, while sports broadcasters started the 2018 season avoiding discussion of head traumas, domestic violence, and especially the anthem protests, doubling down on the escapist framing that had historically served them so well. Commentators focused instead on the league's offensive explosion, seemingly unstoppable teams like the Los Angeles Rams, and particularly exceptional players such as Kansas City Chiefs quarterback Patrick Mahomes II, all reinforcing football's classic mythologies (Porter 2018). This pivot seems to be a direct response to White fans' outrage, fans who, in highly emotional letters, emails, and blog posts, frequently drew fondly on their personal histories of familial bonding over sport that had been "ruined," saying they had had enough of politics mixing with sports, their "little oasis away from it all" and their "escape from all that crap" (*Sports Illustrated* 2017). Viewers' rationales for boycotting NFL broadcasts often reflected Robin DiAngelo's (2018) explanation of White fragility, in which White people who are not accustomed to confronting racism or even their own racial identity tend either to flee from such discussions or to react emotionally with anger or tears. So, in acquiescing to these vocal White dissenters, the league and television broadcasters reacted to those overvalued emotional responses, with the result of centralizing those White viewers' sense of precarity and feelings of loss. In the process, they shore up structural White supremacy in the same way, but from the opposite end of a political and cultural spectrum, as Horrible White People shows do.

The sunnier, less politically engaged discourses surrounding the NFL's 2018 and 2019 seasons seem to have contributed to a rebound in football's TV ratings. Viewership as a whole was up about 5 percent from 15.76 million in 2018, which was the most-watched regular season since 2016, when NFL games also averaged 16.5 million viewers. And even though the NFL has not reclaimed all the audience it lost over the previous two seasons, it has stopped hemorrhaging viewers and remained the surest bet to draw a truly mass audience on US commercial television (Porter 2018, 2020). Of course, an era of drastic change and transformation for the TV industry overall makes it difficult to parse how much of the NFL's ratings decline can be attributed to internet competition versus the incorporation of politics. The important takeaway, though, is that the NFL and broadcast networks that own its TV rights prioritized the emotional needs of vocal White viewers encouraged by President Trump's own hypervisible displays of White fragility. This is the same programming strategy that streaming portals and cable networks developing and distributing Horrible White People shows followed in creating the programming cycle at the center of this book, a programming strategy that propagates an elite transatlantic taste culture and an aesthetics of Whiteness and centralizes floundering White characters.

It is important to note that the NFL was pressured by boycotts from both sides of the political spectrum reacting to anthem protests. For example, "a large crowd protested in support of Kaepernick outside the Chicago Bears–Atlanta Falcons game in Chicago [at the beginning of the 2017 season]. Black-owned businesses from Chicago to Brooklyn, New York, turned off NFL games. Baseball legend Henry Aaron tuned out. A boycott tweet from activist Shaun King was retweeted more than 19,000 times. A #NoKaepernickNoNFL petition on change.org grew past 177,000 signatures" (Washington 2017). High-profile musicians like Rihanna, Adele, Jay-Z, Cardi B, and Pink turned down the 2019 Super Bowl halftime show in solidarity with the protests. And the massively dominant sports brand Nike leaned into the controversy by featuring Kaepernick in its thirtieth-anniversary "Just Do It" campaign. The ad was a tight, black-and-white close-up of a stoic Kaepernick with the words "Believe in something. Even if it means sacrificing everything" emblazoned across his face. While the ad did inspire acts of White fragility from the conservative Right—some people posted videos and photos of themselves burning or destroying their Nike apparel—the company's stock shares surged as much as 9.2 percent in the aftermath of the Kaepernick campaign launch (Bloomberg 2018). The ad's success proved there is another untapped and potentially profitable market of consumer activists for the NFL: the Black urban demographic that Nike prioritizes. But the league and its television broadcasters have so far chosen to overlook those audiences, instead reflecting the stubborn hierarchies of White supremacy.

The NFL's implementation of policies preventing players from protesting illustrates its support of the vocal White fragility that the anthem protests inspired. The league's massness prevented it from reacting with agility when it became embroiled in cultural and political unrest that it could not ignore. It seemed unable even to offer a negotiated response, ending instead by tightening control over its players. Political arguments about racial inequality like the anthem protests cannot be negotiated in the mass-market model of TV's dominant Whiteness, a Whiteness protected by the TV industry's racist legacies of dependence on "structuring [viewer] identifications with the fictions of whiteness" (Lipsitz 1998, 99). But, most importantly, placed in a broader televisual context that includes the cycle of innovative "quality" comedies that are the main subject of this book, the fallout from the NFL protests illustrates the existence of a broad ideological field extending across all forms of television. Representations, programming choices, target audiences, and the public framing of those choices—in both the most mass and smallest niche TV—are an ultimately consistent response to the material realities of a historical conjuncture that includes racial violence, recession, emergent feminisms, and other iterations of and causes of White precarity. And that response, made starker by the Diverse Quality Comedies and the NBA coaches and players who provide contrasting possibilities, is a doubling down on the centralization of Whiteness and the shoring up of structural White supremacy.

Horrible White People

In our authors' note and this book's introduction, we wrote that our goals included being more trustworthy White people, working hard to hold and present complex, challenging, sometimes confrontational conversations about race with and about White people, and contributing to the dismantling of White supremacy by disrupting the invisibility of Whiteness. In this conclusion, we have expanded our conversation from small-market comedies to the most mass-market sports in an effort to make clear that our arguments are not limited to shows you may never have heard of but in fact apply across television's broad ideological field and implicate a far wider swath of consumers than Horrible White People show viewers. We have done this with the same method we have used throughout of applying combined industry studies and cultural studies to critical race theory and studies of Whiteness. This methodology allows us to see the institutionalization of White supremacy as it undergirds both economic and cultural logics in the era of Peak TV. This conclusion could easily grow into the subject of an entire book and thus also nods toward elements we have either cut or had to leave undeveloped in order to produce a bounded, complete study. We had to cut, for example, an entire chapter using affect studies to explore the contrasting presentations of White characters' emotional breakdown versus the consistent resilience of characters of color. The figure of the isolated Black male genius in Diverse Quality Comedies demonstrates the inclusiveness of patriarchy alongside and intertwined with the shifting, heavily policed boundaries of Whiteness, but we lacked the space to analyze gender as thoroughly in chapter 4 as in the rest of the book. Indeed, an entire book could easily grow from that chapter as well. We would welcome other scholars to conduct reception studies in order to add a dimension of audience analysis that was outside the scope of our work here but could help further illuminate how self-critical comedy encourages or forestalls political critique and action. Similarly, scholars might find Horrible White People in parts of the televisual world that were beyond our focus. Yet despite what we were unable to include, we have produced an incisive intervention in Whiteness studies, highlighting a middle-class, self-identified liberal taste culture, putting generic and aesthetic innovation in conversation with Whiteness and TV industrial and technological change. More even than scholarly intercession, we hope that we have made Whiteness more visible and in so doing have offered a small contribution to the dismantling of pervasive White supremacy.

We now return briefly to Horrible White People shows and their own endings to draw our book to a close. In the final episode of *Fleabag*'s first season, the unnamed main character flees her stepmother's art exhibition in tears after admitting her role in her best friend's suicide. The image became the show's primary marketing image, appearing on all its one-sheets and advertisements. The image shows Phoebe Waller-Bridge, the creator, writer, and star of *Fleabag*, in close-up with thick streams and smudges of black mascara running down her cheeks and across her face. In the image, the character is distraught and has clearly been weeping. Although she is alone and in obvious emotional distress, you can guess from her trench coat and a blurred car in the background that she is walking on a public street. When we pitched this project to publishers, we included this image on a mock-up book cover because, even without recognizing Waller-Bridge or *Fleabag*, her face, clothing, location, and emotional state said so much about the collection of programs we had

Figure C.1. Fleabag flees her stepmother's art exhibition in the season 1 finale. (Still from *Fleabag*; screenshot by the authors).

started calling Horrible White People shows. Her clothes and jewelry reveal her upper-middle-class social position; she is White and female and expressing some unnamed or unknown but obviously extremely painful emotion. The black mascara streaks offer the emotional response as big, dramatic, excessive, and explicitly feminine. And the setting, in a city, on a street with cars and streetlights intentionally blurred out in the background, positions this pain in public but places the focus utterly on the character's face. For us, the image encapsulates the cycle's overwhelming bleakness and centralization of white precarity.

Yet the individualized pain and suffering of White women and men symbolized in this image are being salved as the cycle concludes by reconstituting the family and returning to postracial ideologies that have been so challenged by the Great Recession and Black Lives Matter that they helped spur the beginning of this programming cycle. For the demographics represented in Horrible White People shows, access to the markers of middle-class achievement that had disappeared—home ownership and stable, lucrative careers, in particular—are returning. And in Horrible White People programs' endings, families (traditional or alternative) and romance are often reconstituted, offering a return to more familiar generic patterns and a neat package ending to the narrative of White suffering. On *Love*'s series finale, for example, Gus and Mickey invite all their friends to Catalina Island off the coast of Los Angeles to witness their wedding. By returning to classic tropes, narrative conclusions, and individualized answers to social problems, this cycle suggests that, unlike Black suffering, White pain has its limits and comes to a neat conclusion, even in aesthetically innovative and creative programming.

Togetherness, Love, Transparent, Girls, You're the Worst, Girlfriends' Guide to Divorce, Catastrophe, Friends from College, and *Casual* all end by reconstituting the nuclear family. Some of the families are less traditional than others. *Girls* creates an all-female family to raise a mixed-race son; *Casual* breaks up the brother-sister coupling for the brother to move away in order to raise his mixed-race daughter; on *Transparent,* Sarah moves back into her large, idyllic, suburban home with her ex-husband and children, commits to him romantically, but doesn't re-marry her husband; *Togetherness* brings the "errant" wife back to the family, ending the show exactly where it began; and couples get married on *Love, Girlfriends' Guide,* and *You're the Worst.* These marriages are of course a tidy way to tie up messy, complex characters' story lines after multiple seasons, but they also speak to abjection as a temporary condition for these White characters.

Along with relieving the abjection of failed romance or threatened housing, HWP shows' endings also point toward a comforting (for White people) backsliding into a postracial mystique and away from confrontational racial awareness. The production of conflict-free, un-remarked-on mixed-race children and families (in addition to *Girls* and *Casual,* Abby on *Girlfriends' Guide* marries a Black man and becomes stepmother to his daughter; *Friends from College* ends in the gynecologist's office looking at the sonogram of a coming mixed-race baby) be-lies the Whiteness of the rest of these reconstituted relationships. The multiracial children in particular function in a classic postracial mode of assuming that race is simply no longer an issue, that, to quote Ilana from *Broad City,* "everyone's gonna be caramel and queer" so it is not a problem to address. But that return to postracial representations itself reveals the self-centeredness of liberal White protagonists. It individualizes racism, thus defanging the idea of structural White supremacy as a real and continuing threat. If liberal Whites marry and reproduce with happy people of color, these stories imply, racial injustice will simply rectify itself. Equally, these resolutions represent this period of failure and despair as a temporary state through which White women and men suffer but ultimately pass (Wanzo 2015). All these shows' conclusions thus reinforce middle-class Whiteness as a position that might suffer but that is ultimately only *feeling* threatened during a transitional phase before security returns.

As we have moved through the book, we have come back, over and over, to this seemingly inescapable ethos of precarity, despair, or, to use the word aimed at the NFL, crisis. The precarity of Whiteness so evident on 2010s television is also a real, functioning cultural force. It contributes to the election of right-wing politicians, the backlash against emergent feminisms, the backsliding toward postracialism, and a consistent implementation of policy on all levels, from the NFL's new national anthem rules to federal courts rescinding voter protection laws and the Senate confirming a(nother) Supreme Court justice accused of sexual harassment. We have done this in an effort to respond to Joseph R. Winters's (2016) caution against progress narratives and his proposition to present "hope draped in black," by offering a critical-cultural studies model that acknowledges *both* the progressive, to-be-celebrated aspects of these shows *and* their more problematic complicity in enduring structures of power. We also heed Cornell West's (2006) injunction against the threat of nihilism, or the existential loss of hope and purpose for Black communities, which can extend to White allies feeling powerless, burdened, or paralyzed by critiques of their persistent privilege despite their best intentions and the prevailing, resonating affect of cruel optimism that does indeed impact us all. While power structures are exceedingly durable, they do suffer from being made visible, and they do sometimes fall. We have made clear that our research, our writing, and our teaching are our activism. We have pointed toward scholarly work that might grow from ours. We have nurtured the idea of a curious reader learning with us as we write. We hope now that you, reader, will use these tools, that you will see White supremacy operating in the cultural products that surround you, even where it may not be obvious, that you will continue to make it visible, and that, together, we can work to dismantle it.

ACKNOWLEDGMENTS

In the three years it has taken to conceive, research, and write this book, we have been supported by an enormous cast of characters. First, we would like to thank Eric Zinner, Dolma Ombadykow, Lisha Nadkarni, and the entire team at NYU Press for shepherding us smoothly through the whole process. An absolutely central part of that process was the outstanding, thorough, thoughtful, invested, so incredibly helpful peer reviews. We are extremely grateful to the dedicated anonymous reviewers who pushed us to make this book the best it can be. And to Sarah Banet-Weiser, thank you for the essential early support and introduction to NYU Press.

Second, we would like to thank all the early readers, conference attendees, friends, colleagues, *Flow* readers, and everyone who gave us feedback as we presented parts of this project in various venues. Every piece of feedback we got was discussed, occasionally agonized over, and in the end shaped our work. We would especially like to thank Chris Becker and the National Cultures of Television Comedy symposium attendees. We each have a long list of people who have listened to us, questioned us, and supported the project with their friendship and love along the way. Jorie would like to thank Kate Fama, Mary Gilmartin, Paul Halferty, Kylie Jarrett, Ann Mattis, Eoin O'Mahoney, Caroline O'Sullivan, Paul Rouse, Rebecca Stephenson, Janani Subramanian, Sheamus Sweeney, and, most of all, Taylor.

Taylor would like to thank her close friends and extended family Jennifer Rosales, Pip Satchell, Erica Bosque, Kate Casebier, Corey Peck, Katie Cook, Dustin and Allison Nygaard, Jason and Christy Cahill, and her colleagues Diane Waldman, Nadia Kaneva, Sheila Schroeder, Julia Himberg, and Hunter Hargraves. She would like to acknowledge, in particular, her grandmother Patricia Kreuzer for instilling a love of film, television, and pop culture as well as an acute awareness of class and taste cultures and her parents for their unconditional love and support, especially her father for always letting her pick the one (or four) movies or TV shows they would watch on Friday nights and her mother for imparting a love of reading and learning in childhood as well as the generous, intensive care labor she provided in the final months of finishing this book.

Taylor had a son, Clay, during the writing of this book, and his arrival gave her a valuable new perspective and sense of purpose in shaping the arguments and activism tied to this book. He is, quite simply, wonderful. She is thankful for him every day and takes incredibly seriously her responsibility to help him become a responsible, kind, feminist, anitracist, "woke bro." In this effort and more, she is exceedingly thankful of and for her inspiring partner, Coyote. She could not have completed this project without his unending and unwavering confidence in her professionally and personally, not to mention his support, both financial and emotional, through some of the most difficult of life's challenges. She hopes he knows that "U da, U da best." And, last but never least, Taylor would like to thank Jorie for her friendship, wit, and humor, without which she could not have made it through this process.

Together we would like to conclude with a note on collaboration. We refer to each other not as coauthors but as writing partners. We have each touched every word of this book and could never have accomplished this feat alone. Working together made this book so much better. We are grateful to each other and really proud of this work.

Horrible White People Shows and Diverse Quality Comedies Synopses

Atlanta (FX, 2016–): This Emmy- and Golden Globe–winning series created, written by, and starring Donald Glover follows Earn and his friends as they struggle to find stable and fulfilling jobs and relationships in Atlanta. This show's remarkable aesthetic and generic innovations make it hard to describe, since episodes are sometimes surreal and often self-contained explorations of a particular character or theme.

Better Things (FX, 2016–): Created, written, directed by, and starring Pamela Adlon, this aesthetically quirky show follows fifty-ish single working mother and former child actress Sam as she raises her three daughters in Los Angeles.

Big Little Lies (HBO, 2017–): Four women living in affluent, beautiful Monterey, California, become friends because their children go to school together. The series turns dark as it explores the hidden aspects of the women's lives that come to light during the course of a murder investigation.

Bojack Horseman (Netflix, 2014–2020): Bojack is an animated horse, not a white person per se. Nonetheless, the production context, self-professed liberal politics, genre, tone, audience address, and emotional crises mirror all the characteristics of the Horrible White People cycle. The show follows Bojack, a washed-up actor, through existential crisis brought on by his failed career and romantic relationships.

Broad City (Comedy Central, 2014–2019): Based on the webseries created by writer/stars Abbi Jacobson and Ilana Glazer, *Broad City* is a sometimes-surreal episodic comedy following two twenty-something women who smoke a lot of marijuana as they pursue their lives in New York City. The girls find and lose jobs and relationships, while seeing each other through all of life's major and minor struggles.

Casual (Hulu, 2015–2018): Valerie and her teenaged daughter move in with her brother, Alex, after her divorce. He is living in an architect-designed home, off the proceeds of a dating app he designed. All the characters are unmoored; the series follows them as they drift in and out of relationships, homes, and jobs.

Catastrophe (Channel 4, Amazon, 2015–2019): Created and written by Sharon Horgan and Rob Delaney, who also star as the central catastrophic couple, Sharon and Rob, *Catastrophe* follows a couple who get together after an accidental pregnancy and lurch from one family disaster to the next. It is very funny.

Chewing Gum (E4, 2015–2017): Created and written by star Michaela Coel, this British cringe comedy follows early-twenties Tracy through her extremely awkward sexual awakening and other work, housing, and romantic conflicts.

Crazy Ex-Girlfriend (The CW, 2015–2019): Created by writer/star Rachel Bloom, this romantic comedy is also an homage to Bloom's love of musical theater. Characters break into nondiegetic song-and-dance numbers multiple times an episode. The central plot concerns Rebecca Bunch, a successful New York attorney, quitting her job and moving to suburban West Covina, California, in pursuit of her childhood summer-camp boyfriend, Josh Chan.

Dear White People (Netflix, 2017–2020): Created by Justin Simien and based on his feature film of the same name, this series follows a group of Black students at a predominantly White Ivy League college. The title comes from Samantha White's radio show of the same name, in which she calls out White people for their privilege and bad behavior.

The Detour (TBS, 2016–2019): Created by longtime *The Daily Show* correspondents and husband-wife team Jason Jones and Samantha Bee, *The*

Detour follows a spontaneous family road trip instigated by father Nate Parker Jr. after experiencing mysterious professional turmoil. During the family's supposed vacation, a set of crazy, unforeseen circumstances causes them to end up on the run from the FBI.

Difficult People (Hulu, 2015–2017): Best friends and comedians Billy Eichner and Julie Klausner navigate New York City by shouting and making fun of everyone around them. Created by Klausner, the show is cowritten by Klausner and Eichner.

Divorce (HBO, 2017–2019): Sharon Horgan, creator of *Catastrophe*, also created this series about an affluent couple living in the suburbs of New York City and going through an acrimonious divorce.

Easy (Netflix, 2016–2019): This anthology series follows one day or night in the life of various middle-class Chicago couples.

Fleabag (BBC Three and Amazon, 2016–2019): The unnamed main character is grieving her best friend, Boo, and struggling to make ends meet at the café they opened together. Originally a one-woman play, it stars creator/writer Phoebe Waller-Bridge. It is a mystery throughout the first series what happened to Boo. Only in the final episode is it revealed why Fleabag has had such a difficult time getting over her death.

Friends from College (Netflix, 2017–2019): Six Harvard classmates reunite in New York City when they are all in their late thirties. They have affairs with each other and struggle with their relationships and unsatisfying jobs. Notably, this Horrible White People show has four White people and two people of color in its central ensemble. Keegan-Michael Key, a biracial comedian best known for the sketch comedy show *Key and Peele*, is the top-billed star despite the ensemble structure.

Girls (HBO, 2012–2017): Created by writer and star Lena Dunham, this series marks the beginning of the Horrible White People cycle. It follows four affluent White "girls" in their twenties as they repeatedly fail to find satisfying jobs and relationships.

Girlfriends' Guide to Divorce (Bravo, 2014–2018): Relationship-guide author Abby McCarthy finds her career, her brand, and her self-image under threat when she and her husband divorce. The series follows her and her friends through a sequence of fits and starts as they struggle through midlife dating, parenting, and career transformations.

High Maintenance (HBO, 2016–): This webseries turned HBO comedy features miniepisodes in which an unnamed marijuana dealer bikes around New York City meeting and sometimes smoking with his clients.

I Love Dick (Amazon, 2016–2017): A writer and artist couple from New York travel to an art colony in Marfa, Texas, for the husband's fellowship; there the wife becomes both obsessed with and inspired by Dick, a local artist and mentor.

I'm Sorry (TruTV, 2017–): Created by writer/star Andrea Savage, this slightly more traditional sitcom follows the foibles of a happy family (mother, father, and five-year-old daughter) living in suburban Los Angeles.

Insecure (HBO, 2016–): Based on the webseries *The Misadventures of an Awkward Black Girl*, creator/writer/star Issa Rae's TV comedy follows Issa as she breaks up with a long-term boyfriend, loses an apartment, quits a dissatisfying job, and deals with the stresses of comparing herself to her more successful friends.

Lady Dynamite (Netflix, 2016–2017): This slightly madcap sitcom follows creator/writer/star Maria Bamford (playing a version of herself) as she rebuilds her stand-up comedy career after a mental health crisis.

Looking (HBO, 2014–2015): Based on a British series of the same name, this show features three gay male friends in San Francisco. It is much like a gay male *Sex and the City* or *Girls*.

Louie (FX, 2010–2015): This was an artistic, episodic show about Louie, a stand-up comic and divorced father of two small girls. Each episode stands on its own and explores a day or so in the life of the title character. Created by writer, star, sometime director Louis C.K., the considerable overlap between character and creator made viewing the show uncomfortable, to say the least, after C.K. admitted to sexual-harassment accusations in 2017 (*New York Times* 2017). We include it because its generic and stylistic experimentation and its auteur creator, granted complete control over his show by the FX network, is an important precursor to the Horrible White People cycle and a direct inspiration for *Better Things*, created by his frequent collaborator and on which he shares co-creator and cowriter credits.

Love (Netflix, 2016–2018): A beautiful sex and love addict falls in love with the unlikely Gus, a dweeby and rather meek on-set tutor and aspiring screenwriter. The show deviates from standard rom-com tropes by making the two leads insecure, flailing, unlikable characters. The amount of drugs and sex and the Hollywood location are similar to creator Judd Apatow's other work.

Master of None (Netflix, 2015–): Created by Aziz Ansari and Alan Yang, it is written by them and stars Ansari. Mostly about Dev living his life as a working actor in New York City, this show's often vignette-like structure means each episode might have a different aesthetic or focus on a different set of characters in Dev's life. Like all these shows, jobs and relationships are central concerns.

One Mississippi (Amazon, 2015–2017): A character loosely based on creator/writer/star Tig Notaro returns home from Los Angeles to Mississippi to be with her dying mother. After her mother's passing, Tig stays in her hometown, and the series follows her as she starts hosting a radio show and rebuilds relationships with her family and friends.

Russian Doll (Netflix, 2019–): Nadia attends her own drug- and alcohol-fueled birthday party only to die at the end of the night and relive the same day over and over in an existential quest for meaning.

Search Party (TBS, 2016–): Dory is a twenty-something looking for a fulfilling job and relationship in New York City. She suddenly finds purpose when a girl she went to school with goes missing and Dory and her friends become amateur sleuths.

Togetherness (HBO, 2015–2016): Two affluent, suburban couples deal with married-life ennui in this series created by the Duplass brothers and starring Mark Duplass.

Transparent (Amazon, 2014–2019): Mort Pfefferman, a retired professor in his sixties, transitions to become Maura. The series follows her and her adult children as they each struggle with their sexual and gender identity. The show ended in 2019, with a feature-length musical "episode" in which Maura died. Jeffrey Tambor's character was killed off after, like Louis C.K., he was publicly accused of sexual harassment during the height of the visibility of the Me Too movement. Unlike C.K., Tambor denies the allegations.

Unbreakable Kimmy Schmidt (Netflix, 2015–2019): After Kimmy has spent her formative years held captive to a charismatic cult leader in an underground, media-free bunker, she tries to make her chipper, naïve way through New York City. The show's racial politics came under critique in particular for casting the White actress Jane Krakowski in the role of a woman who claims to be Native American.

UnReal (Lifetime, 2015–2018): This melodrama follows best frenemies Rachel and Quinn as they navigate the behind-the-scenes politics of their work on a *Bachelor*-style reality-TV dating-competition show. Rachel's unnamed mental illness features prominently in her characterization and in her relationship with Quinn and her poorly chosen romantic partners.

You Me Her (Audience, 2016–2019): A bored but still very much in love thirty-something upper-middle-class White couple invite a beautiful young escort into their relationship to combat their ennui.

Younger (TV Land, 2015–): An affluent forty-year old mother is going through a divorce and trying to reenter the workforce. To get her dream job in publishing, she passes herself off as twenty-six and attempts to maintain her secret and keep her job for the rest of the show.

You're the Worst (FXX, 2014–2019): This is a bleak romantic comedy about two self-professed terrible people, struggling novelist Jimmy and music publicist Gretchen. The pair get along because they both drink heavily and treat everyone around them, including their best friends, Edgar and Lindsay, abominably.

NOTES

INTRODUCTION

1. Both Abbi and Ilana are secular Jews, coded throughout the show as White. See chapters 2 and 3 for a discussion of *Broad City*'s place within Jewish comedy traditions and the relationship of Jewishness to Whiteness in Horrible White People shows.

2. See, for example, Bell 2013; DeCarvalho 2013; Grdešić 2013; Nygaard 2013; McRobbie 2015; Watson, Mitchell, and Shaw 2015; Ford 2016; Wanzo 2016; Nash and Whelehan 2017; Silverman and Hagelin 2018.

3. This is a trope that is so central to the show's conceit that the title sequences for seasons 4 and 5 end with the show's title in a coaster.

4. Culturally specific characterizations counteract the dominant Hollywood trend of blindcasting, or casting talented actors supposedly without regard to race. In practice, this often means that actors of color are cast in roles written by and about White people, thus Whitewashing any specific histories that might adhere to the actor's racial identity. See Warner 2015a.

5. There is a large body of work about television melodrama, particularly soap operas, their feminine address, social and political content, and heightened emotionalism. The point is neatly summarized by Lagerwey 2018. See for example Feuer 1995; Modleski 1982; Thorburn 2000; R. Allen 2004.

CHAPTER 1. PEAK TV AND THE SPREADABILITY OF TRANSATLANTIC HORRIBLE WHITE PEOPLE

1. The scene was filmed at the Tate Modern art gallery, the view recognizable to anyone familiar with the museum. This is noteworthy because, like so many casual references in Horrible White People shows, it makes no narrative difference if a viewer catches it or not, but it speaks very precisely to the culturally savvy, highly educated, in-the-know, middle- and upper-middle-class taste culture hailed by the cycle.

2. James Collins (1992) describes building a coalition audience by appealing to multiple audience segments with different elements within a show. We borrow his phrase but shift its emphasis toward shared concerns among seemingly disparate audience segments.

3. As we discuss in the book's conclusion, sport programming maintains very large national viewership as an exception to this shift.

4. Toby Miller argues that the history of "quality" discourse surrounding television in the United States is "clearly articulated to a snobby ruling-class doctrine of cross-subsidized elevation" (2008, x). He points to pay-TV advocates in the 1950s and '60s such as the anti-Marxist liberal Left, represented by Americans for Democratic Action, who called for innovation by collapsing a rhetoric of cultural uplift with consumer sovereignty through choice. Moreover, in our special issue of *Television and New Media* about *The Good Wife*, we detail the inherently gendered notions of "quality" and interrogate the biases of hypermasculine discussions of twenty-first-century quality TV (Nygaard and Lagerwey 2016). Ultimately many of these periodically resurgent progressive narratives are elitist and tend to disregard the importance of television to personal, social, and cultural development well before the time period described.
5. See chapter 3 for the cultural impact of the cycle's representations of feminism and chapter 4 for awards and acclaim for the parallel cycle of "Diverse Quality Comedies."
6. Nielsen statistics show that 36 percent of US households subscribe to Netflix (more than forty million US subscribers in all), with Amazon Prime (13 percent) and Hulu (6.5 percent) lagging behind (Lynch 2015).

CHAPTER 2. ALTERNATIVE FAMILIES AND WHITE FRAGILITY

1. These family ideals and their relationship to feminism were never straightforward and often depended on whether one chose to read a program's neat episodic endings or dwell in the much messier, funnier middle. Susan Douglas (1994) has mapped the uneven and contradictory relationship between American sitcoms and feminism, and Patricia Mellencamp (2003) has argued for the transgressiveness of Gracie Allen's and Lucille Ball's 1950s sitcoms. Nonetheless, as Lynn Spigel (2001) argues, feminist containment and reassertion of the dominant family structure were key features of 1950s and 1960s sitcoms.
2. Horrible White People shows are of course not the only White-cast comedies on the air in this era. There are many more generically traditional White-cast sitcoms that similarly reinforce these traditional ideologies, including the nostalgic reboot of *Roseanne* (*The Conners*, ABC, 2018–) and the return of Tim Allen to *Last Man Standing* (ABC, 2011–2017; Fox 2018–) after complaining that ABC had canceled the show because of his conservative political leanings. We note *Black-ish*, *One Day at a Time*, and *Fresh Off the Boat* because they appeared collectively at a time when sitcom families of color had been largely missing from American screens for a period after the 1990s surge of Black-cast sitcoms like *Fresh Prince of Bel-Air* (NBC, 1990–1996) and *Living Single* (Fox, 1993–1998).
3. *All in the Family* was itself modeled on a British sitcom, *Till Death Us Do Part* (BBC1, 1965–1975). The translation reflects an earlier era's version of the movement of comedy between Britain and the United States, and the shows' similarities illustrate a longer history of the two nations' "special relationship" in comedy, described in chapter 1.

4. Several White celebrities have been rightfully harshly criticized for wearing black-face Halloween costumes in recent years: *Dancing with the Stars'* Julianne Hough painted her White face dark to appear as Crazy Eyes from *Orange Is the New Black* in 2013; *Keeping Up with the Kardashians'* Scott Disick, who is White, dressed up as an "Arab Sheik" for Halloween in 2014; and young revelers at the Coachella music festival are routinely called out for appropriating Native American and other cultural styles for their concert garb.

5. Although the critique is dulled by the series' ending, which, in a classic example of the impossibility of ending heavily serialized shows with any kind of satisfaction, has Lindsay remarry Paul.

6. "JAP" refers to "Jewish American Princess." In this musical number, two childhood rivals from wealthy New York City suburbs, now successful lawyers, try to outdo each other with their accomplishments, set to rap beats. Like the *Broad City* girls, they acknowledge their liberal credentials (by literally holding up a card claiming membership in the ACLU) and White-skin privilege, while peppering the rap with Yiddish words ("I'm translating for the goys," says one of the rappers) and Jewish cultural references. The cringey, well-meaning White-lady persona is both claimed ("I spent a semester in Kenya, remember?" and "Well I volunteered in Ghana") and mocked by the structure of the comedy musical number. Much of the comedy also stems from the racial misidentification that comes from well-off White-skinned women engaging in a musical form created by and most associated with African American men.

7. We place "nonnormative" in quotation marks to highlight the contested nature of the term, especially by scholars in fat studies.

CHAPTER 3. EMERGENT FEMINISMS AND RACIAL DISCOURSES OF TELEVISUAL GIRLFRIENDSHIP

1. The hashtag #metoo originated in 2006, the creation of activist Tarana Burke. There was controversy after a group of predominantly White actresses made it go viral in 2017 because the history of Burke's work was largely erased from the conversation. When *Time* magazine named "The Silence Breakers" person of the year, for example, only Burke's elbow made the cover image; readers had to pull open the fold-out image to see her face (Zacharek, Dockterman, and Edwards 2017; see also Brockes 2018).

2. Any self-revelation that Abby may have had about her treatment of Barbara and postfeminist norms of beauty and behavior (which she never understands as racialized anyway) are ultimately undercut since Abby ends up marrying Mike, the baseball coach whom the two meet that night, at the end of the series.

3. Heather's indeterminate race is a running joke on the show until she finally tells everyone that her father is Black and her mother is White.

4. Like so many of the contradictions within this cycle, male producers' allyship is not without its own messy gender politics. In 2018, Louis C.K. confirmed sexual-harassment allegations against him, smudging the reputations of *One Missis-*

sippi and *Better Things*, on which he was credited as an executive producer. That particular contradiction is outside the scope of this book, but Notaro addressed it directly on *One Mississippi* (S2E5) and in subsequent interviews in which she distanced herself from C.K. (Ryzik, Buckley, and Kantor 2017).

CHAPTER 4. DIVERSE QUALITY COMEDIES IN AN ERA OF WHITE PRECARITY

1. Throughout this chapter, we rely on critical race theory that is primarily rooted in African American texts and experiences. We maintain that the United States' and the United Kingdom's colonial histories have created structural White supremacy that makes this body of theory broadly applicable to non-White people in both nations. Richard Dyer (1997) makes a similar argument in his explanation of why he uses the term "non-White" rather than something more specific.

2. The prestige aesthetics of "quality TV," which we describe throughout this chapter as an aesthetics of Whiteness, stem from patriarchal as well as White-supremacist legacies and will accept creators who fit a limited understanding of male genius before creators who are neither White *nor* male. While we signal those distinctions throughout the chapter, detailed intersectional gender analysis is unfortunately outside the scope of this chapter.

3. Aymar Jean Christian (2018) defines "legacy TV" as linear or traditional network distribution in contrast to what he describes as "open TV," web or networked television.

REFERENCES

Adalian, Josef. 2018. "Forget Peak TV: FX Boss John Landgraf Says We're Now in the 'Gilded Age' of Television." *Vulture*, August 3. www.vulture.com.

Adalian, Josef, and Maria Elena Fernandez. 2016. "The Business of Too Much TV." *Vulture*, May. www.vulture.com.

Adichie, Chimamanda Ngozi. 2012. "We Should All Be Feminists." *Ted Talk*, December. https://www.ted.com/.

Affuso, Elizabeth. 2018. "'They're Just Like Us: Celebrity Civilianizing on Social Media," *Flow*, March 26. www.flowjournal.org.

Ahmed, Sara. 2017. *Living a Feminist Life*. Durham, NC: Duke University Press.

Alexander, Michael. 2007. "The Price of Whiteness: Jews, Race, and American Identity (Review)." *American Jewish History* 93 (1): 96–99.

Alexander, Michelle. 2012. *The New Jim Crow: Mass Incarceration in the Age of Color-blindness*. New York: New Press.

Allen, Robert C. 2004. "Making Sense of Soaps." In *The Television Studies Reader*, edited by Robert C. Allen and Annette Hill, 242–257. London: Routledge.

Allen, Samantha. 2016. "*Crazy Ex-Girlfriend*: How Paula and Rebecca's Unlikely Friendship Became TV's Best Love Story." *Daily Beast*, April 18. www.thedailybeast.com.

Alsop, Elizabeth. 2016. "Why TV Needs 'Weak' Female Characters." *Atlantic*, December 4. www.theatlantic.com.

Anderson, Benedict. 1991. *Imagined Communities: Reflections on the Origin and Spread of Nationalism*. New York: Verso Books.

Anderson, Christopher. 2008. "Producing an Aristocracy of Culture in American Television." In *The Essential HBO Reader*, edited by Gary R. Edgerton and Jeffrey P. Jones, 23–41. Lexington: University Press of Kentucky.

Andreeva, Nellie. 2018. "*Catastrophe*'s Sharon Horgan Inks Overall Deal with Amazon Studios." *Deadline*, January 16. http//deadline.com.

Ansari, Aziz, with Eric Klinenberg. 2015. *Modern Romance*. New York: Penguin.

Ansley, Frances Lee. 1997. "White Supremacy (and What We Should Do about It)." In *Critical White Studies: Looking behind the Mirror*, edited by Richard Delgado and Jean Stefancic, 592–555. Philadelphia: Temple University Press.

Bahr, Robyn. 2018. "HBO's Sharpest Comedy Continues to Crackle, Despite Slow-Burn Start." *Hollywood Reporter*, August 10. www.hollywoodreporter.com.

Bakare, Lanre. 2018. "The 50 Best Shows of 2018: No. 9—*Atlanta*." *Guardian*, December 10. www.theguardian.com.

Banet-Weiser, Sarah. 2015. "Popular Misogyny: A Zeitgeist." *Culture Digitally*, January 21. http://culturedigitally.org.

———. 2018. *Empowered*. Durham, NC: Duke University Press.

Banet-Weiser, Sarah, and Laurie Ouellette. 2018. Editors' introduction to "Media and the Extreme Right." Special issue, *Communication Culture & Critique* 11 (1): 1–6.

Becker, Ron. 2006. *Gay TV and Straight America*. New Brunswick, NJ: Rutgers University Press.

Bell, Katherine. 2013. "'Obvie, We're the Ladies!' Postfeminism, Privilege, and HBO's Newest Girls." *Feminist Media Studies* 13 (2): 363–366.

Berg, Madeline. 2017a. "Don't Blame Jemele Hill for ESPN's Ratings Problem." *Forbes*, October 7. www.forbes.com.

———. 2017b. "Note to Networks: Diversity on TV Pays Off." *Forbes*, February 22. www.forbes.com.

Berger, Joseph. 2012. "As Greenpoint Gentrifies, Sunday Rituals Clash: Outdoor Cafes vs. Churchgoers." *New York Times*, May 10. www.nytimes.com.

Berlant, Lauren. 2008. *The Female Complaint: The Unfinished Business of Sentimentality in American Culture*. Durham, NC: Duke University Press.

———. 2011. *Cruel Optimism*. Durham, NC: Duke University Press.

Berri, David. 2017. "Think Women Don't Know Sports? You Don't Know as Much about Sports as You Think." *Forbes*, October 9. www.forbes.com.

Bianculli, David. 2016. *The Platinum Age of Television: From "I Love Lucy" to "The Walking Dead"; How TV Became Terrific*. New York: Doubleday.

Blake, Meredith. 2019. "Rob Delaney and Sharon Horgan Bring Their Funny, Unflinching 'Catastrophe' to an End." *Los Angeles Times*, March 15. www.latimes.com.

Bloomberg. 2018. "Nike's Big Bet on Colin Kaepernick Campaign Continues to Pay Off." *Fortune*, December 21. http://fortune.com.

Bonilla-Silva, Eduardo. 2014. *Racism without Racists: Color-Blind Racism and the Persistence of Racial Inequality in America*. 4th ed. Lanham, MD: Rowman and Littlefield.

Bonner, Frances. 2003. *Ordinary Television: Analyzing Popular TV*. London: Sage.

Bore, Inger-Lise Kalviknes. 2011. "Transnational TV Comedy Audiences." *Television and New Media* 12 (4): 347–369.

Bourdieu, Pierre. 1984. *Distinction: A Social Critique of the Judgment of Taste*. Translated by Richard Nice. London and New York: Routledge.

Brockes, Emma. 2018. "#MeToo Founder Tarana Burke: 'You Have to Use Your Privilege to Serve Other People.'" *Guardian*, January 15. www.theguardian.com.

Brunsdon, Charlotte. 2000. *The Feminist, the Housewife, and the Soap Opera*. Oxford, UK: Clarendon.

Buchanan, Larry, Ford Fessenden, K. K. Rebecca Lai, Haeyoun Park, Alicia Parlapiano, Archie Tse, Tim Wallace, Derek Watkins, and Karen Yourish. 2015. "What Happened in Ferguson?" *New York Times*, August 10. www.nytimes.com.

Bush, M. E. L. 2004. "Race, Ethnicity and Whiteness." *Sage Race Relations Abstracts* 29 (3–4): 5–48.

Butler, Bethonie. 2018. "The 10 Best TV Episodes of 2018, from *Atlanta* to *This Is Us.*" *Washington Post*, December 5. www.washingtonpost.com.

Butler, Judith. 1990. *Gender Trouble: Feminism and the Subversion of Identity*. New York: Routledge.

———. 2011. "For and Against Precarity." *Tidal: Occupy Theory, Occupy Strategy* 1:12–13.

Butsch, Richard. 2005. "Five Decades and Three Hundred Sitcoms about Class and Gender." In *Thinking Outside the Box: A Contemporary Television Genre Reader*, edited by Gary R. Edgerton and Brian G. Rose, 111–135. Lexington: University Press of Kentucky.

CBS News. 2017. "Trump to NFL Owners: Fire Players Who Kneel during National Anthem." September 23. www.cbsnews.com.

Chemi, Eric. 2014. "The NFL Is Growing Only Because of Women." *Bloomberg*, September 26. www.bloomberg.com.

Christian, Aymar Jean. 2018. *Open TV: Innovation beyond Hollywood and the Rise of Web Television*. New York: NYU Press.

———. 2019. "Expanding Production Value: The Culture and Scale of Television and New Media." *Critical Studies in Television: The International Journal of Television Studies*, May 16, 1–13. DOI: 10.1177/1749602019838882.

Cills, Hazel. 2015. "*Broad City* Is a Fearless, Priceless Ode to Female Friendship." *Deadspin*, January 14. http://deadspin.com.

Clark, Tiana. 2019. "This Is What Black Burnout Feels Like." *Buzzfeed*, January 11. www.buzzfeed.com.

Cobb, Shelley, Neil Ewen, and Hannah Hamad. 2018. "*Friends* Reconsidered: Cultural Politics, Intergenerationality, and Afterlives." *Television and New Media* 19 (8): 683–691.

Collins, James. 1992. "Postmodernism and Television." In *Channels of Discourse, Reassembled: Television and Contemporary Criticism*, 2nd ed., edited by Robert Allen, 327–353. London: Routledge.

Collins, Patricia Hill. 2012. "Social Inequality, Power, and Politics: Intersectionality and American Pragmatism in Dialogue." *Journal of Speculative Philosophy* 26 (2): 442–457.

Comedy Central. 2017. "Broad City—Hack into Broad City—Inauguration—Uncensored." YouTube, January 20. www.youtube.com/watch?v=c-d8VP3cuDM.

Cook, Bob. 2019. "High School Football Participation Is on a Decade-Long Decline." *Forbes*, August 29. www.forbes.com.

Coontz, Stephanie. 1993. *The Way We Never Were: American Families and the Nostalgia Trap*. New York: Basic Books.

Cooper, Helene. 2009. "Obama Criticizes Arrest of Harvard Professor." *New York Times*, July 22. www.nytimes.com.

Coulangeon, Philippe. 2005. "Social Stratification of Musical Tastes: Questioning the Cultural Legitimacy Model." *Revue Francais de Sociologie* 46:123–154.

Couldry, Nick. 2003. *Media Rituals: A Critical Approach*. New York: Routledge.

Cramer, Katherine J. 2016. *The Politics of Resentment: Rural Consciousness in Wisconsin and the Rise of Scott Walker*. Chicago: University of Chicago Press.

Crenshaw, Kimberlé. 1991. "Mapping the Margins: Intersectionality, Identity Politics, and Violence against Women of Color." *Stanford Law Review* 43 (6): 1241–1299.

Critchley, Simon. 2002. *On Humour*. London: Routledge.

Crupi, Anthony. 2015. "Sports Now Accounts for 37% of Broadcast TV Ad Spending." *AdAge*, September 10. https://adage.com.

Cullins, Ashley. 2016. "'Gilmore Girls' Producer Sues Warner Bros. over Netflix Reboot." *Hollywood Reporter*, April 11. www.hollywoodreporter.com.

D'Acci, Julie. 1994. *Defining Women: Television and the Case of Cagney and Lacey*. Chapel Hill: University of North Carolina Press.

Daniels, Jessie. 2014. "Lena Dunham and the Trouble with (White) 'Girls.'" *Racism Review*, April 8. www.racismreview.com.

Dauber, Jeremy. 2017. *Jewish Comedy: A Serious History*. New York: Norton.

Davies, Hannah J. 2018. "'It Was Important for Black Women to See Ourselves Normally': How *Insecure* Changed TV." *Guardian*, July 31. www.theguardian.com.

Davis, Angela. 1981. *Women, Race and Class*. London: Women's Press.

DeCarvalho, Lauren. J. 2013. "Hannah and Her Entitled Sisters: (Post)feminism, (Post)recession, and *Girls*." *Feminist Media Studies* 13 (2): 367–370.

Del Barco, Mandalit. 2014. "How Kodak's Shirley Cards Set Photography's Skin-Tone Standard." National Public Radio, November 13. www.npr.org.

Delgado, Richard, and Jean Stefancic, eds. 1997. *Critical White Studies: Looking behind the Mirror*. Philadelphia: Temple University Press.

Demers, Jason. 2017. "Is a Trojan Horse and Empty Signifier? The Televisual Politics of *Orange Is the New Black*." *Canadian Review of American Studies / Revue canadienne d'études américaines* 47 (3). DOI: 10.3138/cras.2017.023.

Denninger, Lindsay. 2018. "*UnReal* Season 4 Pits Rachel & Quinn against Each Other in the Darkest of Ways." *Bustle*, July 24. www.bustle.com.

DiAngelo, Robin. 2011. "White Fragility." *International Journal of Critical Pedagogy* 3 (3): 54–70.

———. 2018. *White Fragility: Why It's So Hard for White People to Talk about Racism*. Boston: Beacon.

Doane, Ashley "Woody." 2007. "The Changing Politics of Color-Blind Racism." In *The New Black: Alternative Paradigms and Strategies for the 21st Century*, edited by Rodney D. Coates and Rutledge M. Dennis, 159–174. Bingley, UK: Emerald Group.

Doll, Jen. 2012a. "The Real War on Brunch in Williamsburg." *Atlantic*, May 9. www.theatlantic.com.

———. 2012b. "The War on Brunch Is Just a War on Gentrification in Brunch Clothes." *Atlantic*, May 11. www.theatlantic.com.

Doty, Alexander. 1993. *Making Things Perfectly Queer: Interpreting Mass Culture*. Minneapolis: University of Minnesota Press.

Double, Oliver. 2005. *Getting the Joke: The Art of Stand-Up Comedy*. London: Methuen.

Douglas, Susan. 1994. *Where the Girls Are: Growing Up Female with the Mass Media*. New York: Three Rivers.

———. 2010. *The Rise of Enlightened Sexism*. New York: St. Martin's Griffin.

Dow, Bonnie J. 1996. *Prime-Time Feminism: Television, Media Culture, and the Women's Movement since 1970*. Philadelphia: University of Pennsylvania Press.

Doyle, Gillian. 2016. "Digitization and Changing Windowing Strategies in the Television Industry: Negotiating New Windows on the World." *Television and New Media* 17 (7): 629–645.

Du Gay, Paul, and Michael Pryke. 2002. Introduction to *Cultural Economy: Cultural Analysis and Commercial Life*, edited by Paul Du Gay and Michael Pryke, 1–20. London: Sage.

Dyer, Richard. 1997. *White: Essays on Race and Culture*. London: Routledge.

Eddo-Lodge, Reni. 2017. *Why I'm No Longer Talking to White People about Race*. London: Bloomsbury.

Fallon, Kevin. 2016. "Is Diversity on TV Really Getting Better?" *Daily Beast*, August 5. www.thedailybeast.com.

Feldman, Keith P. 2016. "The Globality of Whiteness in Post-racial Visual Culture." *Cultural Studies* 30 (2): 289–311.

Ferrier, Morwenna. 2015. "*Girls* and the Trend for Ill-Fitting Chic." *Guardian*, January 15. www.theguardian.com.

Feuer, Jane. 1995. *Seeing through the Eighties: Television and Reaganism*. Durham, NC: Duke University Press.

Feuer, Jane, Paul Kerr, and Tise Vahimagi, eds. 1985. *MTM: Quality Television*. London: British Film Institute.

Fiske, John. 2011. *Television Culture*. 2nd ed. London: Routledge.

Ford, Jessica. 2016. "The 'Smart' Body Politics of Lena Dunham's *Girls*." *Feminist Media Studies* 16 (6): 1029–1042.

Frankel, Todd C. 2017. "'Peak TV' Paradox: Why So Much Great TV Has Become Such Bad News for Writers." *Washington Post*, April 28. www.washingtonpost.com.

Friedman, Sam. 2011. "The Cultural Currency of a 'Good' Sense of Humour: British Comedy and New Forms of Distinction." *British Journal of Sociology* 62 (2): 347–370.

Frontline. 2013. *League of Denial: The NFL's Concussion Crisis*. PBS. Film.

Gans, Herbert. 1974. *Popular Culture and High Culture: An Analysis and Evaluation of Taste*. New York: Basic Books.

Garber, Megan, David Sims, Lenika Cruz, and Sophie Gilbert. 2015. "Have We Reached 'Peak TV'?" *Atlantic*, August 12. www.theatlantic.com.

Garner, Steve. 2017. "Surfing the Third Wave of Whiteness Studies: Reflections on Twine and Gallagher." *Ethnic and Racial Studies* 40 (9): 1582–1597.

Garza, Alicia. n.d. "Herstory." Black Lives Matter. Accessed November 1, 2019. www.blacklivesmatter.com.

Gates, Racquel J. 2018. *Double Negative: The Image and Popular Culture*. Durham, NC: Duke University Press.

Gennis, Sadie. 2016. "How *UnREAL* Pushed the Boundaries of Female Friendships on TV." *TV Guide*, August 14. www.tvguide.com.

George, Kat. 2014. "*Broad City* and the Most Important Female Friendship on TV Right Now." *Thought Catalog*, March 28. https://thoughtcatalog.com/.

Gervais, Ricky. 2011. "The Difference between American and British Humour." *Time*, November 9. http://time.com.

Gilbert, Sophie. 2018. "The 22 Best Shows of 2018." *Atlantic*, December 9. www.theatlantic.com.

Gill, Rosalind. 2007. "Postfeminist Media Culture: Elements of a Sensibility." *European Journal of Cultural Studies* 10 (2): 147–166.

———. 2016. "Post-postfeminism? New Feminist Visibilities in Postfeminist Times." *Feminist Media Studies* 16 (4): 610–630.

Gillborn, David. 2006. "Rethinking White Supremacy: Who Counts in 'WhiteWorld.'" *Ethnicities* 6 (3): 318–340.

Gillette, Felix. 2017. "Commentary: The NFL Has a Woman Problem, and Vice Versa." *Chicago Tribune*, December 14. www.thechicagotribune.com.

Gillota, David. 2010. "Negotiating Jewishness: *Curb Your Enthusiasm* and the Schlemiel Tradition." *Journal of Popular Film and Television* 4 (38): 152–161.

Gitlin, Todd. 2000. *Inside Prime Time*. Berkeley: University of California Press.

Gledhill, Christine. 1999. "Pleasurable Negotiations." In *Feminist Film Theory: A Reader*, edited by Sue Thornham, 166–179. New York: NYU Press.

Goldberg, Lesley. 2018. "*Black-ish* Creator Kenya Barris Plots Exit from ABC Studios Pact after Clashes (Exclusive)." *Hollywood Reporter*, April 4. www.hollywoodreporter.com.

Goldstein, Eric. 2008. *The Price of Whiteness: Jews, Race, and American Identity*. Princeton, NJ: Princeton University Press.

Grady, Constance. 2017. "The Friendship Plot Is Replacing the Marriage Plot: *Crazy Ex-Girlfriend* Subverts Both." *Vox*, January 8. www.vox.com.

Graff, Agnieszka, Ratna Kapur, and Suzanna Danuta Walters. 2019. "Introduction: Gender and the Rise of the Global Right." *Signs: Journal of Women in Culture and Society* 44 (3): 541–560.

Gray, Herman. 1989. "Television, Black Americans, and the American Dream." *Critical Studies in Mass Communication* 6 (4): 376–386.

———. 1994. "Response to Justin Lewis and Sut Jhally." *American Quarterly* 46 (1): 118–121.

———. 1995. *Watching Race: Television and the Struggle for "Blackness."* Minneapolis: University of Minnesota Press.

———. 2005. *Cultural Moves: African Americans and the Politics of Representation*. Berkeley: University of California Press.

Gray, Jonathan, Jeffrey P. Jones, and Ethan Thompson, eds. 2009. *Satire TV: Politics and Comedy in the Post-Network Era*. New York: NYU Press.

Grdešić, Maša. 2013. "'I'm Not the Ladies!': Metatextual Commentary in Girls." *Feminist Media Studies* 13 (2): 355–358.

Gross, Terri. 2013. "'Orange' Creator Jenji Kohan: 'Piper Was My Trojan Horse.'" *Fresh Air*, National Public Radio, August 13. www.npr.org.

Grote, David. 1983. *The End of Comedy: The Sit-Com and the Comedic Tradition*. Hamden, CT: Archon.

Gus P. 2017. "Gregg Popovich Schools Everyone on White Supremacy, Politics, and Protest in Sports." *Kulturehub*, September 26. https://kulturehub.com.

Hall, Ronald E. 2018. "The NFL Plantation: Home to Million Dollar Slaves." *Electronic Urban Report*, May 8. https://eurweb.com/.

Hall, Stuart. 1979. "The Great Moving Right Show." *Marxism Today*, January, 14–20.

———. 1993. "Encoding, Decoding." In *The Cultural Studies Reader*, 2nd ed., edited by Simon During, 507–517. New York: Routledge.

———. 1996. "New Ethnicities." In *Stuart Hall: Critical Dialogues in Cultural Studies*, edited by David Morely and Kuan-Hsing Chen, 441–449. New York: Routledge.

Hamad, Hannah, and Anthea Taylor. 2015. Introduction to "Feminism and Celebrity Culture." Special issue, *Celebrity Studies* 6 (1): 124–127.

Harding, Xavier. 2017. "Keeping *Insecure* Lit: HBO Cinematographer Ava Berkofsky on Properly Lighting Black Faces." *Mic*, September 6. www.mic.com.

Hargraves, Hunter. Forthcoming. *Uncomfortable Television*. Durham, NC: Duke University Press.

Harris, Anita. 2003. *Future Girl: Young Women in the Twenty-First Century*. New York: Routledge.

Harrison, Sheri-Marie. 2018. "New Black Gothic." *Los Angeles Review of Books*, June 23. https://lareviewofbooks.org.

Harwell, Drew. 2014a. "Women Are One of the Sporting-Goods Industry's Biggest-Growing Markets—and One of Its Most Ignored." *Washington Post*, October 14. www.washingtonpost.com.

———. 2014b. "Women Are Pro Football's Most Important Demographic. Will They Forgive the NFL? Female Fans, a Group Beloved by Advertisers, Represent the NFL's Biggest Opportunity for Growth." *Washington Post*, September 13. www.washingtonpost.com.

Havas, Julia, and Maria Sulimma. 2018. "Through the Gaps of My Fingers: Genre, Femininity, and Cringe Aesthetics in Dramedy Television." *Television and New Media* 21 (1): 75–94.

Havens, Timothy. 2013. *Black Television Travels: African American Media around the Globe*. New York: NYU Press.

———. 2018. "Showtime's *The Chi* and the Surge in Black-Cast TV Dramas." *Flow*, February 26. www.flowjournal.org.

Herman, Alison. 2017. "*Broad City* Grows Up in Season 4." *Ringer*, September 12. www.theringer.com.

Hilmes, Michele. 2012. *Network Nations: A Transnational History of British and American Broadcasting*. New York and London: Routledge.

Himberg, Julia. 2014. "Multicasting: Lesbian Programming and the Changing Landscape of Cable TV." *Television and New Media* 15 (4): 289–304.

———. 2018. *The New Gay for Pay: The Sexual Politics of American Television Production*. Austin: University of Texas Press.

Hollinger, Karen. 1998. *In the Company of Women: Contemporary Female Friendship Films*. Minneapolis: University of Minnesota Press.

Holloway, Daniel. 2017. "Almost Nobody Watches Most Emmy-Nominated Shows, Survey Finds." *Variety*, September 15. https://variety.com.

———. 2018. "Kenya Barris Signs $100 Million Netflix Deal." *Variety*, August 16. https://variety.com.

Holmes, Linda. 2015. "Television 2015: Is There Really Too Much TV?" National Public Radio, August 16. www.npr.org.

hooks, bell. 1992. *Black Looks: Race and Representation*. Boston: South End.

———. 2013. "Dig Deep: Beyond *Lean In*." *Feminist Wire*, October 28. https://thefeministwire.com.

Ignatiev, Noel. 1995. *How the Irish Became White*. New York: Routledge.

Iwamura, Jane Naomi. 2017. "The Oriental Monk in American Popular Culture." In *Religion and Popular Culture in America*, 3rd ed., edited by Bruce David Forbes and Jeffrey H. Mahan, 51–70. Berkeley: University of California Press.

James, Kendra. 2012. "Dear Lena Dunham: I Exist." *Racialicious*, April 19. https://racialicious.tumblr.com.

James, Meg. 2015. "2015: Year of 'Peak TV' Hits Record with 409 Original Series." *Los Angeles Times*, December 16. www.latimes.com.

James, Robin. 2015. *Resilience and Melancholy: Pop Music, Feminism, Neoliberalism*. Alresford, UK: Zero Books.

Jarvey, Natalie. 2019. "Netflix under Pressure: Can a Hollywood Disruptor Avoid Getting Disrupted?" *Hollywood Reporter*, August 8. www.hollywoodreporter.com.

Jenkins, Henry, Sam Ford, and Joshua Green. 2013. *Spreadable Media*. New York: NYU Press.

Jenner, Mareike. 2016. "Is This TVIV? On Netflix, TVIII and Binge-Watching." *New Media and Society* 18 (2): 257–273.

Jensen, Peter Kragh, and Matt Sienkiewicz. 2018. "Introduction: Nation and Globalization." In *The Comedy Studies Reader*, edited by Nick Marx and Matt Sienkiewicz, 238–243. Austin: University of Texas Press.

Jhally, Sut, and Justin Lewis. 1992. *Enlightened Racism: "The Cosby Show," Audiences, and the Myth of the American Dream*. New York: Routledge.

Johnson, Carla. 1994. "The Schlemiel and the Schlimazl in *Seinfeld*." *Journal of Popular Film and Television* 3 (22): 116–124.

Johnson, Catherine. 2012. *Branding Television*. New York: Routledge.

Joseph, Ralina. 2018. *Postracial Resistance: Black Women, Media, and the Uses of Strategic Ambiguity*. New York: NYU Press.

Kaplan, Ilana. 2017. "*Chewing Gum*: Meet the Mastermind behind Netflix's Sex-Obsessed Britcom." *Rolling Stone*, April 11. www.rollingstone.com.

Keh, Andrew. 2017. "How a Slave Spiritual Became an English Rugby Song." *New York Times*, March 7. www.nytimes.com.

Keller, Jessalynn, and Maureen E. Ryan. 2018. "Introduction: Mapping Emergent Feminisms." In *Emergent Feminisms: Complicating a Postfeminist Media Culture*, edited by Jessalynn Keller and Maureen E. Ryan, 1–22. New York: Routledge.

King, Cecillia. 2015. "With Shows like 'Empire,' 'Black-ish' and 'Cristela,' TV Is More Diverse than Ever." *Washington Post*, January 29. www.washingtonpost.com.

Krieger, Rosalin. 2003. "'Does He Actually Say the Word Jewish?': Jewish Representations In *Seinfeld*." *Journal for Cultural Research* 4 (7): 387–404.

Kristeva, Julia. 1982. *Powers of Horror: An Essay on Abjection*. New York: Columbia University Press.

Lachmann, Renate, Raoul Eshelman, and Marc Davis. 1988. "Bakhtin and Carnival: Culture as Counter-culture." *Cultural Critique* 11 (Winter): 115–152.

Lagerwey, Jorie. 2018. "The Feminist *Game of Thrones*: *Outlander* and Gendered Discourses of TV Genre." In *Women Do Genre in Film and Television*, edited by Mary Harrod and Katarzyna Paszkiewicz, 198–212. New York and London: Routledge.

Lagerwey, Jorie, Julia Leyda, and Diane Negra. 2016. "Female-Centered TV in an Age of Precarity." *Genders* 1 (1). www.colorado.edu/genders/.

Lagerwey, Jorie, and Taylor Nygaard. 2017. "Liberal Women, Mental Illness, and Precarious Whiteness in Trump's America." *Flow*, November 27. www.flowjournal.org.

Lapchick, Richard. 2018. "NBA Leads Men's Sports Industry in Racial and Gender Hiring Practices." ESPN, June 26. www.espn.com.

Laskas, Jeanne Marie. 2015. "The Brain That Sparked the NFL's Concussion Crisis." *Atlantic*, December 2. www.theatlantic.com.

Lauzen, Martha M. 2018. "Boxed In 2017–18: Women On Screen and Behind the Scenes in Television." Center for the Study of Women in Television & Film, San Diego State University. https://womenintvfilm.sdsu.edu.

Leishman, Rachel. 2018. "Crazy Ex-Girlfriend: Friendship Is the Real Important Thing." *Culturess*, November 19. https://culturess.com.

Leonard, Suzanne. 2014. "Escaping the Recession? The New Vitality of the Woman Worker." In *Gendering the Recession: Media and Culture in an Age of Austerity*, edited by Diane Negra and Yvonne Tasker, 31–58. Durham, NC: Duke University Press.

Leverette, Marc, Brian L. Ott, and Cara Louise Buckley, eds. 2008. *It's Not TV: Watching HBO in the Post-television Era*. New York: Routledge.

Levin, Gary. 2016. "TV's Making Progress on Diversity, but It's Motivated by Money." *USA Today*, November 1. www.usatoday.com.

Levine, Elana. 2011. "Teaching the Politics of Television Culture in a 'Post-television' Era." *Cinema Journal* 50 (4): 177–182.

Lipsitz, George. 1986. "The Meaning of Memory: Family, Class, and Ethnicity in Early Network Television Programs." *Cultural Anthropology* 1 (4): 355–387.

———. 1998. *The Possessive Investment in Whiteness: How White People Profit from Identity Politics*. Philadelphia: Temple University Press.

Lobato, Ramon. 2017. "Rethinking International TV Flows Research in the Age of Netflix." *Television and New Media*, May 19. DOI: 10.1177/1527476417708245.

———. 2019. *Netflix Nations: The Geography of Digital Distribution*. New York: NYU Press.

Lotz, Amanda. 2017. *Portals: A Treatise on Internet-Distributed Television*. Ann Arbor, MI: Maize Books.

———. 2018. *We Now Disrupt This Broadcast: How Cable Transformed Television and the Internet Revolutionized It All*. Cambridge, MA: MIT Press.

Lynch, Jason. 2015. "Here's Why Consumers Love Netflix More than Amazon and Hulu: Clear Branding Is Key." *AdWeek*, June 24. www.adweek.com.

MacDuffie, Allen. n.d. "Seriality and Sustainability in *Breaking Bad*." Unpublished manuscript. Accessed via peer review for *Cultural Critique*, July 2017.

Martin, Alfred L., Jr. 2018. "Notes from Underground: WGN's Black-Cast Quality TV Experiment." *Los Angeles Review of Books*, May 31. https://lareviewofbooks.org.

Marty O Radio Show. 2016. "My Personal Boycott of the NFL." *Marty O Radio Show Blog*, September 15. https://themartyoshow.weebly.com.

Maske, Mark. 2018. "NFL Owners Want Players to Agree to Stand for the National Anthem." *Washington Post*, July 25. www.washingtonpost.com.

Maske, Mark, and Adam Kilgore. 2018. "Two Cases of Player Violence against Women Turn the NFL Season 'Upside Down.'" *Washington Post*, December 5. www.washingtonpost.com.

McDonald, Soraya Nadia. 2018. "Can *Grown-ish* Avoid the Chaste, Safe Reality of *A Different World*?" *Undefeated*, January 2. https://theundefeated.com.

McNary, Dave. 2017. "Netflix Grants Public Screening Access for Ava DuVernay's Documentary '13th.'" *Variety*, February 14. https://variety.com.

McRobbie, Angela. 2007. "Top Girls? Young Women and the Post-feminist Sexual Contract." *Cultural Studies* 21 (4–5): 718–737.

———. 2008. *The Aftermath of Feminism: Gender, Culture and Social Change*. Los Angeles: Sage.

———. 2015. "Notes on the Perfect." *Australian Feminist Studies* 30 (83): 3–20.

Medhurst, Andy. 2007. *A National Joke: Popular Comedy and English Cultural Identities*. London: Routledge.

Mellencamp, Patricia. 2003. "Situation Comedy, Feminism, and Freud: Discourses of Gracie and Lucy." In *Critiquing the Sitcom: A Reader*, edited by Joanne Morreale, 41–55. Syracuse, NY: Syracuse University Press.

Merriam-Webster Online. n.d. "Peak." Accessed March 11, 2020. www.merriam-webster.com.

Miller, Toby. 2008. "Foreword: It's Television. It's HBO." In *It's Not TV: Watching HBO in the Post-television Era*, edited by Marc Leverette, Brian L. Ott, and Cara Louise Buckley, ix–xii. New York: Routledge.

Miller, Toby, Nitin Govil, John McMurria, Richard Maxwell, and Ting Wang. 2005. *Global Hollywood 2*. London: British Film Institute.

Mills, Brett. 2004. "Comedy Verité: Contemporary Sitcom Form." *Screen* 45 (1): 63–78.

———. 2009. *The Sitcom*. Edinburgh: Edinburgh University Press.

———. 2018. "Comedy and the Nation in *The Trip*." In *The Comedy Studies Reader*, edited by Nick Marx and Matt Sienkiewicz, 267–281. Austin: University of Texas Press.

Mills, Brett, and Erica Horton. 2016. *Creativity in the British Television Comedy Industry*. New York: Routledge.

Minow, Newton N. 1961. "Television and the Public Interest." Address to the National Association of Broadcasters, Washington, DC, May 9.

Mittell, Jason. 2001. "A Cultural Approach to Television Genre Theory." *Cinema Journal* 40 (3): 3–24.

———. 2015. *Complex TV: The Poetics of Contemporary Television*. New York: NYU Press.

Mizejewski, Linda. 2014. *Pretty/Funny: Women Comedians and Body Politics*. Austin: University of Texas Press.

Mizejewski, Linda, and Victoria Sturtevant. 2017. *Hysterical: Women in American Comedy*. Austin: University of Texas Press.

Modleski, Tania. 1982. *Loving with a Vengeance*. New York: Routledge.

Monk-Payton, Brandy. 2017. "Blackness and Televisual Reparations." *Film Quarterly* 71 (2): 12–18.

Moore, Jack, and Daniel Levitt. 2018. "The NFL's Rooney Rule: Why Football's Racial Divide Is Larger than Ever." *Guardian*, September 19. www.theguardian.com.

Moraña, Mabel, Enrique Dussel, and Carlos A. Jáuregui. 2008. *Coloniality at Large: Latin America and the Postcolonial Debate*. Durham, NC: Duke University Press.

Morreale, Joanne. 2003. "Sitcoms Say Good-Bye: The Cultural Spectacle of *Seinfeld*'s Last Episode." In *Critiquing the Sitcom: A Reader*, edited by Joanne Morreale, 274–288. Syracuse, NY: Syracuse University Press.

Morris, Wesley, and James Poniewozik. 2016. "Why 'Diverse TV' Matters: It's Better TV. Discuss." *New York Times*, February 10. www.nytimes.com.

Murthi, Vikram. 2015. "Indians on TV: How Aziz Ansari and *Master of None* Navigate the Anxieties of Representation." *IndieWire*, November 10. www.indiewire.com.

Nash, Meredith, and Imelda Whelehan, eds. 2017. *Reading Lena Dunham's "Girls": Feminism, Postfeminism, Authenticity and Gendered Performance in Contemporary Television*. New York: Palgrave Macmillan.

Nathanson, Elizabeth. 2014. "Dress for Economic Distress: Blogging and the 'New' Pleasures of Fashion." In *Gendering the Recession: Media and Culture in an Age of Austerity*, edited by Diane Negra and Yvonne Tasker, 136–160. Durham, NC: Duke University Press.

Negra, Diane. 2004. "'Quality Postfeminism?': Sex and the Single Girl on HBO." *Genders* 39. www.colorado.edu/genders/.

Negra, Diane, and Yvonne Tasker. 2014. Introduction to *Gendering the Recession: Media and Culture in an Age of Austerity*, edited by Diane Negra and Yvonne Tasker, 1–30. Durham, NC: Duke University Press.

Negus, Keith. 2002. "Identities and Industries: The Cultural Formation of Aesthetic Economics." In *Cultural Economy: Cultural Analysis and Commercial Life*, edited by Paul du Gay and Michael Pryke, 115–131. London: Sage.

Newcomb, Horace, and Paul M. Hirsch. 1983. "Television as Cultural Forum." *Quarterly Review of Film Studies* 8 (Summer): 45–55.

Newman, Michael Z., and Elana Levine. 2012. *Legitimating Television: Media Convergence and Cultural Status*. New York: Routledge.

New York Times. 2017. "Louis CK Responds to Accusations: 'These Stories Are True.'" November 10. www.nytimes.com.

Ngai, Sianne. 2007. *Ugly Feelings*. Cambridge, MA: Harvard University Press.

Nielsen. 2017. "For Us by Us? The Mainstream Appeal of Black Content." February 8. www.nielsen.com.

Nilsen, Sarah, and Sarah E. Turner. 2014. Introduction to *The Colorblind Screen: Television in Post-racial America*, edited by Sarah Nilsen and Sarah E. Turner, 1–14. New York: NYU Press.

Noble, Safiya Umoja. 2018. *Algorithms of Oppression: How Search Engines Reinforce Racism*. New York: NYU Press.

Norton, Michael, and Samuel Sommers. 2011. "Whites See Racism as a Zero-Sum Game That They Are Now Losing." *Perspectives on Psychological Science* 6 (3): 215–218.

NPR Staff. 2016. "The 'Girl' in the Title: More than a Marketing Trend." *Moring Edition*, National Public Radio, February 22. www.npr.org.

Nudd, Tim. 2015. "Always 'Like a Girl' Adds the 2015 Emmy Award to Its Haul of Trophies." *AdWeek*, September 15. www.adweek.com.

Nussbaum, Emily. 2013. "Difficult Women: How *Sex and the City* Lost Its Good Name." *New Yorker*, July 29. www.newyorker.com.

———. 2016. "Laverne and Curly: The Slapstick Anarchists of *Broad City*." *New Yorker*, March 7. www.newyorker.com.

———. 2017. "Definitely Not a Top Ten List: The Best TV Shows of 2017." *New Yorker*, December 18. www.newyorker.com.

Nygaard, Taylor. 2013. "Girls Just Want to Be 'Quality': HBO, Lena Dunham, and *Girls'* Conflicting Brand Identity." *Feminist Media Studies* 13 (2): 370–374.

———. 2018. "'I'm Cool with It': The Popular Feminism of *Inside Amy Schumer*." In *Emergent Feminisms and the Challenge to Postfeminist Media Culture*, edited by Maureen Ryan and Jessalyn Keller, 57–72. New York: Routledge.

Nygaard, Taylor, and Jorie Lagerwey. 2016. "Broadcasting Quality: Re-centering Feminist Discourse with *The Good Wife*." *Television and New Media* 18(2): 105–113. DOI: 10.1177/1527476416652485.

Obaro, Tomi. 2016. "What *Girls* and *Broad City* Teach Us about Female Friendship." *Buzzfeed*, May 10. www.buzzfeed.com.

O'Donnell, Victoria. 2007. *Television Criticism*. Thousand Oaks, CA: Sage.

Oliver, Melvin. 2008. "Sub-prime as Black Catastrophe." *American Prospect*, September 20. www.prospect.org.

Ouellette, Laurie, and Sarah Banet-Weiser. 2018. Editors' introduction to "Media and the Extreme Right." Special issue, *Communication Culture & Critique* 11:1–6.

Paskin, Willa. 2016. "The Brutal Romantic." *New Yorker*, April 25. www.newyorker.com.

Patterson, Troy. 2018. "Issa Rae's Breakthrough in *Insecure* Season 3, Episode 4." *New Yorker*, September 2. www.newyorker.com.

Pedersen, Erik. 2016. "'Gilmore Girls' Revival Triggers WBTV Lawsuit by Producer Gavin Polone." *Deadline*, April 11. www.deadline.com.

Pegg, Simon. 2007. "What Are You Laughing At?" *Guardian*, February 9. www.theguardian.com.

Petersen, Anne Helen. 2014. "The Unruly Stoner Girl: What Makes *Broad City* So Radical." *Los Angeles Review of Books*, March 31. www.lareviewofbooks.org.

———. 2015. "In *Trainwreck*, Amy Schumer Calls Bullshit on Postfeminism." *Buzzfeed*, July 18. www.buzzfeed.com.

Petruska, Karen, and Faye Woods. 2018. "Traveling without a Passport: 'Original' Streaming Content in the Transatlantic Distribution Ecosystem." In *Transatlantic Television Drama: Industries, Programs and Fans*, edited by Matt Hills, Michele Hilmes, and Roberta Pearson, 49–68. Oxford: Oxford University Press.

Pham, Jason. 2017. "Why Lena Waithe Almost Didn't Write Her Emmy-Winning *Master of None* Episode." *Variety*, October 25. www.variety.com.

Polan, Dana. 2007. "Cable Watching: HBO, *The Sopranos*, and Discourses of Distinction." In *Cable Visions: Television beyond Broadcasting*, edited by Sarah Banet-Weiser, Cynthia Chris, and Anthony Freitas, 319–337. New York: NYU Press.

Poniewozik, James. 2015a. "*Empire* and *Black-ish* Show Why Diversity Needs to Be Deep, Not Just Broad." *New York Times*, September 24. www.nytimes.com.

———. 2015b. "Review: Aziz Ansari, in 'Master of None,' Negotiates Technology and Social Mores." *New York Times*, November 5. www.nytimes.com.

———. 2018. "Review: 'Grown-ish' Comes into Its Own-ish." *New York Times*, January 9. www.nytimes.com.

Porter, Rick. 2018. "TV Long View: NFL Ratings Up While Broadcast Nets Bleed Viewers." *Hollywood Reporter*, November 16. www.hollywoodreporter.com.

———. 2020. "NFL TV Ratings Grow for 2nd Straight Year." *Hollywood Reporter*, January 2. www.hollywoodreporter.com.

Post Staff. 2008. "Stuff White People Like." *New York Post*, July 6. www.nypost.com.

Projansky, Sarah. 2014. *Spectacular Girls: Media Fascination and Celebrity Culture*. New York: NYU Press.

Rabinovitz, Lauren. 1999. "Ms.-Representation: The Politics of Feminist Sitcoms." In *Television, History, and American Culture: Feminist Critical Essays*, edited by Mary Beth Haralovich and Lauren Rabinovitz, 144–167. Durham, NC: Duke University Press.

Radway, Janice. 1984. *Reading the Romance: Women, Patriarchy, and Popular Literature*. Chapel Hill: University of North Carolina Press.

Ramos, Dino-Ray. 2017. "Asian Americans on TV: Study Finds Continued Underrepresentation Despite New Wave of AAPI-Led Shows." *Deadline*, September 12. www.deadline.com.

Raphael, Amy. 2009. "'There's No Moral Centre to *Pulling* Because We Don't Have One!'" *Guardian*, May 15. www.theguardian.com.

Reid, Eric. 2017. "Why Colin Kaepernick and I Decided to Take a Knee." *New York Times*, September 25. www.nytimes.com.

Rich, Adrienne. 1980. "Compulsory Heterosexuality and Lesbian Existence." *Signs* 5 (4): 631–660.

Richardson, Adam. 2011. "Netflix's Bold Disruptive Innovation." *Harvard Business Review*, September 20. https://hbr.org/.

Richardson, Michael. 2017. "The Disgust of Donald Trump." *Continuum* 31 (6): 747–756.

Rorke, Robert. 2015. "How *Empire* Changed Prime-Time Diversity for the Better." *New York Post*, October 29. www.nypost.com.

Rosenberg, Alyssa. 2014. "*All in the Family* and the Limits of Satire." *Washington Post*, April 1. www.washingtonpost.com.

Rothstein, Richard. 2017. *The Color of Law: A Forgotten History of How Our Government Segregated America*. New York: Liveright.

Rowe, Kathleen. 1995. *The Unruly Woman: Gender and Genres of Laughter*. Austin: University of Texas Press.

Rowe Karlyn, Kathleen. 2011. *Unruly Girls, Unrepentant Mothers: Redefining Feminism on Screen*. Austin: University of Texas Press.

Roxborough, Scott. 2016. "America's TV Exports Too Diverse for Overseas?" *Hollywood Reporter*, March 30. www.hollywoodreporter.com.

Ryan, Maureen. 2016. "Showrunners for New TV Season Remain Mostly White and Male." *Variety*, June 7. www.variety.com.

Ryan, Shannon. 2016. "Start Taking Female Sports Fans—and Their Impact—Seriously." *Chicago Tribune*, December 3. www.chicagotribune.com.

Ryzik, Melena, Cara Buckley, and Jodi Kantor. 2017. "Louis C.K. Is Accused by 5 Women of Sexual Misconduct." *New York Times*, November 9. www.nytimes.com.

Sandell, Jillian. 1998. "I'll Be There for You: Friends and the Fantasy of Alternative Families." *American Studies* 39 (2): 141–155.

San Martin, Nancy. 2003. "Must See TV: Programming Identity on NBC Thursdays." In *Quality Popular Television: Cult TV, the Industry, and Fans*, edited by Mark Jankovich and James Lyons, 32–47. London: Bloomsbury.

Santo, Avi. 2008. "Para-television and Discourses of Distinction: The Culture of Production at HBO." In *It's Not TV: Watching HBO in the Post-television Era*, edited by Marc Leverette, Brian L. Ott, and Cara Louise Buckley, 19–45. New York: Routledge.

Saponara, Michael. 2017. "Michael Smith and Jemele Hill's Top 5 'His and Hers' Moments." *Vibe*, February 6. www.vibe.com.

Saraiya, Sonia. 2018. "TV Review: 'Atlanta: Robbin' Season.'" *Variety*, February 28. www.variety.com.

Scharff, Christina. 2013. *Repudiating Feminism: Young Women in a Neoliberal World*. Farnham, UK: Ashgate.

Schilling, Dave. 2014. "Brunch Is America's Most Hated Meal Because We All Ruined It." *Vice*, April 16. www.vice.com.

Scott, Darieck. 2010. *Extravagant Abjection: Blackness, Power, and Sexuality in the African American Literary Imagination*. New York: NYU Press.

Seitz, Matt Zoller. 2013. "Seitz Asks: Should Netflix Shows Be Considered 'Television'?" *Vulture*, June 5. www.vulture.com.

Semuels, Alana. 2019. "The White Flight from Football." *Atlantic*, February 1. www.theatlantic.com.

Sender, Katherine. 2007. "Dualcasting: Bravo's Gay Programming and the Quest for Women Audiences." In *Cable Visions: Television Beyond Broadcasting*, edited by Sarah Banet-Weiser, Cynthia Chris, and Anthony Freitas, 302–318. New York: NYU Press.

Sepinwall, Alan. 2018. "The 20 Best TV Shows of 2018." *Rolling Stone*, December 4. www.rollingstone.com.

Serazio, Michael. 2019. *The Power of Sports: Media and Spectacle in American Culture*. New York: NYU Press.

Shelburne, Ramona. 2017. "Warriors Get Shunned by President before There Could Be a Dialogue." ESPN, September 24. www.espn.com.

Siino, Sal. 2018. "The Future of Traditional Television Survival Relies on Live Sports." *Business of Sports*, October 2. www.thebusinessofsports.com.

Silman, Anna. 2016. "TV's Most Gloriously Twisted Female Friendship Is Back." *Cut*, June 7. www.thecut.com.

Silverman, Gillian, and Sarah Hagelin. 2018. "Shame TV: Feminist Antiaspirationalism in HBO's *Girls*." *Signs* 43 (4): 877–904.

Smith, David. 2013. "'Racism' of Early Colour Photography Explored in Art Exhibition." *Guardian*, January 25. www.theguardian.com.

Smith, Stacy L., Marc Choueiti, and Katherine Pieper. 2016. "Inclusion or Invisibility? Comprehensive Annenberg Report on Diversity in Entertainment." USC Annenberg Media, Diversity, & Social Change Initiative. www.usc.annenberg.edu.

Spigel, Lynn. 1992. *Make Room for TV: Television and the Family Ideal in Postwar America*. Chicago: University of Chicago Press.

———. 2001. *Welcome to the Dreamhouse: Popular Media and the Postwar Suburbs*. Durham, NC: Duke University Press.

Spivak, Gayatri C. 2011. "General Strike!" *Tidal: Occupy Theory, Occupy Strategy* 1:8–9.

Sports Illustrated. 2017. "The Fans Who Say They're Walking Away from the NFL." September 27. www.si.com.

Squires, Catherine R. 2014. "Introduction: Welcome to Post-racial America." In *The Post-racial Mystique: Media and Race in the Twenty-First Century*, edited by Catherine Squires, 1–16. New York: NYU Press.

Stacey, Judith. 1987. "Sexism by a Subtler Name? Postindustrial conditions and Postfeminist Consciousness in the Silicon Valley." *Socialist Review* 17 (6): 7–28.

Stewart, Kathleen. 2007. *Ordinary Affects*. Durham, NC: Duke University Press.

Stratton, Jon. 2006. "*Seinfeld* Is a Jewish Sitcom, Isn't It? Ethnicity and Assimilation in 1990s American Television." In *Seinfeld, Master of Its Domain: Revisiting Television's Greatest Sitcom*, edited by David Lavery and Sara Lewis Dunne, 117–136. New York: Continuum.

Streeter, Thomas. 1997. "Blue Skies and Strange Bedfellows: The Discourse of Cable Television." In *The Revolution Wasn't Televised: Sixties Television and Social Conflict*, edited by Lynn Spigel and Michael Curtin, 221–244. New York: Routledge.

Taylor. Ella. 1989. *Prime-Time Families: Television Culture in Post-war America*. Berkeley: University of California Press.

Television Academy. 2018. "70th Emmy Awards: We Solved It!" YouTube, September 17. www.youtube.com/watch?v=J74hHQgCjrc.

Thompson, Derek. 2013. "Sports Could Save the TV Business—or Destroy It." *Atlantic*, July 17. www.theatlantic.com.

Thompson, Robert J. 1997. *Television's Second Golden Age: From "Hill Street Blues" to "ER."* New York: Continuum.

Thorburn, David. 2000. "Television Melodrama." In *Television: A Critical View*, 6th ed., edited by Horace Newcomb, 595–608. Oxford: Oxford University Press.

Ticineto Clough, Patricia, and Jean Halley, eds. 2007. *The Affective Turn: Theorizing the Social*. Durham, NC: Duke University Press.

Turchiano, Danielle. 2017. "Donald Glover Wins Emmy for Lead Actor in a Comedy Series." *Variety*, September 17. www.variety.com.

Turner, Sarah E. 2014. "BBFFs: Interracial Friendships in a Post-racial World." In *The Colorblind Screen: Television in Post-racial America*, edited by Sarah Nilsen and Sarah E. Turner, 237–260. New York: NYU Press.

Ugwu, Reggie. 2018. "Why the Creator of 'Dear White People' Is Doubling Down on Identity Politics." *New York Times*, May 2. www.nytimes.com.

Vagianos, Alanna. 2015. "The Reaction to #LikeAGirl Is Exactly Why It's So Important." *Huffington Post*, February 3. www.huffpost.com.

Valenti, Jessica. 2014. "Beyoncé's 'Flawless' Feminist Act at the VMAs Leads the Way for Other Women." *Guardian*, August 25. www.theguardian.com.

Van Luling, Todd. 2017. "Donald Glover Is First Black Director to Win an Emmy in Comedy." *Huffington Post*, September 17. www.huffpost.com.

Vernon, Polly. 2015. *Hot Feminist: Modern Feminism with Style without Judgement*. London: Hodder and Stoughton.

Wanzo, Rebecca. 2015. "Brown Broads, White TV." *Los Angeles Review of Books*, March 16. www.lareviewofbooks.org.

———. 2016. "Precarious-Girl Comedy: Issa Rae, Lena Dunham, and Abjection Aesthetics." *Camera Obscura* 31 (2 [92]): 27–59.

Warner, Kristen. 2015a. *The Cultural Politics of Colorblind TV Casting*. New York: Routledge.

———. 2015b. "The Racial Logic of *Grey's Anatomy*: Shonda Rhimes and Her 'Post–Civil Rights, Post-feminist' Series." *Television and New Media* 16 (7): 631–647.

———. 2016. "[Home] Girls: *Insecure* and HBO's Risky Racial Politics." *Los Angeles Review of Books*, October 21. www.lareviewofbooks.org.

———. 2017. "Plastic Representation." *Film Quarterly* 71 (2). www.filmquarterly.org.

Washington, Jessie. 2017. "The NFL Is Being Squeezed by Boycotts from Both Sides over Anthem Protests." *Undefeated*, September 13. www.theundefeated.com/features/.

Washington Post. 2016. "How One Scholar's Arrest Tainted the President's Image as a Racial Healer." April 22. www.washingtonpost.com.

Wasserman, Robin. 2016. "What Does It Mean When We Call Women Girls?" *Literary Hub*, May 18. www.lithub.com.

Watching Staff. n.d. "Convincing Female Friendships." *New York Times*. Accessed March 11, 2020. www.nytimes.com.

Watercutter, Angela. 2019. "What Ryan Murphy's Netflix Show Should Say about Hollywood." *Wired*, February 26. www.wired.com.

Watson, Amy. 2018. "Revenue of Television Production (NAICS 51211b) in the United States from 2009 to 2018 (in Billion U.S. Dollars)." Statista, June 28. www.statista.com.

Watson, Elwood, Jennifer Mitchell, and Marc Edward Shaw, eds. 2015. *HBO's "Girls" and the Awkward Politics of Gender, Race, and Privilege*. Lanham, MD: Lexington Books.

Weiss, Suzannah. 2016. "4 Problems with How We're Talking about 'Female Friendships.'" *Everyday Feminism*, March 23. http://everydayfeminism.com.

Welk, Brian. 2018. "LeBron James Calls Out 'Slave Mentality' of 'Old, White Men' NFL Owners." *Wrap*, December 22. www.thewrap.com.

West, Cornell. 2006. "Nihilism in Black America." In *Crime and Violence in American Film*, edited by Aaron Baker, 205–209. New York: Pearson Learning Solutions.

Williams, Matt. 2013. "Trayvon Martin Protests Being Held in More than 100 US Cities." *Guardian*, July 20. www.theguardian.com.

Winch, Alison. 2013. *Girlfriends and Postfeminist Sisterhood*. New York: Palgrave Macmillan.

Winters, Joseph R. 2016. *Hope Draped in Black: Race, Melancholy, and the Agony of Progress*. Durham, NC: Duke University Press.

Woods, Faye. 2019. "Too Close for Comfort: Direct Address and the Affective Pull of the Confessional Comic Woman in *Chewing Gum* and *Fleabag*." *Communication, Culture & Critique* 12 (2): 194–221.

Yahr, Emily. 2015. "Amy Poehler's 'Difficult People' Slammed for Blue Ivy–R. Kelly Joke: Here's Why It's Extremely Meta." *Washington Post*, August 19. www.washingtonpost.com.

Yuval-Davis, Nira. 1993. "Gender and Nation." *Ethnic and Racial Studies* 16 (4): 621–632.

Zacharek, Stephanie, Eliana Dockterman, and Haley Sweetland Edwards. 2017. "The Silence Breakers." *Time*, December 18. www.time.com.

Zarum, Lara. 2016. "The One Authentic Relationship on *UnReal*." *Huffington Post*, August 6. www.huffpost.com.

Zhou, Jingqiong. 2006. *Raymond Carver's Short Fiction in the History of Black Humor*. New York: Peter Lang.

—

INDEX

activism. *See* Black Lives Matter; feminism; national anthem protests

Adichie, Chimamanda Ngozi, 129, 136

aesthetics. *See* non-White aesthetics; prestige aesthetics; quality TV

All in the Family, 90, 107, 167, 232n3

Amazon Prime Video, 45, 49–53, 56–59, 61–63, 66

Ansari, Aziz, 159, 183–84. See also *Master of None*

Ansley, Frances Lee, 14–15

Arnaz, Desi, 80–83. See also *I Love Lucy*

Atlanta: and diversity in TV industry, 9, 69–71; economic insecurity in, 24–25, 158, 175, 195; non-White aesthetics of, 170–72, 177–81; and quality aesthetics, 155, 161; and racialized conflict, 27, 164, 188–90; structural inequalities in, 159–60, 165

awards shows. *See* Emmy Awards; Oscars

Banet-Weiser, Sarah: and capacity versus injury, 10–11, 104–105; and mediated taste communities, 62–64, 199; and popular feminism, 33–34, 103, 126–28, 137–38

Barris, Kenya, 69, 83–84, 166–67. See also *Black-ish*

Beadle, Michelle, 208–11

Being Mary Jane, 25, 70, 158, 164

Berkofsky, Ava, 180–81

Berlant, Lauren, 87, 133; and "cruel optimism," 17, 22, 66, 78, 177, 184, 202

best Black friend forever (BBFF) trope, 29–31, 141–42

Better Things: creator of, 151, 233n4; and domestic dystopia, 112–13; girlfriendships in, 137–38; and taste cultures, 40; transgender experience in, 33–34, 103–104

Beyoncé, 33, 67, 93, 128–29

blackface, 92, 179, 190, 233n4

Black-ish, 25, 70–71, 83–84, 157–59, 166, 232n2

Black Lives Matter, 26, 129, 165, 182, 195, 200, 204

Blackness: and friendship, 29–31, 128–29, 132, 139, 141–44; and housing inequality, 23–24, 199; and racist oppression, 25–30, 146–48, 153–54, 160–61, 172, 200–204, 210–11; and sitcom genre, 82–85, 91–93, 157–59; and "televisual reparations," 28, 164–65; and TV aesthetics, 174–182; and TV industry, 70–73, 162–71, 183–84, 187–96

blindcasting, 71, 165, 231n4. *See also* plastic representation

Bourdieu, Pierre, 42–44

Brexit campaign, 8, 44, 62

Broad City: centering Whiteness, 1–2, 14, 103, 152; cringe humor in, 146–48; economic insecurity in, 35, 118, 122–23; and feminisms, 18, 32–33; girlfriendship in, 124, 126, 134–38; hyperawareness of race in, 27–29, 218; and Jewish humor, 13, 96–97, 157, 231n1, 233n6; producers of, 151

Brown, Sterling K., 163, 165

Taylor Nygaard is Faculty Associate in the Department of English's Film and Media Studies division at Arizona State University. She writes about identity, television, digital culture, and media industries. Her work has appeared in *Feminist Media Studies*, *TV and New Media*, *Flow*, and elsewhere.

Jorie Lagerwey is Associate Professor in Television Studies at University College Dublin. She writes about race, gender, genre, celebrity, and television. She is the author of *Postfeminist Celebrity and Motherhood: Brand Mom* (2016). Her work has appeared in *Cinema Journal*, *TV and New Media*, *Celebrity Studies*, *Flow*, and elsewhere.